i

In the Lap of the Widow-Maker

In the Lap of the Widow-Maker

Extreme Events That Closed Down a Mountain

VIRGINIA BUCHANAN

Clockface Publishing © 2019

Clockface Publishing © 2019

Clockface Publishing,
Wall Grange, ST9 9QD,
clockface1066@gmail.com

First published 2019

ISBN: 978-1-9160040-0-9

For Gemma and Rhys

Contents

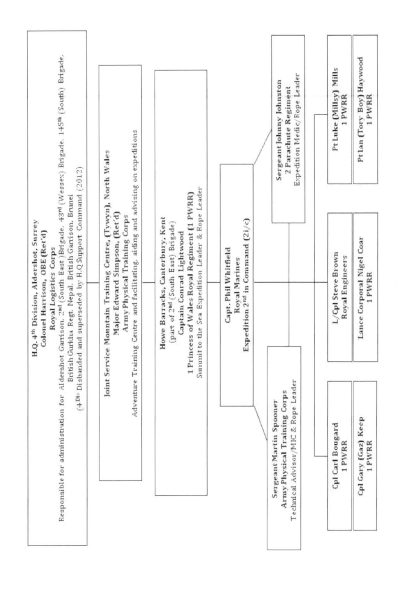

H.Q. 4th Division, Aldershot, Surrey
Colonel Harrison, OBE (Ret'd)
Royal Logistics Corps

Responsible for administration for Aldershot Garrison. 2nd (South East) Brigade. 43rd (Wessex) Brigade. 145th (South) Brigade. British Gurkha Regt. Nepal. British Garrison. Brunei
(4Div Disbanded and superseded by H.Q Support Command (2012)

Joint Service Mountain Training Centre, (Tywyn), North Wales
Major Edward Simpson, (Ret'd)
Army Physical Training Corps
Adventure Training Centre and facilitating, aiding and advising on expeditions

Howe Barracks, Canterbury, Kent
(part of 2nd (South East) Brigade)
Captain Conrad Lightwood
1 Princess of Wales Royal Regiment (1 PWRR)
Summit to the Sea Expedition Leader & Rope Leader

Capt. Phil Whitfield
Royal Marines
Expedition 2nd in Command (2i/c)

Sergeant Martin Spooner
Army Physical Training Corps
Technical Advisor/MIC & Rope Leader

Sergeant Johnny Johnston
2 Parachute Regiment
Expedition Medic/Rope Leader

Cpl Carl Bougard
1 PWRR

Cpl Gary (Gaz) Keep
1 PWRR

L/Cpl Steve Brown
Royal Engineers

Lance Corporal Nigel Coar
1 PWRR

Pt Luke (Millsy) Mills
1 PWRR

Pt Ian (Tory Boy) Haywood
1 PWRR

PREFACE

In Alaska, just 300 miles below the Arctic Circle, Denali, formerly Mount McKinley dominates the entire landscape. North America's biggest mountain, the coldest mountain, the wildest weather, the exquisite land and skyscapes, and the exceptional opportunity for technical Alpine climbing. Climbers from every continent are drawn to the high-risk game of Denali allowing them to pass to the summit...and back down to safety in one piece. It is not known as 'The Widow-maker' for no reason. -40 degrees Celsius, 160kmh winds, 3 long falls, crevasse falls, injured and trapped at 19,000ft with no food, water, tent or sleeping bag. How would you survive in body and mind? Cut-off from everything except the enormous bullwhip end of a storm from El Niño racing up around the Bering Straits to your tiny, sloping ledge. Now what?

Those involved ranged from novices to highly qualified and experienced mountaineers and other specialists. Only a series of exceptional circumstances allowed the 10 man British Army expedition to even leave the UK to climb Denali. Warning signs appeared early on the mountain until close to the summit one man collapsed and set into motion a series of falls, injuries, acts of bewildering confusion, of bravery and the biggest and most expensive mountain rescue in US history.

Roger Robinson, the Head Ranger of Denali National Park, and Head of the rescue operations edited the story for accuracy.

The story tells of the extreme flying skills and bravery shown by the award-winning helicopter pilot, Jim Hood. Reports from the U.S State Department of the Interior investigation and a statement taken by the Special Investigation Branch of the Royal Military Police are used in support of the telling of this expedition. The story tells of the subsequent Board of Inquiry and how it sparked concerns amongst some team members regarding the way the questions were posed and the interpretation of the information. There is also the telling of medical treatments administered from the best available at the time to the barbaric and shocking.

This is a human-interest story of those left at home. Service spouses learn how to display apparent self-reliance and fortitude they do not always feel. They are married to soldiers and they know the score. Within hours of the first fall, the press agencies gathered and the story went around the world. It was the number one news story for Summer Solstice weekend that year. Worldwide news teams conducted many interviews, even documentaries were made. Conditions were so appalling on the mountain that immediately after the rescue, Denali was 'shut down' for the rest of that climbing year.

All things can get skewed over time, so here is the story, as told in the first person by the technical expert on the expedition, Martin Spooner. The man who was injured and survived four nights and three days when the rescuers were organising 'log-grabbers' to bring the bodies down when the weather cleared. He is a holder of the Mountain Instructor Certificate, the highest mountaineering qualification in the U.K. and is a long-experienced adventurous training instructor. The story is also supported by other injured expedition members with their versions of the events given through interviews and hand-written statements. These men also donated photographs, including those of the frost injuries taken at the hospital in Alaska.

INTRODUCTION

This book is a compilation of stories surrounding a mountaineering expedition that took place in Alaska during the summer of 1998. There were several stories unfolding from the organisation of the British Army expedition to its long-term aftermath and other stories of other climbers 'In extremis' and the outstanding feats of the rescuers and the decisions they made.

For some involved it was just another day, another dollar but for others its impact continued to shadow them physically, mentally and/or emotionally. The story brings together people from all backgrounds, skill-levels and experience on both sides of the 'pond' as they say.

The story has been written in the first person to aid its continuity and it is through Martin's experiences and those of the various friends that have lived and worked around him that it is told. It is these people that appear to have been affected most chronically.

Martin joining the Army as a Junior Leader at sixteen opened his eyes to how society was really working but he had a long battle as a young man with the way his character had been developed.

Martin was quiet, not gregarious at all, sometimes shy but resolute when he had made his mind up about anything or anyone. If he thought someone was truly wrong, there was no pacifying him until the matter had been cleared up and put to bed.

Fortunately there were many that could see through this occasionally abrasive manner to find a talented, tenacious and dedicated young man who could take one by surprise with his sensitivity, tenderness and sometimes unnerving insight.

Martin eventually ended up teaching, which he does with competence, charm and excellent results. He had a great deal of practical experience under his belt and finally went on to obtain his Mountain Instructor Certificate, which is the U.K.'s highest mountaineering qualification. He had coaching qualifications in various sports but he made most use of the skiing, climbing and kayaking ones to work as an

Adventure Training instructor for many years at various centres in different countries. This role entails teaching all ranks and abilities from apprentices and novices to the highest ranks and Special Forces in small one day courses to extreme and remote locations and expeditions. He has organised, led or taken part in many various types of expeditions or adventurous training exercises in Kenya, Japan, Austria, Germany, France, Italy, Switzerland, Spain, Cyprus, Norway, Canada, and U.S.A. and all over Scotland, Wales and England.

This story follows Martin to one of the most hostile mountains in the world where his experiences bring together some of the toughest, most compassionate, and bewilderingly brave people it could be anyone's most fortunate fate to meet. He also has dealings with some of the most apparently inept or perhaps calculating and sadly ambitious of people. One or two of whom will later, sour, for him his last few years of Army life. This is not a crime, of course and when a career or professional reputation is in balance it appears it is every man for himself. This saddened Martin rather than embittered him because the Army gave him so much in so many different ways and certainly shaped the man he grew into but there are lessons here on moving on and finding a new way.

There was one particular Army Physical Training Corps officer who was astute enough to see early on that there was a story to be told and Martin had quite readily trusted his judgement. He had stood by Martin in the past and proved to be fair, just and professional, which is all Martin appeared to need and look for in a boss. As this man said, "It's easy to be popular." Martin was not socially ambitious, but had a particular charm once he was in his own comfort zone, which was usually out of most other peoples'.

There have been many documentaries and articles regarding this story and even decades on if one cares to 'Google' Rescue on Denali it is still there, such was the size of the operation.

It should also be noted by American readers that the story is told from a British perspective, so spelling and some phrasing are used accordingly. It is hoped that this will not make the reading of it irritating or halting in any way. The intention from the start is to use everyday language and show that humour can be found anywhere and that it is possible to move on from anything with lessons learned and positive outcomes.

Martin will never settle. It is in his nature to want to escape to the wilderness and spend his time amongst the elements he finds. It doesn't matter what the remoteness is, hills and mountains, forests and valleys or a new love; the blue, green, grey and foaming, white sea. Mountains would be his first choice if he could but the sea comes a very close second. He works in the forests now. He'll divert his skills to anywhere but it must be alongside nature.

A great many people I have spoken with want to know this story and keep asking, 'When are you going to write it?' Why they want to know after all this time is still beyond Martin's comprehension. I believe the reminders of human nature and the natural spark, both good and bad, are justification on their own.

The title of the book is taken from two national newspaper headlines and comments on the story as it was unfolding that expressed the circumstances very well; 'In the Lap of the Gods' and 'Clinging to Life on the Widow-Maker'.

GLOSSARY

I am introducing a glossary here at the beginning for reading ease, as with all the services, military and civilian, acronyms etc. are part of the everyday vocabulary and would certainly cause confusion for the lay reader. I find it maddening to have to keep flipping to the back of a book to understand what I'm reading when I could have picked up a bit of information at the start. It is also copied to the back for quick reference.

AMS   Acute Mountaineering Sickness (Altitude Sickness)
APTC   Army Physical Training Corps.
ATFA   Army Training Form (Alpha), mainly concerned with any adventurous outdoor activities in the UK or worldwide from a simple ramble to extreme activity. It is pronounced 'At-fer'.

Mountaineering Qualifications in order both military and civilian:
UEL   Unit Expedition Leader
ML (S)   Mountain Leader (Summer)
ML (W)   Mountain Leader (Winter)
JSMEL (S) Joint Service Mountain Expedition Leader (Summer)
JSMEL (W) Joint Service Mountain Expedition Leader (Winter)
MIA   Mountaineering Instructor Award
MIC   Mountain Instructor Certificate
MoD   Ministry of Defence
MO   Medical Officer
HACE   High Altitude Cerebral Oedema
HAPE   High Altitude Pulmonary Oedema
PXR   Post Exercise Report
SIB   Special Investigation Branch (Royal Military Police)
TAIT   Training Accident Investigation Team
USNPS   United States National Park Service

Before the MIA, a JSMEL can be taken; this is pronounced 'Jes-mel'. Each qualification must be supported by a completed logbook with minimum criteria of experience in terms of time, breadth of experience, weather and terrain conditions and assessments. If an assessment is failed then a minimum time must pass before re-taking the assessment with the logbook further supporting extended training. This list is typical of what would be expected in the profession at the time of the expedition.

DENALI

Denali National Park and Preserve is located just over a hundred miles north of Anchorage, Alaska and was established to protect the Denali Mountain and the surrounding lands, wildlife and ecosystem.

Set in the stunningly dramatic landscape, the Alaskan Range runs for 650 miles, rising out of the sub-arctic tundra. Constantly layered in snow and creaking with centuries-old ice, the monoliths feed the mighty rivers of the Yukon, Susitna and Kuskokwin. They are truly wild waters set in and travelling through truly wild country. With heavy volumes of water roaring down through the land and boulders the size of houses littering the routes, the rivers are magnets for the most intrepid and experienced kayakers. Cutting through the foothills to the tundra, a vast area of marshy lands about 2,700ft above the tree line, supports the hardy wildlife, which not only scrapes out their existence, but also thrives.

Huddled to the ground are abundant arrays of vegetation; lichens, mosses, grasses, sedges and berries growing down amongst the small shrubs that are dotted about. This feeds and provides homes for the fauna.

The vegetation provides the perfect diet for what is probably nature's greatest land nomad, and Bev's favourite, the reindeer (caribou). Although they are essentially herbivores, they have been known to eat the odd lemming in Scandinavia when times are hard! Grizzly bears wander through in search of berries and the weasels and foxes find their prey in voles, lemmings and other small mammals. Dall sheep, marmots and ground squirrels are other hardy Denali dwellers.

The tundra gives way to the command of the mountains at about 7,500ft where movement of the tectonic plates have heaved up one of the greatest vertical rises on the planet, the peak of Denali at 20,310ft, (6,190m)

The mountain range sits on the Denali Fault System, which stretches right across Alaska, 1,300 miles making it the largest break in the earth's crust in North America. Denali is also the third most remote mountain on the planet.

Previously Mount McKinley, or again, now Denali, a native Athabaskan name meaning 'The High One', is the giant of Alaska. It is the highest peak on the North American continent. Imposing by its isolation, it rises out of the tundra, enabling it to be viewed from a very great distance.

The mountain has the greatest vertical height from base to summit of any mountain in the world above sea level, including Mount Everest, which, is only higher due to the elevation of its base above sea level. Denali's North face rises a sheer 14,000ft, (Peters Glacier to the summit of the North Peak), making this feature the greatest single rise of any mountain in the world. Mount Everest rises from the Tibetan plateau 12,000ft vertically.

One factor that makes Denali such a demanding and sometimes frightening challenge is the weather. With a latitude of 63 degrees North, it is just 200 miles South of the Arctic Circle, which situates it in the sub-arctic climate zone of the arctic tundra. It is known to be one of the coldest mountains on earth. Exacerbating this is the weather that moves in from the Bering Sea and the Gulf of Alaska, causing rapid and dramatic changes on the mountain. The wind races across the tundra, increasing in speed. The mountain's height and latitude create wind speeds in excess of 100 miles per hour, (170kmph) and temperatures as low as – 40 degrees C/F. Due to its colossal size and the effect this has on the air streams that meet it, Denali, infamously creates its own weather.

The first non-native to claim to have discovered Denali was George Vancouver, in 1794. Dr Fredrick Cook and Edward Braille claimed to have made the first ascent of Denali in 1906. This claim was disputed and the photographic 'evidence' of Cook standing on the summit with the US flag, was proved to be a fake. It was seven years later in 1913 that the summit was reached for the first time, by the leader, Reverend Hudson Stuck, Harry Karstens, Walter Harper (Alaska Native and first person on top) and Robert Tatum.

It's hard to imagine on a supposedly bitter winter's day in the UK, what it must have been like to climb a mountain like Denali back then with their equipment and resources.

The climbing season runs from mid-April to early August, with over a thousand climbers tackling the mountain each year. Out of this thousand, only 50 - 60% will make the summit. May and June are very busy, but temperatures still frequently drop below -22 degrees Fahrenheit, (–30 degrees C), and deep falls of snow are common. It is still climbed throughout July and August, but as summer goes on and autumn approaches, there is a greater risk as the terrain becomes more unstable due to open crevasses and increased avalanches.

The mountain has beautiful flows of sculpted ice, spreading 14,000ft down the mountainside. Still on the move on its timeless journey, it is thought to be thousands of feet deep in places. Dotted with glaciers, crevasses, ice-falls, sharp ridges and huge vertical rises, it is a good technical mountain, which increases the attraction for climbers from all over the world, especially those who enjoy 'Alpine' climbing.

There are routes for everybody, from guided, novice climbers to experienced adventurers and routes yet to be tackled or carefully considered. As it is still a mountain that can offer new adventure, it is becoming more and more popular.

With the support of the Mountaineering Rangers of the United States Park Service, helicopter evacuations and an emergency medical tent at the 14,200ft Camp, a great many lives have been saved. Also a good number of people have attempted to climb that may not have tried had the support not been there if they needed it. Some say that this is a great way of helping climbers to seek their potential and offers peace of mind to those who have doubts, knowing that they have at least a bit more than an outside chance of surviving if they have an accident or fall foul of the conditions. It has certainly made many feel that the summit is more accessible if they feel they can relay messages to an expert if need be.

There are also a great many that feel passionately that the summer throngs that 'invade' the mountain should rely on their own resources and perhaps some of the reasons people climbing are not doing so for the true wilderness experience, but to add Denali to their list of summits.

For my part, I can empathise with both sides. An adventure like climbing Denali is a lifetime ambition for some and their lives are enriched and changed forever by such an experience. They may have to rely heavily on advice, guides and the security of knowing that emergency medical help may be within reach to help them make it. It is also true that some will not try to rely on themselves first when they get into trouble.

Some will litter the mountain with their waste and packaging and not have a true appreciation of the whole environment they are in.

Most climbers try their best to adhere morally to the environmental needs of the mountain and want to face the challenge of self-reliance. Ten climbers would either climb in ten different ways and for ten different reasons, so I leave the politics of climbing Denali to those who can cope with the headaches of the arguments.

In poor weather, Denali is a savage and desolate place to be. It is not a mountain to be caught on over night without shelter, even in the best of weather. There have been many fatalities on the mountain and some routes are more notorious for claiming lives than others. During the 1998 season, which is the time written about in this story; the conditions were exacerbated by a phenomenon known as 'El Niño'. The storms whipped up with such ferocity that the mountain was closed down to climbers early that year. But in good weather, the changing light of the sky reflecting off the faces of the mountain makes for the most breathtaking, beautiful images. From the golden mountainside in the evening sun to the magenta, peach and azure sky of the dawn at summer solstice it leaves many to sit and contemplate the wonders of this place.

It was now about 19:20hrs. It had been a slow day but we still had a lot of daylight, excellent visibility and plenty of it left for the descent after the summit. Ready to move, we'd had a good little break and we were all three up on our feet. Steve had taken his helmet off during the break probably because he was so hot maybe and we waited while everyone got their kit back on and sorted. I stood still until I felt we were ready for the cut through, waiting for Steve and Phil to sort themselves out and I looked up at the solid wave of snow that rolled above us. I made up my mind just where to make the first cut, while Phil and Steve secured their last bits of gear. As I reached around for my other ice axe I said to the other two "OK guys, you'll need your other ice…" the instruction was left in mid-air as I saw Phil sit back as his harness was pulled hard from behind pulling him right off balance.

The horror shot through me in the blink of an eye as I saw what was about to happen "Shit!" was all I had time to say as Phil's face tensed to a shocked grimace and his eyes widened, startled as he toppled and stepped out with his right foot into thin air. Steve wasn't there, he was gone. I immediately twisted round to the front to brace myself and hold their weight. The tension built up on the rope and the snow-pack started to give way beneath my feet. Immediately I threw myself into an ice-axe arrest. The pick had barely bitten into the surface when I felt the tension pulling me on the rope and was plucked from the steep slope in a way I can only describe as like being shot from a catapult and down the face of the mountain.

The pick of the axe was whipping through softened ice and snow. All I could see was the white rush of the ice spraying all around me as the pick tore it away. I held the axe hard into my body, my arms locked into position as I waited for it to start biting into the ice. All I could hear was the rush and roar and scraping that our fall was creating then; 'Bang!' my axe was wrenched from my hands and wrist so quickly, I didn't see it go, it had hit hard ice. My teeth were biting together so hard I thought they would smash. My arm was momentarily deadened from the ice axe being ripped away with the weight of three men on it.

A new sensation I was suddenly aware of was that of the rope somehow being above me at some point and I felt as though I was slowing down. Then the rope came whipping past me and again I was catapulted down. Obviously the other two were tumbling out of control and not arresting with their axes. There was nothing to slow us down.

I was clawing frantically at the surface, embedding my hands as hard as I could at the unstable ice on the near vertical surface. The rope jerked again as the weight of the two men below pulled at me and sped the descent again. We were falling a long, long way.

The fall was lasting so long that I had time to think to myself, "What can I do now?

All I could do now was a desperate act that would either flip me over so I was free-falling up-side-down or break both ankles but slow our fall. If I didn't try something, we were dead anyway, no kidding, it was two-miles down from where we were. I desperately felt for contact with the surface again and as my body closed in to meet it I dropped my lower legs to dig my crampon points into the ice.

I was braced ready for the pain as my points bit at the surface. They rattled at the rough surface at first, as I continued plummeting at speed feeling the hard vibration travel through my body. Then it came, within a few long seconds. The crack was clearly audible even above rushing sound that was filling my ears.

The pain shot through my body like a hot and freezing blade. With the full capacity of my lungs, I screamed out with the pain. I knew my boots would hold my ankles in place regardless of the pressure I applied. I continued to dig in now with my mind now in full combat against my pain. All my effort was in digging my toes into roughened ice and hoping I wasn't going to be flipped over if I hit something big. In my mind the worst was to come because I knew I had to do it again with the other foot. I did it and there was the same pain, the scream across the sky and gasping but I heard no crack this time. Don't pass out, please don't pass out. I was grasping at the surface, I was panting, gritting my teeth.

Suddenly, a new and terrifying realisation came to me; everything lightened and I was lifting away from the surface of the mountain. With fresh air between me and the mountain, I wasn't going to stop falling. Startled now I whispered "Oh God, No!"

Martin's Story
Chapter1 - The Waste, Leek, England

I suppose my love of climbing goes back to the age of around ten when, as a school boy I would race through my daily routine, to make time to go up 'The Waste' with my mates Moggs, Mugs, Check, Rozzer and my younger brother Micky, (Mick now that he's a grown up).

Most towns have a 'Waste' and they are all called something different I expect. This one is a small copse of trees and bushes with wonderfully steep mounds and ditches - a perfect scrambling track for 'Choppers' and 'Tomahawks'; the seventies and early eighties versions of BMX bikes. The kids with racing bikes were at a definite disadvantage; their bikes were too cumbersome to compete with this gang as we prepared for the ultimate chase - Tree Tick! (Or Tag, depending on where you live). We would take to the trees, chancing the finest limbs in our attempts to escape swinging and leaping from tree to tree with what we thought was the agility of apes. Our over-confidence didn't deter us in the slightest, even when one of us would land flat on our backs from a great height and be so badly winded that one could almost see a football-sized lump of air getting thumped out of the six stone, gangly body. After the tears of pain and embarrassment from the victim, accompanied by the howling hysterics of the rest of the gang, the incident would make a tale to be told in future years, fading and mingling into countless similar ones as old stories often do.

My climbing 'career' progressed from The Waste to an adventure playground on my doorstep. My father, John worked for Severn Trent Water Authority and my mother Barbara had worked as a secretary at a dental surgery before going on to work at the local swimming baths. For a short time, when money was tight they came home from work and went out again until about 22:00hrs bagging up coal for a few more shillings an hour. Both have always worked. They bought a terraced house in a small cul-de-sac called Nelson Street just near the town centre of Leek.

Leek is essentially a rural market town on the edge of the Peak District on the Staffordshire Moorlands, but had an overspill of the mills and potteries industries of nearby Stoke-on-Trent. Nowadays, most of these mills are home to smaller businesses working out of small sectioned off areas of a mill or they are the smart, new apartments advertised in the estate agents with 'good sized bedrooms.'

We were fortunate, as Micky and I saw it back in the early 1970's to have a small factory at the head of the street. Ma was busy working at the 'baths' and later in an old folks home and Pa worked out and about all over the Moorlands and we, (the children) often went to Nanna's for our lunch. Most days after school we would pop along to the baths for a swim. We are all good, strong swimmers as a result. Pa sometimes worked on the house making constant improvements that didn't always work out and Ma would clean up the mess.

I remember the bathroom being tiled over two days of a weekend then later everyone hearing the tiles pop off the wall one by one and falling into the bath. Then there was the ill-timed soot fall from the chimney just after Ma and Pa had wallpapered the sitting room and then Ma 'going up' like a shaken bottle of pop when Pa decided to bring a motorbike into the sitting room to strip down and re-build when she was out at work. Home repairs by 'Bodgit & Scarper'. Yes, we laugh now...

We children, all needless to say 'played out' a great deal. We were the same gang with the same game; we just had a new and exciting venue, the factory roof! As we never did any damage, we didn't see the harm in what we were doing nor the danger of it. It was perfect for tick and most especially 'Werewolf', as it got dark, a howling version of 'tick', we found quite scary and thrilling. The Leek branch of the Staffordshire Constabulary didn't agree and gave chase on more than one occasion, in vain, luckily for us. We would have had a proper hiding if we had ever brought a policeman to the door.

As time went by, my friends and I turned our attention to other roofs in the area, discussing the lead from which we discovered could turn into extra pocket money. I have never been what can be described as a church goer, but I didn't want to tempt fate with that line of work, so I never got involved and was quite scared at the thought of the trouble it would bring on one or two of my friends.

The closest we ever got to it was when Moggs and I made a pretty weedy grappling hook in metalwork at school with big plans to check out a roof and make our master plan. Moggs cast it up into the air and it bit into its target after several attempts. He began to climb. Suddenly the tines completely buckled and gave way and the grappling hook 'pinged' off the roof gutter. Moggs plummeted to the ground and landed flat on his back. The bent up and twisted grappling hook and rope thumped down nearby. Moggs was lying there unable to take a breath but making little creaky noises like a swinging gate. When he was eventually able to stand, we inspected our grappling hook and were bewildered that our schoolboy metalwork talent hadn't been able to hold his weight.

The thought of going to court and borstal was deterrent enough for me, let alone facing Ma and Pa with a policeman holding me by the scruff of the neck and I turned my attention from climbing buildings to climbing rocks.

The Roaches are gritstone crags that rise from the hills at the edge of the Peak District. They offer excellent quality climbing at all levels. There are plenty of boulders to play on and plenty of 'classic' routes. It is a place that attracts sightseers and climbers alike, as the crags can be viewed from the top by walking the pathways behind them. The open aspect of the view shows the countryside sprawling away from the foothills and the far off Tittesworth reservoir to look like nothing more than a large pond.

These crags are about three or so miles from the edge of town. The gang would cycle up to them on the notoriously tricky A53, down and up 'Solomon's Hollow', which is a nasty long dip in the road with a bend. It didn't matter that it took so much energy to get to the Roaches and we would scramble and tear around them all day playing 'tick' on bikes and on foot then cycle all the way back to Leek. I would never allow my kids to cycle on that road but there was no sense of danger for us at the time.

Before I joined the Army as a boy soldier, I went to earn my keep as a farm labourer one summer. Apart from the fact that I witnessed the pleasing and magical event of a foal being born in one of the fields, I also learned that farming was a profession that held no appeal for me. It was farming or factory, if I stayed in Leek and if I'm honest, probably trouble if I didn't have some excitement and adventure to my life.

After working for some time with Severn Trent Water, Pa was offered the opportunity to take a cottage in the grounds of a rural pumping station in a picturesque village called Longsdon a couple of miles from the town. The offer was taken up and this enabled Pa to work in the pumping station on the property and Ma to tame the huge garden that ran as far as she chose.

This place lies in the bottom of a valley between two branches of a canal at the edge of a country park. There is a tree-lined track about a quarter of a mile long that leads from the village lane. It opens out into about three acres of lawns, marsh, rhododendrons, wild flowers and small trees with two red-bricked, buildings that housed the pumps. They look like small churches with their tall arched windows and large double doors although one is much larger than the other.

About a hundred metres away are two cottages with the huge lawn in front of them, which is the roof of the underground reservoir. Beyond the lawn and hedgerow is the marsh. A young forty-year old copse borders the bottom edge of the site and then there is a brook, which is a tributary of the River Churnet. Beyond that is a disused railway line and the other side of that is another canal through the beech, birch, willows and oaks. The hills beyond all this are the Country Park and farmland.

Seeing this place after long absences is like it was the first time, like stumbling across the secret garden. There was so much land for us children to play on and so much wildlife, that the whole family has grown up with a love of the outdoors and a deep respect for the environment.

The pumping stations have been closed for many years now and have been converted inside for other uses. Wildlife is plentiful with a wide variety of birds, mammals including bats and we have a healthy population of grass snakes.

Before a weir was built in the Churnet, the brook at the end of the garden would sometimes burst its banks enabling Micky and I to be able to kayak right up to the gate that adjoins to the farmland. This no longer happens, but 30 years ago there were still waist deep floods along the track to the village, which were always an adventure if our children or nephews and nieces were around. Even that has changed and the water is much better behaved and now and the children are all grown up with families of their own.

In the summer the gang and I would still play tree tick in the grounds or build rafts or go scrambling on my motor-crosser.

Beverley came on the scene when I was twenty-three and right up until I was around thirty or so I still played tick either in the trees or inside the dis-used pumping station with Micky and Moggs. One particular occasion that comes to mind was when I was around twenty six we all ran off to the pumping station for a game of tick.

Many people would think that we had no business playing like this at our ages, but there is more than enough of the serious side of life for us to be mature adults, so who cares what people thought when we played our games. In the roof of the tallest building was a gantry and crane that works on a girder. One simply pulls one side of the chain and the girder will move one way, pull the other side to bring it back. The same went for the girder that moves from the front of the building to the rear. Bev had chickened out of the game in the girders, as she didn't want to fall 20ft onto the huge, cast iron pumps if she lost her footing, (strange girl!).

Micky, Moggs and I were old hands at the game, so dodgy bits of ropes were thrown and secured over the fixed girders and the game commenced. It was fast, noisy and exhilarating, even to watch. We were swinging and climbing on the ropes and the gantry beams slid back and forth on their enormous cogs.

Micky slid down to the ground to operate the chain that would enable me to evade Moggs who was shuffling his way towards me. At this point I sat in between two of the cogs and had my attention on the shuffling Moggs who was getting a bit too close but I wanted him to have a sense of hope. Micky, probably too excited to notice my precarious position yanked the chain with all his might in order to help me move across on the girder that I was no longer sitting on.

My scream echoed around the walls of the building as the great industrial cogs chewed into my backside, pulling my buttocks into them. There was a moment's stunned silence as the echo died out and ears stopped ringing, then they all realised what had happened. I drew a long breath and screamed an unrepeatable stream of names at poor Micky, who didn't know whether to take flight or stand and stammer out his apology. I called him every damned name I could think of. I don't know how I got down; I was burning hot with anger, embarrassment and so much pain.

Bev had hidden behind a locker due to her unfortunate habit of laughing in shock situations that aren't funny. She did find it funny even though I was hurt, but the guilt she felt helped her to control her breathing enough to take away the grin, which was now an involuntary reaction. She stepped out from behind the locker and followed me, sniggering with the others as I was now walking like John Wayne in a fury back to the house, effing and jeffing at my brother. Micky and Moggs followed in silence between their uncontrollable tittering. Bev dropped behind further, obviously losing control altogether.

In the kitchen I lay face down along the bench with my pants round my ankles, in an absolute state of agony and anger, while Bev tended my four-inch bite marks on each cheek from the cogs with antiseptic fluid. In her haste she poured copious amounts of it onto the cotton wool and applied it to the broken skin. This was breath-takingly painful as I sank my teeth into the end of the bench. However, as she had used so much antiseptic fluid, it ran between my legs and onto my wedding tackle. After a few seconds the cold fluid turned to stinging and fire. I let out a shriek, leaped up from the bench and plopped my tackle into the washing up bowl full of soapy water and lunch dishes. I moaned and groaned in relief with my eyes to the ceiling, and then to further my horror I dropped my gaze to the window in front of me where Micky and Moggs were watching the whole event and howling with laughter with their heads just visible over the window sill from outside. Well, as I said before, it's funny now.

That was the last game that was ever played in the girders so the venue reverted back to The Roaches and I issued Bev a lifetime ban from administering first aid. (Funnily enough, 20 years on she was responding for West Midlands Ambulance Service as a Community First Responder. Off she went with her bags of drugs, needles, dressings and gasses with her little blue light flashing to torture some other poor soul already in distress!)

Decades on from that time, we still played as far as the injuries from the accident dictated. Whenever the mood took us we became unruly and rowdy children, playing tick, having water fights with Ma yelling "Mind my plants, get this dirty ball out of here!" Scolding us for tearing the place up, except now it's with our dogs. My ankle injury would swell up and I'd be written off for the next few days, but hey ho, I say, we've got to live. The only advantage to my injury on everyone else's part is that I am so much easier to catch now! That and age.

Chapter 2 - You're In The Army Now

I joined the army as a boy soldier and spent most of that at Dover. I went on to adult service and was posted to my first Unit, 25 Engineer Regiment, Iserlohn, Germany. Although I enjoyed being in the Royal Engineers, I had expressed a wish from the outset to join the gym. I was therefore tasked to report to the Military Transport Section (MT). I had been with my Unit little more than a week at this point and 'they' had been wondering where to put me; so this was as a good a place as any.

It became quickly clear that things were a bit different in adult service. Upon my arrival at the MT I rounded the corner to the office to be startled by a furious yell from within and closely following this a body being ejected through the swinging doors. The unfortunate soldier skidded across the workshop floor but before he could regain his footing, lost balance and disappeared down the nearby vehicle inspection pit. This wasn't enough, even then he was pursued by the snarling, spitting corporal who followed him into the pit and dragged him back out by the scruff of the neck. Upon seeing me standing there looking aghast, the corporal himself looked slightly taken aback and regaining his composure mumbled, "Don't let it happen again." The unfortunate private scuttled off quickly to his duty.

I quickly settled in to be part of the team and following a few clips around the ear and kicks up the backside learned to play my part well.

The Falklands conflict arose and along with countless others, I volunteered but my Unit weren't to go. My time in Germany was spent much the same as many other single soldiers' there. Weeks on exercise were spent laying bridges and taking them back up again, falling asleep at the wheel of four ton trucks in convoy with all my mates in the back. Stand to, stand down, stand to, and going to town at weekends to wind down if I wasn't 'spammed' for a duty.

My friends of course played the usual 'new boy' tricks on me. I was sent to the HQ to ask for a 'long stand' and it was only after standing in the corridor for some considerable time that I realised what I was doing. Another occasion I was sent to the fast food wagon (Schnelly) outside the camp for "Ein grosse pimmel mit pomme frites, bitte!" (A large penis with fries, please.) There were countless others but these are two that are probably familiar to many soldiers.

I also made quite an impression with my driving skills by miscalculating the space at the entrance to the Regiment. One gate was open, the other closed. I drove my four-ton, Bedford lorry straight through what I thought was the gap, nearly taking the closed gate with me. After I had taken the truck load of lads to the ranges for the day for weapons training, I noticed that the keys to the Bedford were missing. I had everyone looking and eventually had no alternative but to use the foil from a gum wrapper to hotwire the truck and hope it stayed in place for the trip back to camp. The keys were never found. As I drove the truck towards the camp gates later that day I was a little embarrassed to see a prisoner from the guardroom grumbling under his breath as he repainted the buckled gate.

Whilst serving out my first tour, I took to climbing with a sergeant from Soest at a place called Honnetal. These were good technical limestone crags that were set back from the road high up on wooded banks. It is a very pleasant area, access is good and the area is frequently climbed so there was often someone else to watch to pick up tips on tricky moves.

I climbed in running shoes for some time. That was until I lost my footing and slipped. The bolt holding my protection shot out and hit me square on the forehead. I fell nearly 40 ft. This prompted me to start buying my own equipment. (Bev is still waiting for me to be prompted to stop). My first purchases were a Whillans harness and a pair of Boreal Firé Classic rock boots. I still own a pair.

A posting to the U.K. followed and I found myself serving with 38 Engineer Regiment in Ripon, North Yorkshire. Soon after my arrival there, my squadron was posted on a four-month tour of Kenya. Here I experienced such delights as touring the Valley of the Kings on a rest and recuperation, (R & R) weekend, trips to Mombasa following vehement warnings by the medical officer, for all soldiers to beware of the hazards inherent with fraternising with the local women. Sadly, Mombasa was an HIV and AIDS hot spot in those days. As we now know it it's a curse that has spread beyond belief with such tragic consequences.

I now have associations with an organisation called Explore Trees which is partly administered through the Amorentia Estate in the Politsi Valley in South Africa and the lovely Espach family but is the brain-child and is run in the UK by my good friend David Wiles. They help a tiny school on the estate in South Africa. So many of the children are born with HIV. Every one of them smiling and happy with so little in life or do they just understand a gift in living?

One of the most vivid experiences I recall from my tour of duty in Kenya is being chased by a furious baboon that took exception to me taking a few photographs of a nearby herd of elephants. I got out of the Land Rover to take some shots. I crossed a ditch and strolled a few paces and spotted the baboons at some good distance off to one side. They grunted, snarled and barked even though I was quite a long way off. I ignored them and concentrated on the elephants. Suddenly the barking from the baboons became more vehement. One of them ran and bloody quick too. I turned and sprinted, but the baboon closed the distance between us with very alarming speed. I cleared the ditch in one leap and shot back into the truck with my backside twitching and my heart thumping. I take my hat off to Sir David Attenborough (always), but really, this baboon crossed a distance so fast it was startling, or was that just fear?

There was also the daily slog of working through the blazing heat day after day, week after week either in enormous plant vehicles or building scaffolding etc. Dust, heat and sweat. A friend of mine walking past me one day had a bottle of pop in his hand. I asked my mate for a good swig. "No, you don't want this." He said.

"I really do," I replied.

"Go on then." He said happily and obligingly passed me the bottle. I glugged and glugged and glugged then wretched, spat, snotted and belched up the detergent he'd put in there.

One of the most memorable aspects of the tour was the whole squadron going down with a violent bout of dysentery. When somebody tries to describe projectile vomiting and diarrhoea and you assume they may be exaggerating the violence of it, don't. It is quite shocking to witness and even worse to succumb to its assault on the alimentary canal.

I did have a good tour in Kenya, with dozens of really amusing stories but I must move on. Part of the tour was an ascent of Mount Kenya. I suffered from AMS (Acute Mountain Sickness), commonly known as altitude sickness but managed to summit. I was very young and it's an expedition I sometimes overlook, but I thoroughly enjoyed it. It is fantastic that the atmospheric pressure changes so much over such a relatively short distance and we trudged through snow and ice when the heat a few thousand feet below was blazing and inescapable. One of the reasons why altitude sickness is a problem around the equator is the sense of false security that the higher temperature gives. Climbers often feel that because the weather is warmer, they are not that high in the atmosphere and climb too quickly and don't take the long breaks required for acclimatisation. The African continent has a great deal of magic about it. I look back upon it all very fondly but was glad to be home when it was over.

I have another great passion in my life, Martial Arts. Since I was a boy, I have worked at different disciplines. I then went on to Karate in which I have practised several styles. My martial arts were an intrinsic part of my fitness training and my philosophy. As I travelled into my twenties I became quieter and extremely fit.

An interest in Ninjutsu developed and I then began to spend time developing skills in this art. Ninjutsu is much abused in the film industry. Indeed, there is an American practitioner and author of the art who has flouted and criticised the teachings of the Grand Master so publicly in the United States that he is now unable to return to Japan, for if he does he is unlikely to survive the wrath of trained and discreet ninja.

In Japan, the traditional dojos, (schools) take their art seriously and it is part of the daily life for many Japanese who treat their art with great respect and reverence. Most dojos have a Kamidana or altar area for praying and meditation.

I continued my training and during my first tour of Ripon, Yorkshire, had the opportunity to take leave to travel to Japan. I saved hard and travelled on a military indulgence flight to Hong Kong with a colleague from the same gymnasium also practising Karate and Kung Fu. I spent a few days sight-seeing before flying to Tokyo.

The experiences gained during this trip had a profound effect on me. Travelling around and camping in different areas I observed a culture that I could relate to and understand in a manner that made me feel as if the experience were a kind of homecoming.

It wasn't easy. Japan was not so set up for foreign travellers and there was hardly any Romanised signage, let alone English signage and I didn't know any Japanese characters.

I was also able to tie in my love of climbing here. Although I was travelling alone once I got to Japan, I took the opportunity to climb Fujiyama. It was quite different to my other climbing experiences and was not demanding on me. It was just a thoroughly enjoyable trip.

In Noda Shi province, the training was hard and brutal, but the people were gentle and generous by nature. The culture overwhelmed me. I learned so many new techniques that no other type of martial art would hold such an interest with me. There was a long history associated with the art and a survival discipline not found elsewhere. These were the people whom I could relate to; focused, gentle, laughing people who knew how to live. Time was allotted to work and training as well as meditation, relaxation and fun. It was difficult for me to return to the UK after such a profound experience. I had been invited back and I intended to go back.

I returned a couple of years later for a six-month trip and was received very well. By this time Bev was on the scene back in the UK in our ramshackle cottage and with a growing belly. I left for the six-month trip with just £800, which was all on the credit limit of my Access card. It was hard going. To make ends meet, I cleared out the lofts of the dojo, swept the dojo floor and walked the Grand Master's dogs. I had to make my money last, so I took lodgings with one of the senior instructors, Ishizuka and his family. I had a small room over some outbuildings with a tatami mat and a sleeping bag for a bed and a hosepipe in the yard for a shower. Sometimes the old grandmother of the house would take pity on me and bring me a bowl of boiled rice and vegetables. Every penny I had was going on training and postage to write home. I would sometimes go to the local post office with a handful of tiny yen coins and tip them on the counter and count out a pile enough to buy a single postage stamp. It was very expensive there for anything.

My frugal living and dedication paid handsome rewards to me. I was invited to take part in a documentary about the school for German television. It was a little disappointing as they filmed the rehearsal instead of the actual demonstration and they called me Jim instead of Martin, as I told them I worked in a gym and they had got a little confused. Still, it's great to show the kids, (now adults) sometimes. I was also asked to participate in a large demonstration in the local town, which I enjoyed immensely.

The training was full contact and it took its toll. I sustained a shoulder injury that I couldn't shake off. I daren't rest because I knew I only had limited time in Japan. The Grand Master, Dr. Masaaki Hatsumi, is also an osteopath, so he offered to treat my shoulder. I went to his little practice, which was lined with books and very small. As Dr. Hatsumi was treating me, he said "You Shodan!" I was a bit bemused and Dr. Hatsumi said again. "You, Shodan, work good." It was like winning a gold medal. I was being offered my black belt by the Grand Master himself and without being in a grading session. The gesture has meant more to me, even after all these years, than anything else I have worked for.

I did have regrets at not pursuing the SAS selection for a while but I was too close to the age bracket to go back after yet another injury right on 'Test Week', which had me limping for nearly eighteen months before I finally had surgery but my only real regret is not returning to Japan.

I arrived home from Japan a few weeks before our first child was born and we both got a shock. Bev wasn't expecting me home at all for a few days, when my face appeared at the window. She was startled to see a scrawny; haggard-looking man with wild hair peering at her, until recognition finally broke its way through. She waddled to the door and as I reached the doorway I stepped back in surprise. At three months pregnant, she had no hint of a bump, but now she looked like she had shoplifted a medicine ball. Bev said I was so thin it looked pitiful, but she couldn't get over how much hair I had. It must have been growing like a privet hedge. That was nothing to now, as I've got a head full of dreadlocks I've had for the last decade.

Life got back to normal and after Gemma was born in June, I lost no time getting us out and about. We were out on our bikes with Gemma in a papoose with a terry nappy wrapped around her neck to keep her head upright and we cycled everywhere. We made trips to the Roaches, the superb gritstone crags and boulders I had climbed as a boy. We left Gemma with unsuspecting climbers in the queue for some routes with instructions to give her a bottle of milk or some rusks if she became fretful while we climbed. It's not as bad as it sounds. A lot of the Roaches is one pitch climbing and many of the climbers were regulars. We used to lash the pushchair to a tree and Bev fed Gemma rusks while she was supposed to be belaying me. She'd have one hand on the rope and one on a feeder cup of milk and she'd be looking from Gemma to me throughout the climb. I just had to make sure I didn't slip when Gemma had her attention. Gemma climbed her first route at three years old in Norway and named it 'Burger' as that is pretty much what it resembled.

My climbing bug was back in full force and it would take me to the Alps, Norway, Austria, Canada and the USA over the coming years. I opted to specialise in adventure training and secured a posting to Norway in 1991. I learned an awful lot there and in little over a year gained qualifications across the board. I was still not keen on kayaking at that time due to a very bad experience during my PT Corps training when I was dumped out of my kayak in some heavy, white water in Wales as a novice and sustained a pretty rough hip injury from the rocks as I was swept off. It was just a bad judgement by the instructor with Grade 3 water and a group of novices who swam more than paddled. It took a long time but the kayaking confidence came back and I coached that for a while too.

A short while after my trip to Japan, I was accepted at the Army School of Physical Training in Aldershot. If I passed the year-long course, I would be re-badged from the Royal Engineers to the PT Corps and wear the 'crossed swords' cap badge and have the same emblem on my uniform. I was sorry in a way to leave the Royal Engineers behind. I loved being part of 38 Engineer Regiment. If I got through this, I was going to be posted out alone each time and 'attached' to regiments but not be wholly part of them. I did pass and I was posted to Dortmund in West Germany. It was a huge camp in a suburb called Brackel. There were two Royal Artillery regiments there, sharing the facilities. I was gym-based but still did what adventure training I could in my free time. The social-life was almost non-stop and exhausting. The terrorism from a campaign that was going on at the time was very unsettling, as it was very much aimed at families as well as combatants and it was also exciting as we were there when the Berlin Wall came down. Car horns blaring, people in the streets cheering and laughing, car lights flashing well into the night. This continued for weeks if a Trabant was seen driving through the city anywhere, car horns blaring and lights flashing again, people waving at the car's occupants. It was very special to be there then. By the time my next posting came through I wasn't leaving West Germany, just Germany.

Bev and I were ecstatic to be posted to Evje in Southern Norway. This tour was a real turning point for us. Our son was born in Lillehammer and given names that were popular with favourite mountaineering regions of ours; Rhys (Wales), Kyle, (Scotland) and our favourite, Håkon, which was suggested by the team of midwives at the hospital and had special significance for the Norway-UK bond as our Royal families are bound by marriage and it is a traditional name for their Crown Princes.

This was an Adventure Training post. I was learning more and teaching skiing, ski-mountaineering, rock and ice climbing and kayaking.

We made friends with a British geologist called Paul McCormick, who taught us a great deal about the country as well as its geology, which for Bev and I tied in nicely with our love of climbing. We began to see the appeal of life in 'Civi Street' and we both became restless. We were bound by financial commitments and the security we felt we had in the Army. It was heart-breaking to leave 'This Shining Land'. Indeed, Bev was truly inconsolable on the trip from Evje all the way to the ferry at Stavanger. She cried the entire way and I had to stop the camper at one point to try and get her to control it. She was heartbroken and was bereft for quite a long time after our return to the U.K.

We were posted back to Ripon, which we weren't pleased about initially, but it was a good adventure training opportunity. I started to really enjoy kayaking for the first time thanks to some training and tips from a friend and colleague, Frank Mingay. Here I was also taken under the wing of my adventure training and nature guru, Sandy Sanderson. Sandy had retired from the Army and was employed as a civilian instructor at the adventure training centre in Ripon. He was my confidant and an excellent teacher, my mentor in what was a difficult posting for us.

We were posted then to Joint Services Mountain Training Centre, (JSMTC) Kingussie in Scotland. It was a dream posting for us as far as the UK was concerned. We had always yearned for a posting back to Norway, which was impossible now, as cutbacks in defence spending had closed the Norway centres down. Our other dream posting would be to Canada, but I didn't have the rank for it yet probably due to my habit of not being 'backwards when coming forwards' or as Bev would say, perhaps slightly lacking in tact.

We loved the Highlands and I threw myself into my work with great zeal. I made some very close friends, funnily enough, civilians again, Wes and Kirsten. Wes worked at the centre as a store man and was my closest friend and was a man to bring perspective to life when things went wrong. We climbed together, got drunk together, escaped pub brawls together by literally crawling on our hands and knees behind the bar and out of the back door before the police arrived and spent time talking away the hours at weekends after Kirsten and Bev passed out on the sofa with their heads full of wine. We were sorry that those defence cutbacks caught up with us there too.

Bev had a wonderful job in the foothills of the Cairngorms as a reindeer herder and guide for the Cairngorm Reindeer Company and met many visitors that came to see them. It was the first time that she had really had experience in the hills on a daily basis and she loved it all year. The people who ran the two farms and centre (The Smiths) were lovely and helpful and lived for their herds and were generous to all the volunteers and staff in sharing their home and lives.

It was spectacular in the winter with racing, biting winds and not a soul to be seen anywhere. They all used to complain that it was like uphill step aerobics going out to find the herd when the snow drifted, but none of them would have swapped a single day of it.

The reindeer were a magical sight racing down the hillside with frosted ice covering their antlers and the whole herd coming to rest with steamy breaths puffing from their nostrils in the calm moments waiting to be fed a line of supplemented food so the herders could count and check on each of them. Each reindeer was named, which is unusual in agriculture, especially with 150 of them but this helped identify them and their calves and who they usually stood near so it was easier to spot if one was missing or sometimes trickier as antlers grew or fell off or winter coats moulted.

The climbers and hill walkers would pass by en route out to Cairn Gorm or the technical ice routes in the Corries and call out their greetings as they went. The reindeer largely ignored the throngs of skiers, but mainly because crowds and reindeer don't mix if the crowd is not under control, or would feed one of the reindeer a fatal sandwich or bag of crisps. Their diet was strict as they are ruminants and have very sensitive digestive systems.

In summer the hills were warm and thick with fragrant heather and the visitors would pour in by the hundreds. It was still lovely, but it didn't have the same atmosphere that the winter had. It was a case of nature allowing us to be there on sufferance in winter. Bev realised for the first time what it was that drew me to the lifestyle of climbing and mountaineering even though she had been climbing so much herself by now.

Bev later described that job she had to a very smartly dressed and glamorous young lady at the Sergeant's Mess Christmas Ball in Pirbright, Surrey. The young lady looked horrified at the whole story and said, "Why on earth would anyone want to work in a place like that?" Well, Bev by that time had done nearly twelve years worth of work at various desks and says 'you can keep it'. Each to their own, but she realised then that there are some things that just cannot be described to people who do not have a kind of empathy for what one is trying to tell. It's not that there is anything wrong with that, we all see other people doing things that we have no enthusiasm for nor understanding of.

Anyway, JSMTC, Kingussie was another victim of MoD cutbacks and closed. We left behind the mountains with the reindeer and our dear friends Wes and Kirsten. We moved to Wales and another adventure training centre. This time it was part of the Army Apprentice College at Arbourfield.

The Wales centre was annexed to it and I found it a little difficult to settle. I was under used and as I was dealing with recruits although I enjoyed seeing them develop their skills and character, was becoming restless for something more challenging in between

I walked and did basic rock climbing and grade I – II kayaking. I took every opportunity to make use of my skills, which I wasn't able to do on a day-to-day basis. I needed something to tax me here. I was very restless and talked about leaving the Army again.

Things were changing fast, and we felt that the changes were not going to do these young men and women any favours when things turned nasty. For instance, our unit was picked to try out a pilot scheme for the penalty cards.

If one of the staff started bawling out an apprentice for whatever reason and the apprentice felt aggrieved, they would hand the staff member a yellow card. That staff member would then have to 'be nice' for so many hours or stay away altogether. If they were shown the red card then that was it for the instructor for the rest of the day. No contact with the student was permitted for 24 hours. It seemed a bit like some of the modern parenting methods where the child seems to be in charge and the parents are afraid to say 'No!' What most people were wondering at the time was what would happen when these kids went to war, which of course they did with further problems in Iraq and Afghanistan thanks to the need for power changes, financial control, arms deals, infrastructure contracts and lithium. What a waste of life on all sides. Disillusion and realisation was flooding in on us.

In the end, I started buying boating magazines with some pipe dream of owning a yacht and sailing away. It was around now that a trip abroad would have been good for me or some staff training expedition in the Alps. I was discontent and beginning to mope and politically, we were opening our eyes and starting to feel very uncomfortable.

Chapter 3 - Alaska Calls

I had lately started a new dream to own a cruising boat, preferably a yacht. Occasionally I would buy a yachting or boat owner magazine and sigh over the articles and glossy photos. I had attended a RYA (Royal Yachting Association) Competent Crew Course at Gosport a few years before and had loved every minute. I toyed with the prospect of owning a real boat, not what was seen as a warm-up project with 'Wonky', a 14-foot shell of a fishing boat we accepted as a cast off and later off-loaded as a part finished project. We already knew that renovation and repair was expensive from that fiasco.

In early January 1998, I was away in fairyland with my magazines going through the classified ads. I came across an ad for a twelve metre converted fishing vessel, which I decided was my destiny to own. Bev had heard this scenario over and over so she paid me the usual lip service and went along with my enquiries although her thoughts were 'No Way!'

There was no possible way we could afford it, Bev told me. She was working as secretary in a psychiatric nursing home and her workload was increasing week by week as her manager had left. There was no time nor energy for a second job and childcare was scarce to non-existent back then. My work commitments were such that if she could get an evening job, I wouldn't be home all the time to take care of the children. Our bank manager, who was actually marvellous at juggling our commitments and salary, told us that we couldn't get a loan for the asking price and as the boat hadn't had a full survey and valuation we couldn't get a mortgage for it either. That was that. Bev actually felt quite sorry for me by then as I had my heart set on it. We looked around for something else.

The following month I asked Bev to call the owners of the boat we had asked about before. The way things were for Bev at work, she could do without discussing this matter again. By the time she got home every day she didn't even want to read her own mail anymore. I can remember Bev sighing heavily to let me know she was doing this under protest. The owners said it was still for sale. A feeling of dread went through Bev, as she knew this would lead to another search for a loan and some more bickering between us occasionally getting to a warmed up discussion and a positively volcanic row on a couple of sessions.

Bev passed the phone to me and I was looking very pleased and arranged a visit to see the vessel. Bev was now in what most couples would call - a mood! She huffed and stomped around while the discussion went on. I then hung up and told Bev that they had dropped the price by £3,000.00 and that we were going to see the vessel this week. I knew Bev was still reluctant about the debt but didn't push her too much, as I knew she was still a little prickly but she would come around. After managing to wriggle a day off work, she went along with it to keep the peace and that was enough for me.

We travelled down from Wales to Hayling Island to a pub a few miles from the boat yard and met the owner. We followed him in the thickest fog we have ever driven in to the scruffiest looking boat yard. The boatyard had around a hundred boats out of the water. The pontoons looked really dodgy and there was equally dodgy looking electric cabling strewn all over the yard and pontoons, sometimes different gauges of it carelessly taped end to end to keep a kettle going or try to run a crackly, fizzing television on the live-aboards that really shouldn't have been lived on all year but who cares as long as they paid their bill eventually. From this it didn't really set the best impression. I suppose like the promise of a very smart car at a bargain price but you find it tucked away at the rear of a breakers yard. It doesn't instil confidence.

This was all new to Bev and not that familiar to me and she was astounded to see 35ft yachts just propped up on a few logs. The owner told us that he was sorry we had come when the tide was out, as 'she' looks lovely afloat. (As if that was making any difference to Bev). We walked off down the pontoon skipping over broken or sagging planks trying to see which one it might be. Bev said she could have fallen off the pontoon when she saw her.

Last Freedom was a forty-foot motor vessel made of marine-ply on pitched pine with a full epoxy sheath that had been completed in the last season. She was freshly painted and had quite a substantial wheelhouse as well as a forward saloon below. The galley was a good size, the engine room was quite roomy and there was a single cabin opposite the galley and a double cabin aft. There was also a shower room with basin and large surface and a sea toilet. There was even a small automatic washing machine. The bilge was freshly painted and looked dry.

Bev and I went out on deck to discuss the matter seriously in private. We burst out laughing and exclaimed, "Bloody hell!" then returned to the wheelhouse to tell the owner that we would take it.

The hull alone as a shell was worth the asking price. I would like to point out at this stage though that it still needed a lot of work on it. We also had little clue what we were doing back then. We didn't get a survey done. The 240volt and 12volt electrics had to be re-done and there is no plumbing at all so we still needed water tanks, plumbing, seacocks and piping as well as holding tanks and a shower.

Our first night aboard after the sale was a shock. Water poured, not dripped onto our bunk and when Bev unplugged the toaster in the galley, the entire bulkhead panel came with it. "Martin dearest, I'm standing here holding a fucking wall in my hand!" Oh, she was so funny that day.

A year on we were still using head torches and candles in part of the boat and we still had to carry containers of water aboard and heat it on the stove. It was perfectly cosy and comfortable especially when the showers in the boat yard were working! When agreeing to buy the boat I promised that there would be no more expeditions, as I wouldn't feel the need if I had the boat to work on. I also told Bev that I would no longer need to buy any more equipment so we should scrape through the re-payments.

It had been a very steep learning curve, as neither of us had a nautical bone in our bodies. To my credit, I have taken a competent crew course (very basic qualification) and navigation of course is already very good but on land, not marine navigation. To Bev's credit, she did grow up by the sea in Hastings and Brighton so she would be good at sun bathing on the deck by the time we get to 'The Med' and beach combing on the islands (dream on!).

We heard second hand a quote made by many boat owners. "Owning a boat is like taking a cold shower, fully clothed whilst tearing up twenty pound notes!"

It's true! We'd hardly been out in the bloody thing since we had it. In winter it was freezing until we put on the diesel heater in the evening and if the wind kicked up, the heater reversed the flow of the fumes and sucked the smoke into the boat, so we opened all the hatches and we were freezing again. In summer it was wonderful, the milk went off, we all got wood shavings in our eyes or glued ourselves up in resin. We ripped through a list of renovating tasks, drank wine, talked to other boaties all day, rowed around the marina in the dinghy and sat on deck with paint and wood stain on our hands and feet until the dew came in. Everything 'BOAT' costs double what it does for 'CAR' even though much of it can be used for either. The mooring fees are crippling and we would have fought in the street with anyone who wanted us to part with her.

I had resigned myself to small home-based expeditions for the next four years whilst Bev was resigning herself to feeding the family on beans on toast for four years. Now bearing in mind this was only February 1998 when all this started with the boat and the promises were still fresh. Incidentally, the boatyard as it was is nothing like that today. The Hayling Yacht Company has scrubbed up extremely well and we'd be happy to moor there again if it suited the boat we have now.

I was then contacted in early March 98, (This is four weeks after the promise to stay home!) by Captain Conrad Lightwood of 1 Princess of Wales Royal Regiment based in Canterbury. He gave me a brief outline of the expedition he was putting together in Alaska. The aim was to climb to the summit of Denali (Mount McKinley, as it was officially titled at that time) make the descent then go on to a glacial river, the Susitna and paddle by kayak in Grade iv-v water the 150 miles to the Cook Inlet.

Denali was a mountain that I had wanted to climb for a number of years, but I was well aware of the mountain's very serious reputation having spoken of it with climbers who had made expeditions there. I asked for the literature to be sent on so that I could look at it in more detail before I made a decision.

Bev thought there was absolutely no point in bringing up the subjects of boats and promises. She knew that as long as the expedition was sound and my Unit approved loaning me to another Regiment that I would be going. Bev told me later that she was thinking to herself at the time that of all the expeditions that could land in my lap, it had to be an attempt at Denali. Bev was resigned to it immediately and also a little concerned, as she knew it was a serious mountain. We'd muddle through financially. Bev's only real concern at this stage was whom I would be going with. She didn't know of any of the team members, never heard of them, (Nor had I for that matter), and pointed out that every past expedition had at least a couple of members that I knew and had climbed with. I said we would both have to wait and see.

As I agreed to join the team at the eleventh hour the expedition had already been set up and told Bev I was confident that everything was in hand already and that the team had been vetted by the Subject Matter Expert at divisional level. If the ATFA (Adventure Training Form Alfa) was completed, everything was covered, most of it already organised and only being three months away, probably a great deal of the kit required was already sitting there waiting to be distributed. Bev felt a bit easier but not comfortable.

The paperwork arrived and it all seemed OK. The ATFA requirements looked to have been covered and most of the finance was in place but with personal contributions required towards the costs. I had very little gear that I needed to purchase, so it wasn't so bad. If I was really pushed for any kit, I could draw kit from the Thatcham caves. As it was, I had gear spilling out of boxes all over the garage.

The idea was to take a team of suitably pre-selected soldiers, who had met the minimum requirements of the ATFA for the expedition for further expedition training and raise some money for charity in the process. Bev read through the paperwork with me and wasn't at all pleased when she saw the nominal roll, which included the date of birth for each member. Some of the team members seemed awfully young that she doubted how much experience they could have gained even at novice level. To her way of thinking there are degrees of novice. There are those who don't know an ice axe from a set of crampons to those who have had some minor expedition experience and those that have a fairly comfortable working knowledge and experience of their equipment and remoteness and are working towards their next level.

Bev went through the unrestricted press release again. Some of the names had changed now from the original nominal roll on the Restricted documents dated 05 March 1998. Sergeant A.R. Alexander had been replaced by Sergeant Johnny Johnston and I had been such a late addition that it did not include my Army number nor date of birth. So Johnny Johnston was also a late-comer to the expedition. One member was only 18 years old. Questions were streaming from her but until I met the team and liaised with Captain Conrad Lightwood I was unable to answer many of them.

One of the criteria was that it was a partial training expedition, so of course there had to be less experienced personnel taking part. The emphasis was on training, remote, hostile, leadership, team-building, endurance, survival, yah-di-dah...

The itinerary was dated Dec 1997 and had a start date of 30 May 1998 for the 2 man advance party and 1 June 1998 for the main party with all returning together at Heathrow on 11 July 1998.

The total estimated expenditure was to be £18,944.43. This included transport, (transfers, flights, taxis, ski plane hire et al.), insurances, permits, accommodation, food and some equipment hire.

Also in the package was some information about the routes on the mountain, specifically The West Rib and The West Buttress. There was also an expedition report by two climbers: Dean James and Simon Adshead dated 1988.

What made interesting reading was the profiles of each of our team members, which becomes important later.

The Summit to the Sea information disseminated included information such as:

Leadership:

i/c*: Capt C Lightwood has wide experience of white water kayaking and mountaineering in the U.K. and overseas and intends to take his ML(W) assessment in the 97/98 season.

This means that as of the document publication date of 8 Feb 1998, he is still not winter qualified and therefore not able to lead a rope team. He must qualify before the expedition and in winter conditions or he will not meet the requirements of the ATFA. (This was not missed when Bev read the document and sat shaking her head almost imperceptibly.)

2i/c*: Sergeant Alexander is the 2nd instructor.

This one was more interesting in that it cites clearly right at the beginning of the profile that he is not winter qualified. He has worked as an instructor on various expeditions and is 'Summer' qualified. He has a wide personal experience on snow, rock and ice.

Bev said that this actually says nothing, explains nothing, and is a non-statement. I could see the warning signs in Bev; we were heading for a real bust up. She was quiet and fault-finding as if she were merely reading a draft report that needed editing by her. Is he a skier, has he done summer work in Chamonix and walked on the Mer de Glace? It says nothing of actual winter mountaineering skills whether qualified or not.

Sergeant Alexander was not going now anyway, so who was the 2i/c going to be in the end? It was a fair question. I knew it wasn't me. It would be Sergeant Alexander's replacement, (Johnny or the other officer in the team if he had some experience). I couldn't answer her question then. The bust up didn't come, she just seemed to fizzle out and brood a while, the silence was safer for now like she was letting it marinate.

I said she was finding things to worry about now and asked what the matter with her was. She said she honestly didn't know and put the uneasiness aside. I explained that Conrad Lightwood had climbed on Denali before so he knew from experience how to deal with the mountain and he knew what he was doing when he put the team together.

Conrad hadn't reached the summit on that occasion but that was quite a common occurrence. That began to worry her too. Was this chap putting together the expedition for his own personal ambition to reach the summit no matter what? She kept this rather uncharitable thought to herself for a while. She didn't want to bring me down into a black mood about the whole affair and decided she was being unreasonable in her opinions.

Being fair to Conrad at that point, his previous expedition report had said he had made it to 20,000ft, just below the summit. That was an extremely close summit bid and that experience is not to be sniffed at.

There were at least half that don't make it that far. It was far too premature to speculate on anything, Bev and I would have to wait until I had met Conrad and the team before she got her answers. Regardless of the concerns, I was going and that was that. It was just a matter of smoothing things domestically before I left. Whatever was lacking in the expedition at this point could very soon be put into place. I knew I'd be fine, so did she. It was just the usual build up of anxiety before a big trip or tour.

As it was, the suggested experience of the team would make up a typical guided party and offer some fantastic training experience for them all.

* i/c - in command, 2i/c - 2nd in command, ML Winter - Mountain Leader, (Winter) Award through the MLTB (Mountain Leader Training Board).

As the date for expedition closed in, more paper work arrived. Conrad and I built up a good rapport by correspondence. I was put at ease by the amount of information coming through and feeling more confident in Conrad as a leader. It really made a nice change not to keep chasing information on minutiae as well as all the major hurdles.

I was invited for a two-day dry training session at Canterbury where I would meet the other team members. Bev was very relieved that I went along, as she wanted my mind, (and hers) put at rest regarding the experience of the team. She also wanted her mind put at rest when I came home to tell her everyone is up to the job and everything is being well organised and the expedition leader isn't a maniac who is going to lead everyone over the edge like lemmings.

The Princess of Wales Royal Regiment (PWRR) had been on a tour of duty in Northern Ireland for several months. The platoon commanded by Captain Conrad Lightwood, spent their off-duty hours passing the dragging hours by watching television, writing letters to home, listening to music and planning for an expedition beyond their imagination.

Conrad had a passion for adventure. His ideal world would be to hop from one expedition to another. It wouldn't matter whether it was climbing, walking, exploring or kayaking. He is not alone in this. Anyone in the 'adventure world' would understand this. It is the ultimate challenge to head into the unknown, whether it is in location or one's own abilities. There is a sensation of freedom in being in a remote place with a rucksack and a few like-minded pals to share the 'fun' and being outside one's comfort zone from time to time makes memories and is great old-fashioned character-building stuff.

Conrad had been part of an expedition to Denali, in the Denali National Park, Alaska some time before. It gnawed away at him that he hadn't made the summit. He felt sure that it was within his capabilities to get to the top. It would really be something to lead an expedition on the mountain.

The seed was sown and he put his mind to thinking about how he would put an expedition together and whom he could interest with his idea. He chatted with the men about the idea and found that some of them were very keen. Although none had any idea how to climb or kayak, they were prepared to apply for a place and learn a few skills in readiness for their new adventure, and Conrad is very charming and persuasive.

Adventurous Training in the Army is an ideal vehicle for bringing to the fore many qualities that are difficult to assess in military training alone, which is why it has been such a powerful training tool for so long. During the Adventure Training phase of basic training, recruits and apprentices are put through their paces with rock climbing, kayaking and hill walking expeditions. Their leadership and initiative is far more easily assessed, as is their attitude and aptitude for teamwork. It gives the new soldiers a chance to step out of the military environment and allow their own individual personalities to come to the surface. It is the only area of training where moral behaviour and development can be observed and assessed.

Soldiers of all ranks can be put together into a team and military rank can also be side-lined for the duration of an expedition. The expedition leader and his/her second in command make the decisions and pass on the instructions. These are positions of qualification and experience not rank, although the usual respectful addressing observations are supposed to be continued they tend to be far less formal in the field. Another unusual factor with adventurous training is that it combines the forces, as the skills very frequently cross over. This also enables the funding to be spread. Although essentially the MoD is all one pot, each of the services allocates finances differently.

Many courses and their centres are run as 'Joint Service' operations. Indeed, in Norway before its closure, the British Mountain Training Centre had instructors from the Navy, Army, Royal Marines and Air Force (Personal note to ex-submariner friend, Navy is listed first as the Senior Service!) The forces also employ civilian instructors with the appropriate requirements, which gives the training a very different 'feel' to other military training.

An expedition could be a simple, locally based, one day affair of any activity, climbing, walking, caving, sailing, sub-aqua diving, skiing et al. Or it could involve greater logistics for something of the nature of this story; international travel and visas, weeks or months away from one's unit and costs of several thousands of pounds.

At the other end of the scale, Adventurous Training provides excellent training and experience for specialists and Special Forces and Martin is fortunate to have done a lot of work in this area and made many friends over the years. The higher-level training is executed through expeditions and specific courses, many with qualifications at the end of them. The training is conducted in more remote and hostile environments for much longer periods and demands higher levels of competence, skill and stamina both physical and mental, which comes with the years of experience the Army (and other services) allowed in this job.

The instructors too, are more highly qualified and experienced, usually moving beyond the qualifications that the forces are able to offer. Many are qualified through civilian centres, where their experience is scrutinized through their logbooks and previous qualifications. Their practical skills are tested with little margin for error, as the candidates would be responsible for students or clients exposed to various levels of hazards.

Achieving qualifications in this area of work is much like university, in that more credibility is often given to those who have trained and qualified through the most prestigious centres. This may not be the right way to look at the centres but it happens. Those who qualify through smaller centres deserve no less merit than those who go through the big national centres. Adventure Training though is an area where weaknesses and strengths of all kinds are soon found out. It requires good emotional balance.

Martin was also very fortunate that the Army sent him to Plas-y-Brenin, Glenmore Lodge and Ballachulish and for his Mountain Instructor Certificate (MIC) he was very proud to have been tested and passed by Alan Fyffe, who by reputation was a fearsome task master and Martin was the only Army candidate that Alan passed first time up to that point.

The use of civilian centres and direct employment of civilian instructors is common and sensible, as there is a wealth of knowledge and experience amongst civilians to pass on and it's good to get a non-military presence to keep things integrated. It's easy to lose touch with civilian life, even living amongst it.

Most outdoor pursuits governing bodies in the U.K. have very stringent guidelines regarding their qualification remits. Their assessments are set up to prevent anyone not capable of gaining a qualification from slipping through the net. Subsequently, the candidate would have to re-train and return for reassessment, usually after a reasonable length of time and more experiences recorded in their log book.

Most of these organisations have a high number of military candidates on their courses. The military help to fund these pursuits, and occasionally, will allow them to be conducted during duty time. All qualified instructors gained will, eventually become assets to various regiments or units. The activities cover all kinds of outdoor activities such as climbing and mountaineering, alpine skiing, Nordic skiing, kayaking (both river and sea), sailing, caving, survival etc. In some conflict theatres, adventure training has been without question, invaluable.

It is historical fact that the armies of foreign countries have never succeeded in Afghanistan in over 200 years of conflicts, as they just cannot overcome the pockets of resistance in outlying areas and the mountainous terrain and the myriad of political and religious factions. However, being able to operate in these areas and gather intelligence, carry out smaller operations in hostile terrain is essential to Allied Government aims and objectives, especially in training the local forces and authorities to self-manage. Funding of these conflicts is well supported but we won't go into that here, just suffice to say that we are all much better aware of how wars are 'made' and the only winners are the bankers.

The modern Armed Forces of the West recognise this type of experience and adventure training is now of more importance in shaping a soldier for a combatant role overseas. Whether or not these problems will ever be overcome by the UN etc. is not for us to say. Everyone knows it has more to do with assets, which are switching from oil to lithium, cobalt and other precious, industrial metals and minerals. Perhaps geology is the new career of choice to bring the human planet to its knees and sod everything else about its eco-system.

If these problems will ever be overcome we cannot tell, it is a complex and geographically spreading problem but the skills gained in 'Adventure Training' are clearly not about being on a woolly-hatted 'jolly' for a few weeks, they are utilised as deadly serious applications of experience.

Many adventure trainers spend more than usual amounts of time away from their units, homes and families and still have to meet their mainstream military training requirements throughout the year.

An expedition idea can be submitted by anyone of any rank. It is not always a requirement of a regiment or corps to put one together for its personnel.

Back in Northern Ireland Conrad made his decision and on return to Canterbury put his energy into the expedition. The expedition wouldn't do his career any harm if it went well. It was a big under-taking and involved a great deal of administrative juggling. Organising something of that magnitude, leading it, completing it and retuning with soldiers that could well go on to become active adventurers themselves as a result of the climbing and kayaking would be a 'Brownie Point' for most. Anyone would like it on record and raising some money for charity is good publicity for the military and the charity involved; everyone's a winner. There has been a lot of money raised for charity through the military not just for the military.

Conrad had a few hurdles to get over before he could fly off to Alaska with his team. The expedition needed its passport – the ATFA, the all powerful document of many pages and tasks.

I had asked about it and Conrad had told me it was all in order but in fact it wasn't, as we all discovered much later. The powers that be at 4 Div. Aldershot, who issued the ATFA and expected all aspects to be covered, required three rope leaders, which is quite right. A rope leader is a properly qualified and experienced climber who supervises those on his/her rope team. The rope team is chosen, which is most usually three people and that team usually stays the same throughout the climb, though changes do have to be made for various reasons sometimes.

Conrad put himself down as one on the express condition that he passed his Joint Service Mountain Expedition Leader (Winter) course, (JSMEL(W)) referred to as 'Jesmel-winter'. The forces love initials and acronyms. This condition was essential and became very important later.

Conrad went to Scotland, as he promised Colonel Harrison, (who was part of the power we are referring to at the time) he would and took his JSMEL (W) course but failed it abysmally. In fact the course report read so poorly that the assessor remembered him as one of the worst candidates he had ever had. Perhaps it was the pressure of the dates looming up when he needed to be ready or that he didn't want to miss out on a second crack at the summit, he had already got so far and everyone else was preparing too.

He really didn't want the expedition to fold before it had begun. Conrad clearly knew he was capable, he must have felt that he had just had a bad course or assessment. We've all had set-backs and it hasn't upset his subsequent career with adventure training. Indeed, most of us know our failures are some of our most excellent lessons in life.

Another body who was involved in the background of the expedition was Joint Services Mountain Training Centre, Tywyn, North Wales, Major Edward Simpson, who was running the centre had some association with Conrad's training and had spoken with Colonel Harrison about the expedition.

Conrad's failure of his JSMEL (W) seemed to go un-noticed by Major Edward Simpson at the time although it was he who had to read and sign the course reports for the candidates, including Conrad's. This is the safety net. This is perhaps one of the biggest flaws there was in the system. This is significant in that now is the time the expedition is stopped in its tracks. This should have been reported to Colonel Harrison at 4 Div. Aldershot. If Simpson didn't pull the plug at this stage, then Colonel Harrison could have, if he'd known. Still in the training stage, still in the UK, still before kit issue, before time, expense, permissions, requests, before money is spent and families start to fret and keep looking at the countdown on the calendar. It only need be a postponement. If everyone is enthusiastic it can go a couple of weeks later, it can go next summer, when everyone has trained thoroughly and gelled as a team.

Nobody knows what went wrong here. This is where we draw our own conclusions, speculate, calculate, imagine and 'think' we know exactly what went wrong. Everyone who was doing wrong got worse here. How and why is long past and isn't difficult to work out but why label it, name it and go on? Moving on.

Edward Simpson curiously enough was said to be a 'Subject Matter Expert' for the same expedition and knew perfectly well the ratios for rope teams in winter mountaineering and knew the implications if Conrad failed. Edward Simpson had long experience in adventure training and loved it too. He was a very popular fellow, very social and deadly self-preserving.

Somehow, the information that Edward Simpson now held about Conrad's JSMEL failure did not reach Colonel Harrison even though he and Edward Simpson were often in communication together. Edward Simpson has been part of an official governing body for some time and during the Board of Inquiry regarding this expedition did not fail to ensure his solicitor was right at his elbow. Regardless of that, these are the facts related to Bev during her enquiries and they cannot be denied as they are a matter of record and there are plenty of documents to find that have to disappear, as did the PXR (Post Expedition Report) that Army records seem to have decided does not exist any longer. Bev tried to use the Freedom of Information Act to try to retrieve the PXR in 2013 but was told that there was no record of any expedition called Summit to the Sea. It did, of course exist because so many people were involved and the press sent the story of it around the world.

Bev did not sign anything, so anything she was told was given freely and with full knowledge of the fact that it would be passed on and used to support this book. She was overwhelmed by what people gave her from restricted documents to information on confidential phone calls. It just seemed to a lot of people at all levels in the system that what eventually happened after return from the expedition was as wrong as what happened on the mountain and before.

Edward Simpson's part in this is crucial (or his lack of it). Perhaps in the day to day running of his centre, he just forgot the report or made a terrible error in not reporting it. Whichever it was he had to cover it up, which exacerbated the whole thing. Only Edward Simpson can know but he recovered his career thankfully, if not his memory of the important report. But back to the expedition prep.

Another condition to be met for the ATFA and 4 Div. was that 'all' team members pass their Introduction to Winter Mountaineering at the Joint Services Mountain Training Centre in Ballachulish, Scotland. The centre there is excellent and so is the staff, so a winter course there stands any novice in good stead for an expedition. I know the syllabus very well and it is an excellent vehicle for moving into more challenging mountaineering. The staff there, like all centres want a candidate to pass, so will help them as far as they can to do that but they cannot control the climate.

The problem here was that only Steve Brown and Gaz Keep from the group went to Scotland and on top of that there was not a snowflake on that side of Scotland when they arrived so they had to follow the syllabus for the summer course instead. It is better than nothing according to a spokesperson at 4 Div, but nothing like what was required for the expedition to leave the country, let alone a mountain like Denali. It certainly didn't cover the ATFA. All these little draw backs were somehow hidden from 4 Div via the centre at Tywyn.

The way this happened was that Conrad in Canterbury would call Colonel Harrison in Aldershot to give him an up-date on the progress of preparations and by 'adapting phrases' to suit the question, Conrad was able to avoid having to confirm the aspects that would halt the expedition. That he had failed his course and was therefore not able to lead a rope team and that none of his men had actually done the winter mountaineering training. For example, Colonel Harrison may ask, "Have you been to Ballachulish to do the JSMEL training?"

To which, Conrad would be able to answer truthfully, "Yes."

And then be able to continue saying things about the course and weather etc. but not actually be required to say that he failed. Colonel Harrison would be happy, thinking that, as a fellow officer, Conrad was being diligent in his communications and up-dates and he trusted Conrad's word. This was also the scenario for the failure of the rest of Conrad's men slipping through the net. Conrad would communicate by phone, not have to lie about anything and keep 4 Div informed. The safety net part was what was not forth-coming from Edward Simpson's Dept. in Wales, which is the 'written confirmation' part - the reporting or warning that 4. Div should have had. The Board of Inquiry later would or would not have the answers as to why the rest of the team didn't go to Scotland or any other centre for training.

Fortunately, what happened over the expedition and following investigations and inquiry was the catalyst for change throughout the MoD, in that evidence must be provided to support any such application. The 'gentlemen's agreement' type of communicating ceased to exist, as did a few careers but only those of the injured, sadly and they were damned lucky.

A lot of kit had to be borrowed from the stores at Thatcham, a vast Aladdin's Cave of equipment that anyone in the military may ever need for any occurrence. The equipment had to be insured at the expense of the expedition and personal equipment had to be insured under a separate policy within the expedition costs. Conrad was acutely aware of the fact that any more increases in the personal contributions from the team would put the whole thing into jeopardy. Mountaineering like many other extreme activities is expensive and he was asking novices and lower ranks on very modest wages to put up a lot of cash, many of whom were on a lot less each month than he. Conrad knew he was asking a lot and he did his best to keep costs down for everyone.

We were to stay in the States for over a month with only around $250 each spending money. The funding from H.Q. 4 Div. would be 1/3, 1 Princess of Wales Royal Regiment and/or sponsorship would be 1/3 and personal contribution would be 1/3.

To make matters worse one chap who was to be a rope leader withdrew. He was a chap from the RAF and I don't know why he backed out, although I did make a few enquiries through my colleagues in the network, I was unable to get any information. Conrad was in danger of seeing the expedition fold. He trawled for a rope leader on the signal network. We found out after the exped, a couple of my friends and previous colleagues had been approached but had turned it down. One of them was a Scottish colleague I had worked with in Norway and I wish he had told me why he backed out.

I'm not saying that I would have withdrawn, I don't know that but I certainly would have taken a stronger stance with regard to my role. I was a guest on someone else's expedition and that is very different to being within one's own team. I may be needed but I am still there on sufferance of the leader.

After the RAF man withdrew Conrad turned to his friend in the system, Edward Simpson for some suggestions. Eventually, it seems I was recommended, though if I had known who it was that came up with the recommendation it would have set alarm bells ringing with all of us.

I wouldn't trust Edward Simpson any further than I could spit. He may be many good things to a good many people but my personal experience leads me to think he's thoroughly unscrupulous and untrustworthy. I had been under his command in Ripon and in Canada and on both occasions found him to be two-faced and his word unreliable. He had no problems with me when he was in Ripon. On the contrary, I was keen, ambitious and reliable. I did my job, went home and kept out of trouble. I had a lot to learn and benefitted from the experience of my friends and colleagues there.

My arrival in Canada for four months was different. I had only been there a day and hadn't even arrived at my final destination. I was in a kind of transit camp at what is known as BATUS (British Army Training Unit, Suffield) in Medicine Hat and was invited out by a few guys there before I travelled on to Trail's End near Canmore in the Rockies. I ended up in trouble for hitting a Warrant Officer who had spent several hours running me down and my Corps. I cannot drink, I was fit and metabolise alcohol quickly and end up sick within a few hours.

We were both drunk and the Warrant Officer picked up a fork and moved towards me. It was too late for the other guy; he was on the floor before he knew what had happened. I walked out with the praise of the waitress for dealing with the guy who was heading for trouble with her. As far as I was concerned, I had put up with a great deal of extreme verbal provocation over some hours and I didn't actually do anything until I was being physically attacked for answering back at last. My mistake was to hit up the ranks and it got me a reputation for not respecting or accepting authority. A big misconception, as I do respect it but with me it's conditional, which isn't a great attitude for a soldier.

I saw through a few people, as being bullies, untrustworthy and blinkered by their own ambition. Quite rightly, these people shouldn't hold these positions of rank or authority but we all know people like that and it's not a perfect world. I am by no means a loose cannon as I was described but I don't suffer fools gladly, especially when the affect is widespread. I tended to avoid these people but didn't hold back anything of my opinions if they crossed me. I feel I stayed true to my own character and scruples and I admit I was unyielding when I could have given a little. Call it tenacity or stubbornness, it did me no favours, and it cost me promotion for a good number of years. I can see things from different angles now and sometimes yield under pressures of a more subtle kind from family nowadays. I'm not surrounded by a vast network of ambition and its pressures.

Edward Simpson was one of those officers I felt shouldn't have been where he was. According to Noel Godfrey, who was a P.T.Corps man during Edward Simpson's earlier days, Edward came to the P.T.Corps through the back door so to speak by way of policy changes meaning that his role was swept up when the P.T. Corps included individuals in Army education. He didn't have to go through the twelve months of courses and final selection to get in. A change in policy and he was there. It wasn't his fault, he was just lucky but it rankles with a lot of people.

The P.T. Corps is not open to recruits. The course is now much shorter but candidates (or probationers, as they're called) still have to be released from Army units all over to be allowed to do the course and if they make the grade they pass in. They have to be 'squeaky clean' in their administration, do lots of extra duties like stagging on guard and working the bar in the mess regardless of what rank they are in their previous unit.

These are duties usually performed by them in the past at lower ranks but they still need to get their course notes done, lectures prepared and perform physically at their peak throughout the months.

My feelings about Edward Simpson were not based on his transfer to the Corps, as I didn't meet Noel Godfrey until long after the accident and I was close to leaving the Army, so I didn't know how he came to be a P.T.Corps officer. I only know from my experience of his management that I knew not to trust him myself. However, he's a popular man and many others have been lucky enough to know his gregarious and social side. No doubt I will have crowds of supporters and fondest friends wanting to beat my door down in his defence but I am talking about me and my experience of him, nobody else's.

I felt he was not true to his word, insincere in his working relationships and not brave enough to look after his own men when a different Warrant Officer was misappropriating their funds and proof provided. Edward wanted a smooth passage; I can understand that, I just didn't like it.

My arrival in Canada caused a great deal of trouble. It was only one punch. I didn't see myself as a crook. It was an honest punch; I didn't steal anything or cheat anyone. Although I hated to admit it, I was in the wrong for the punch and had let myself down. I got my dressing down from Edward Simpson when I finally arrived at the camp and under his command again. I thought that was that and moved on. I spent the next several months there thinking we were getting on well. I worked hard and did my job thoroughly, met a load of great friends and thought the tour had gone well apart from a series of incidents which put me in a sticky situation. A group of the staff approached me as their line manager (for want of a better description) complaining that our boss in camp, (another non-commissioned officer of higher rank than myself) had been stealing funds, rations and making excessive personal use of the camp vehicles leaving staff stuck in camp. This was a big deal but they were sure of their facts and had been gathering evidence before approaching me.

So, here I was already in trouble about to cause more but I had no choice. I reported the concerns and offered the evidence to Major Edward Simpson officially and hoped it would be dealt with without fuss. I made enquiries a week or so later on behalf of the guys in camp and was told to leave it alone and get on with my job. We all just got on with it and watched small amounts of money disappear and listened to the frustrated cook about minor raids on his stores. I was told again to back off and it was clear we could do nothing. We just didn't understand why Major Edward Simpson didn't act.

I got a damning report from Edward Simpson after he had told me to my face just before I left Canada what a great job I had done during the tour and how pleased he was with me and the little 'bar fracas' would blow over. The report sowed the seed for an undeserved reputation for flouting authority and also sowed the seed for a Court Martial and certainly helped to 'feed' the prosecution preparations.

For eighteen months, my Commanding Officer in the U.K. did what he could to help me fight the charges and help to redress the report from Major Edward Simpson. My C.O. helped to find witnesses and obtain reports from Canada and give support to Bev who was very worried by the possible bleak future. He really went out of his way to help. It was far beyond his duty and we are grateful to him. I was in serious trouble at this point. They were talking a two-year prison term in Colchester Military Prison and Dishonourable Discharge for one un-premeditated punch.

The support was extremely helpful and put me back onto an even keel with my career in adventurous training. The inflated charges against me dwindled as witness after witness came forward on my behalf and statements were submitted. In the end there was no Court Martial. I was on the carpet in front of my Commanding Officer for a sound 'bollocking' and I was fined four days pay. If the prosecution had its way, I could have been looking at two years. It turned out that I had enough objective witnesses to support my plea of self-defence and it was only one punch. I didn't try to hit him again. I just walked way.

This was a blow for Edward Simpson and the Intelligence Corps Warrant Officer but as the events that followed the expedition unfolded both Edward Simpson and the Intelligence Corps were going to cross my path again.

If this part of the story doesn't seem relevant to anything now, I make connections later to it, especially with the Intelligence Corps.

So, I came to be on the expedition through the normal system but on recommendation of somebody that would have caused me to feel very uncomfortable if had known he was involved, but I didn't find this out until Canterbury.

I arrived in Canterbury to find the kit being issued. I sat on a chair in the corner of a two-tone grey room. There were quite a lot of boxes in it. They were all addressed to Capt. C. Lightwood; I thought they were all from Thatcham. I told Conrad that I would not need anything from Thatcham, as I prefer my own gear.

There was certainly nothing wrong with the Thatcham equipment, it was fit for its purpose and in pretty good condition, even if some of it had been used before, a lot of it was new. I had a look at some of the gear and it was no different to anything I'd pay good money for in a climbing shop. It's just that when you are in a 'trade' you prefer your own tools.

There were various team members hovering around in the room waiting for their kit but I wasn't introduced to anyone. The whole thing looked to be a real muddle with gear all over the place and people coming and going. I sat and waited for something to happen and began to wonder why I was here, especially as my boss was pushed for staff back in Wales and had 'indulged' me with the meet.

Conrad was in the room generally over-seeing things and making some conversation with the lads and myself. I felt that I wasn't involved in anything and wasn't asked anything about my climbing or background.

Come lunchtime, we went for a bite to eat and returned to look in on the first aid lecture. It was taken by one of the unit medics from what I could gather and seemed to be pointing out the basics of altitude sickness and hypothermia. It didn't bear much relevance to high level mountaineering to the degree we would be experiencing, just the run-of-the-mill kind of thing that would be given on any exped. lecture. About two-thirds of the way through the lecture they took a break. I seized upon the opportunity to ask Conrad the questions that had been forming in my mind before and since my arrival.

We stood by the widow-sill and I gestured over to Luke Mills (Millsy). "What's with the guy with the lip?" I was concerned because Millsy appeared to have his bottom jaw slightly protruding and didn't seem to have very articulate speech. His bottom lip looked a bit swollen and I thought it would be a problem with frost injury and infection.

"Yeah, don't worry, he's fine," replied Conrad. "He's always been like that, he'll be O.K." He went on, "They've all done their training up in Scotland over the winter at Ballachulish." This was a big reassurance to me, as I knew the guys up there and the syllabus. It pretty much put my mind at rest that they all had a good in-depth knowledge at a basic level for the task ahead, or so I thought. I had no reason to believe that Conrad had just 'misled' me in exactly the same way he had done with Colonel Harrison.

Conrad then pointed out that Johnny and Gaz had done some extra training and that Johnny had his Mountain Leader (Winter), ML (W). Johnny was in fact with the Parachute Regiment and not part of 1 Princess of Wales Royal Regiment.

I went on, "I noticed that you didn't have helmets on the kit list, how come?"

"I've been in touch with the Rangers over there and they told me that it wasn't necessary to take them to reduce the burden of weight."

This surprised me a good deal because it was something I always took; in fact I had never climbed on a mountain or a rock without one whilst working. All my students wore them; everyone I knew in climbing wore their helmet. I did say I would be taking mine.

Then I got an even bigger surprise. "How did you get my name for the trip?" I asked

"Oh, Major Edward Simpson said you'd be a good rope leader now that you've calmed down a bit." Said Conrad.

I bit my lip and was a little disconcerted by the recommendation. It puzzled me. Of course he'd be fair in the recommendation, I knew that but the reference to my long past and brief behaviour I thought unnecessary and I expect that Conrad had probably got the whole of Edward Simpson's version before I met him. I didn't feel at a disadvantage, I just thought that Conrad would have the wrong impression of me but I took a moment to consider whether I cared or not and decided I didn't. I remembered thinking that I truly didn't care and felt lighter in myself as a result. It hadn't occurred to me to be bothered about it before apart from the time I was waiting for the non-existent Court Martial.

I said that I was fairly comfortable with what was going on and that as I wasn't involved in any of the teaching at this stage; I might head back to Wales. Conrad said that would be fine and invited me to a training session if I could make it in Somerset before the exped.

Meanwhile, Corporal Carl Bougard was hanging, suspended from the ceiling in the gym with some of the other guys when Conrad came in to see how they were getting on with their gear. Carl's harness slipped undone so that he nearly came out of it because he didn't know how to fasten it and nor did the others there. A few months later, Bev asked Carl what Conrad had said at the time. He told her that Conrad was pissed off with him and said, "It's a good job Sergeant Spooner's gone back!"

Carl (Bougard) told Bev later that Conrad knew that if I had witnessed it then I would have realised then that something was drastically deficient in the training and I would have pulled out and Conrad needed me. He simply would not have been able to find another rope leader so close to the expedition date. I was already starting to feel like a last resort as it was, though time to get away from a Regiment at short notice is not always that easy, so I could understand Conrad's difficulties.

Carl also told Bev and I later that he was down as the kayak expert on the team and had only been in a kayak twice in his life on a lake and had never done any level of moving water let alone white water. The training weekend in Somerset was a bit of local kayaking near Conrad's parent's home. It's incredulous to think that was all the pre-training a couple of the guys had for a raging Alaskan river 150 miles long. How the Susitna at any time of year could bear any resemblance to anything in Somerset at the end of May, literally a week or two before the expedition beggars belief, (again). Somehow all this was slipping through the system. The all important ATFA was becoming a piece of fiction.

Major Edward Simpson or his clerks would have had the reports of all 'two' team members that went to Ballachulish and certainly had the scathing report of Conrad's failure on the JSMEL (W). Of course let us not forget all the team members that must have gone to Ballachulish at some stage before the expedition, though there is of course no record of it because they didn't actually go at all.

Major Edward Simpson, very sadly, later suffered a catastrophic memory loss that was specific and isolated to the Summit to the Sea Expedition.

The memory loss was satisfyingly successful for him and frustratingly infuriating for everyone else because really, what could they do? Very well done indeed. We've heard rosemary tea is good for memory enhancement. This is very scathing and may seem very harsh on Edward Simpson but these are the reported facts and Edward has had a happy, long career and retirement. I've even changed his name, so he can continue his 'smooth passage'.

4 Div wanted to know from Conrad if there was any problem with the requirements of the ATFA. Conrad was extremely convincing, he sent more correspondence than most expedition leaders and could really 'talk a good game.' He was likable as much as anything. One wanted to make it right for him. The boyish enthusiasm was there as well as the efficient professionalism, (apparently). Conrad knew they had the go ahead to leave the UK with the ATFA intact if they had the rope leaders, insurances and training. If he could scrape by on the information, he could scrape his way onto the mountain at last.

I called Conrad in Canterbury and I asked him directly about the ATFA, as the departure date loomed up. I didn't want any last minute bit of forgotten red tape or any other colour to stop us leaving now. He told me the ATFA was all O.K. so I trusted in the system. Conrad told me and others that the team had been to Scotland for their winter training, giving the impression that they had all been and completed the winter assessment and that he had done his JSMEL (W). He had indeed done it; he just omitted to tell me that he had failed. The same story he gave to 4 Div. delivered in a way that left me to make the incorrect assumption too.

Somehow he had to have the backing of someone else in the system to pull it off. I suspected after the accidents that it was Major Edward Simpson but of course, it could have been someone else in a responsible position in the system too but from our enquiries, nobody else could come up with any other suggestion. There was no evidence to support there was any actual help given to Conrad to hide his JSMEL (W) failure, just a lack of action and reporting. It was only my assumption that Edward Simpson had to be involved otherwise he would not have been involved in the Inquiry as Subject Matter Expert would he?, Though he did end up being questioned by the Board with his solicitor present so he shouldn't have been part of the Inquiry Board team. You see, it's all wrong isn't it?

The insurance the team and individuals held was the absolute minimum, though it was our understanding that rescue reimbursement was included. In fact for the thousands of pounds worth of equipment that I took, as an individual I found out that it was only insured by the company Conrad used for £1,000. My clothing alone came to more than that. My ice-tools that Bev bought me for an anniversary gift in Chamonix, on an Army Alpine meet, I don't even want to talk about them.

So, with a veil over the truth and no lid on his enthusiasm for the adventure Conrad put himself down as a rope leader. With Johnny and I as the other two, insurance cover scraped together and only two of the team with their summer training during the winter in Scotland and no suitable or relevant experience for the kayaking at all the exped. Was cobbled together. The visas were done, passport details complete and he had his dodgy ATFA and was nearly ready for the off. By this stage, I was probably as excited as Conrad to be going. I'd be in my element on a good Alpine climb.

What some may ask here, as they did at the Board of Inquiry was why didn't I check the ATFA myself? Well, the answers are that Conrad was the leader of the expedition, a Captain and was organising it all through a different Regiment outside the Principality. I was merely a guest on the expedition as technical advisor for the work on the ground; I was a Sergeant, just a team member.

I had an unofficial title of 'technical expert' and could advise but I was still only part of a team and not even 2nd in command. Most crucially, I had no physical access to the document before the expedition. It wasn't my place to question an officer about his job when not only he's leading; (managing) and I had no reason to suspect there was anything wrong. Also, it would have seemed very odd for me to ask for a copy. It may seem strange but soldiers didn't go asking their superiors for documentary proof that they had been doing their job properly. We were soldiers he had his tasks, I had mine.

I had already asked if everything was in order with the administration, the ATFA and the men before. Why should I have not taken his word at that time when there was nothing to suspect? Also, I was brought into the expedition at such a late stage that I assumed it would have already been in place by now with just a few loose ends to tie up. It is something I said I would always ask for in future, even if it gave offence.

Things calmed down in South Wales where I prepared for the expedition and I don't know what the atmosphere was like in Canterbury.

Chapter 5 - Midsummer Madness

One sunny afternoon in mid-May Bev wandered across to the play park to see if the kids were OK. She found a gang of wifeys (Bev's expression!) sitting on the grass. She had never seen them together like this before so she went over and joined them.

It was really refreshing, as she has pretty much been a self-confessed and contented loner. They chatted and joked and the only gossip was good-natured chaffing. Bev was asked about work and she said that she was scouring the 'Sits Vac' ads every Thursday looking for a better job along with the rest of the staff. Bev had been working as an administration assistant in a psychiatric/geriatric nursing home. She loathed it. Not because of the nature of the business but the role she had. She was left without a manager, an ever-increasing workload, no other administrator to help and a tyrannical, bonus-chasing old dragon of a regional manager breathing her bitterness down Bev's neck every time she visited the home. Bev admitted she was out of her depth and was only staying because if she walked the staff would only have a locked office door every day. The residents were looked after but the staff were virtually high and dry.

Bev had got to the stage where she had reported money missing that had been kept quiet and informed the inspector of the local health authority that the residents of a second home she had to look after were living off fish and chips day after day from a local chippy because there were so few staff there was nobody to cook for them. She had been requested by the nursing staff to report it but she realised she didn't want to be working for a company where absolutely everyone was unhappy.

Bev reported the problems and gave a month's notice and the guilt and panic of this subsided when she found out she was in the front of a queue. She sat out the last month with the fallout of her calls and told the manager what she had done and waited for her time to finish.

The problems of the home were more than a temporary slide in standards but if you do nothing about neglect then you can be seen to condone it. Head office were swift and improvements slowly took hold.

In the care industry, many staff stay because they feel guilty about leaving simply because they care about their service users and friends at work.

Bev used to be a person who felt guilty about everything and was afraid to speak up. She does seem to have moved on somewhat as I have discovered at my peril.

On top of my going away and the worry of a new debt with the boat, she felt she had enough on her plate. Rats and sinking ships came to mind. Happily for the staff and residents, the regional manager resigned from the company and the home had a new matron who soon settled things down. Bev wound up her work and set up a guide for her replacement and enjoyed the last days in her job.

Bev quickly got a job in the camp just along the hall from my own Unit's offices. She only needed to see the kids off on the school bus, give the dog a run about and walk in through the back gate of the camp to get to work. Bev was happy as a lark to be working for the MoD as a clerk in the offices next to my Unit. She was due to start a few days after I flew out to Denali. A new job was just the thing to distract her and lift her mood while I was away.

Another late afternoon after school finished, Bev went to look for the kids and found the wifeys in the park again. They were all pleased for her with her new job and she had one of the girls, Helen to thank for bringing the new job to her notice. Helen was a cleaning supervisor on camp and not a lot escaped her. She was bright, cheery and always busy. Cindy, the fitness freak; asked about me and how things were going. Bev rolled her eyes and groaned. There was only the little gang left, Helen, Cindy, our good friend and next door neighbour Elvy and Ann our other next door neighbour and saintly mother of two 'extremely active and loud' children called Cara and Callum (Whom we called Frogmella and Turbo-man to their great amusement).

Bev complained that it felt wrong but she couldn't put her finger on anything that would really be a reason to stop me from going aside from her own worries about the motive of the expedition leader or the inexperience of the team. They all suggested she tell me how she felt. All the girls have been there before. She knew that would be the wrong move. If she stopped me going away and the team succeeded, she thought

I would feel bad and maybe resentful to her even if I didn't mean to. She thought this to be her own selfishness at an imagined predicament in our relationship. If I stayed and it went wrong, she thought I would be frustrated at feeling I may have been able to help it succeed or get someone out of trouble.

Things were going wrong between us. That intensity that builds up in a relationship when there is going to be a long tour or a 'dodgy' one. The anxiety builds up, the anticipation builds and you both want the actual parting bit to be over even though the approach is dreaded but you want things to get back on track before that. It's horribly conflicting emotionally.

It's a row waiting to happen. Heightened emotions are held back for the sake of each other when tenderness should be in their place.

The phone calls when we servicemen and women are away are bad enough when they go wrong, she thought 'without me whining at Martin before he leaves'. We've all been there before.

The phone calls that go wrong are horrid. Things get said in the wrong context or tone or instead of feeling relaxed a phone call can sound unintentionally formal. One will start to get uptight with the other and the phone call will get cut short or ten minutes will be wasted listening to crackles on the line waiting for the situation to be resolved or worst of all someone will hang up with no return number to contact them. Remember, this was 1998 and just a few of us had mobile phones and we certainly didn't try to use them abroad. There was no easy email, no Skype, Snapchat, Facebook, Facetime, nothing. There were public call boxes and bad connections, expensive charges and time delays in dialogue, echoes and time differences.

We have had years of this happening from time to time. It's one of the hazards of this half-separated marriage that so many of us lead in the services and other similar jobs. There are welfare worries, financial worries, doubts and insecurities that arise over the years. Some years have been really hard but they fade, no matter how bad or painful they are they do fade. Even most of the pain of this story has faded. At the time though we couldn't see anything beyond it.

Anyway, back to the sunny park. Cindy chirped in "Never mind Bev, just 'up' the old insurance and if he pops it we'll all go to the Bahamas for a holiday!" They all laughed at her and had a group fantasy about what they'd do with the money. Cindy loved us to bits so Bev didn't feel in the slightest bit sensitive about what she said. However, just as they were still giggling Bev says that she remembered seeing me as I strode across the grass with a slow relaxed lope and a big smile of greeting on my face. A moment Bev's sure some of them will remember.

We greeted each other and I stopped for a chat with the girls, which was unlike me at the time, a group of women together would usually have me running for the kitchen, the hills or anywhere else. It's just an awkwardness that I never seemed to grow out of.

One of the children managed to kick a football over the perimeter fence and into the trees beyond. Gallantly, I ran across to rescue it. I leaped up the loose, chain-linked, 12 foot fence, missed the post, swayed backwards as the loose section of fence sagged, strained with all my might to regain my dignity and peeled off it altogether and sat neatly onto my backside in slow-motion. They were all delighted and squealed with giggles and raucous laughter. I took a bow and succeeded on my second attempt at the 'peak.' Obviously, climbing abilities and up-coming expeditions came into the jokes.

More re-packing and final phone calls and we were all set. There were no more changes to the team:

Captain Conrad Lightwood (1 PWRR - Expedition Leader - Rope Leader)
Captain Phil Whitfield (Royal Marines - 2 i/c)
Sergeant Martin Spooner (APTC - MIC Technical Advisor - Rope Leader)
Sergeant Johnny Johnston (Parachute Regiment - Medic - Rope Leader)
Corporal Gary Keep   (Gaz) (1 PWRR)
Corporal Carl Bougard (1 PWRR)
Lance Corporal Steve Brown (RE)
Lance Corporal Nigel Coar (1PWRR)

Private Luke Mills	(Millsy) (1 PWRR)
Private Ian Haywood	(Tory Boy) (1 PWRR)

A few days later we were on our way to Gatwick airport. We were very fortunate here because London, Gatwick is actually a very long way from London, Heathrow. We both checked the letter again to make sure it was Heathrow with the flight details and timings but Bev wanted to be sure, so she phoned the airline at Heathrow to check the timings and found out that the details I had been given were wrong. This was the afternoon before I was due to leave. The information desk could find no details. She checked Conrad's message letter again. The Heathrow information desk suggested Gatwick. Of course, it was Gatwick, an easy enough mistake we supposed but we would never had made it from one to the other in time for a flight, even missing the check-in times. It was just a routine that we check and very luckily we had kept the habit of it. At least that would have been one way out of it, Bev thought – turning up at Heathrow instead of Gatwick and it wouldn't have even been her fault, bonus!

As you can imagine, Bev already had the breaking strain of a chocolate biscuit at that time and she was looking anxious. We had a few less than cool words or rather I had to wrestle the phone off her before she phoned Conrad and we calmed down again.

I can't remember much about the trip except that the conversation didn't flow. Everything felt a strain and Bev was aware that the clock was ticking and she felt she had only a three hour drive and an hour or so at the airport to put right all the fractiousness and a slight distance that had developed in the previous weeks. We both knew that it was that this expedition was different in many ways, especially in the organisation with team changes so late on, which wasn't building confidence.

I remembered the strain of the conversation in the car and was anxious to get the goodbye over with. I didn't know what was wrong with her. I just wasn't that sensitive back then I suppose. I know now I hate to be parted from her but my focuses are different. I'm not saying my attitude was right or wrong but that life is pressured and different. You don't stroll into work late and say you missed the bus or pull a 'sicky' because you've got a cold from the kids. Everything in the Forces can follow you around. You always have to be 'performing' and doing it well. I never even held her hand in public until after this expedition.

When we arrived at the airport, we had a look for the team but couldn't find them. We went for breakfast and wandered around the shops chatting. We both felt better at the airport, as if some of the waiting and anxiety was already over. We went for a coffee and sat watching the passers-by and making comments on what type of people they were or what jobs they did. A kind of game we played for a feeling of self-satisfaction that compensates for short-comings we perceived in our own life-style. We were feeling better. Suddenly, I announced that I hadn't packed any underwear. "You're kidding, after all that re-packing you've done in the last week." Bev exclaimed.

"Yes, I know but don't worry, forget it; I'll get some the other side when we land."

"OK, if you're sure because there's a Sock Shop right here?" She pointed to the left of the coffee bar.

"No, don't waste the money here, I'll get them later."

"Yes, OK" She said as she picked up her bag and went into the shop. One thing she knew was that I wouldn't remember to go shopping once I get my head into climbing gossip and the in-flight movie. She grabbed a few multi-packs of boxers and was just about to take them to the checkout when she realised that she had no idea what size I was. I'm the type that buys my own or get them from mum, along with socks and beer mugs I never drink out of with my name on for Christmas. She had bought some a few years before but they were so big they looked like a baggy nappy on me and I asked her not to buy me any more. She thought she had better not buy me 'small' even though I was slim because I'll curse her if I have to go up Denali with a permanent wedgie. She opted for medium and came back to the coffee bar. "Here are your knickers." She said as she dropped the bag full of packets into my lap. I smiled and complained half-heartedly that she was fussing. Bev was pleased that I could now get run over by a bus in the States without embarrassing her as a shoddy wife and I had to go on a flight with nine pairs of underpants in my hand luggage.

So I had to pack my new 'knickers' in my hand luggage and hoped I wouldn't have them spilling out of their shiny packets on the plane in case someone thought I had an unfortunate medical problem and would sit grimacing at me as I passed them to visit the toilet.

We moved off from the coffee bar and looked over the balcony to the check-in desk. "There they are!" I pointed out the team in a queue below us. Bev looked at them for a few moments and wasn't pleased I could tell you. "You're not flying out with that lot!" She demanded.

"Why, what's up?" I asked, somewhat surprised at the outburst.

"Well, look at them for goodness sake, half of them look like they are still at school and look at the bloody state of him with the beer-belly. How's he going to drag himself up there, are they going to install a chair lift? What does he think he looks like with the headphones and his cap on backwards, how old is he?" Oh, Martin, you can't go with them." She looked crushed and whined about them all, pulling them all to bits in less than a minute. I laughed out loud and gave her what I hoped was a big, reassuring hug. "Come down and meet them, you'll feel better. They only look young because you're so old you moaning old bat!" I felt good that we were both smiling. She was OK really.

It was clear before now, without Bev having to tell me that she really didn't want me to go. She had been morose for a few weeks, nothing short of sulking really, which she admits to. We did argue quite furiously once or twice about the expedition but no mention was actually made either side about not going until that moment. I didn't want to back out now, as I felt part of the expedition and a late withdrawal really would put a spanner in it all. Bev didn't want to say she didn't want me to go because she didn't want the finger pointed at her for years to come every time Denali got a mention.

We did argue badly, like kids bickering, not constructively like adults. Even our own kids, now grown up tell us to "Grow up!" and we are good parents, we listen to our kids and take their advice.

I picked up my bag and herded us into the lift. She had to admit that they didn't look so startlingly inadequate at ground level. The guy with the beer-belly didn't have one at all. He was stocky and solidly built, not wiry-looking and weathered the way she is used to seeing climbers of all kinds, it was Johnny, the Para, who later was a huge asset to the team and rescue operations. I greeted them and introduced Bev to one or two of them, they were all very polite with each other but Bev didn't let go of my arm, she clung on like a barnacle with one hand and shook hands with the other.

Then we met Captain Conrad Lightwood, the expedition leader. Bev thought him to be a gentle-eyed, relaxed and charming man with a twinkle of mischief in his expression and enough easy, self-confidence to calm her inner turmoil.

Bev no longer felt that Conrad and the team was a conspiracy to kill her husband by incompetence. She liked Conrad on first impression and felt easier when we left to spend the last half an hour on our own. I was more at ease now that everyone was there.

I said, "It's not easy leaving someone you don't know in charge of something like this. I'm not used to not having some control of the organising but it all seems alright. At least we're at the right airport." I joked. "I'd like to know who sorted that out; I'd have been well pissed off if I'd turned up at Heathrow this morning!"

It was the only time Bev heard me express any concern but she knew it was because I was feeling that things were running smoothly. Bev appeared to be anxious and ready to bite most of the time before this day arrived but this was unusual for her. It is actually the other way around. I can go from 'Flash to Bang!' and it used to be over some minor issues but Bev's fuse is longer and slower, the explosion soon dampens and her memory of any disagreement, like most women's is loooong! Also, we're not in those circumstances any more. Life is much more laid back and so are we.

Bev says she can't remember anything else about the time we spent from then except that suddenly my flight was called. We went to the entrance to the gates. It was really crowded. I hugged the kids and gave Bev no more than a peck and a quick hug and told her not to worry. I didn't want the whole thing to get emotional now.

Gemma and Rhys clung onto me and my clothes and were suddenly crying, which neither Bev nor I expected from them. Bev looked at me with her mouth open and a look of desperation on her face, as if she was about to grab me back. Before we knew what was happening, I was swept in with the flow of people pouring in towards the desk, passports and boarding cards in readiness. I looked back to wave and was lost in the crowd. Bev said she felt cheated that it was rushed on us. She had wanted to pull me back and say she was sorry for being so sour in the past weeks and for being distant all day, she didn't mean it. She just couldn't find her own way back in. I was oblivious to all this in the chaos around me. I was so focused on the expedition I didn't realise I and my departure had been the main focus for her.

Bev couldn't speak or breathe, her throat was tight and she could hardly see through the tears that suddenly welled up in her eyes. She caught herself and took a deep, shuddering breath. She swept the children in front of her and was out of the terminal building in what seemed like a few seconds.

I was swept away with the crowd and was caught unawares by the emotion that welled up in me from seeing Gemma and Rhys so upset. I didn't put much thought to Bev's emotion at the time because I thought we were on a slightly bad footing with each other, which I knew would only be temporary. Neither of us had the sense to just say what we felt and it had all gone wrong. I loved her but felt we had reached a point and nobody knew what that point was.

I had met up with the team in the departure lounge but still felt a little on my own. I hooked up with Steve Brown for the flight, a Royal Engineer like myself in his past and 'attached' to the Regiment. His trade was electrical engineer.

* * *

Bev got all the way back to the car and realised she hadn't paid the parking fee at one of the machines in the terminal. She drove to the exit in a whirl of frustration. She parked near the exit and ran up to the ticket machine. She had no change, just a creased up fiver. She flattened it out and inserted it over and over. It wasn't having it.

She went back to the car and dug down the sides of the seats. She found a pound coin and a twenty pence piece. With the other bits of car park change she keeps in the ashtray, she had just enough.

She slammed the door shut and nearly screamed in a tantrum at the queue that had suddenly appeared in front of the machine when her head was in the car. She stood in the queue with a strained smile at the man in front, grinding her teeth and looking at her watch every few seconds. Finally! She got her ticket, bumped over the speed bumps on the way out of the car park and told the kids to not speak before they got to the M25, as she needed to concentrate on where she was going. She was as stiff as a plank from head to foot and physically had to sway from side to side to relax and start breathing. She didn't know her way back to the motorway or even the terminal. She tried in vain to force calm on herself.

The kids sat looking grim in the rear view mirror. Although they had recovered quite quickly after I had disappeared into the crowd. They had skipped and played on their way through the terminal to the car park and had been 'sorting out' who was having the central armrest in the back seat before Bev realised her 'fiver' wasn't working in the machine. She felt a pang of shame and started to come down out of orbit.

"Sorry, I didn't mean to be all ghastly, I just hate all this hassle of doing this on my own." What a selfish thing to say, she thought. She wasn't on her own, 'you self-pitying cow, get yourself sorted out' she told herself. She changed the subject and told the kids they would be home in about three hours.

They played some of our usual driving games to pass the time and sang some songs for a while. The kids would do 'There's a hole in my bucket' and 'There was an old lady who swallowed a fly,' several times on one journey so that when we woke up the next day Bev and I would report that we'd had the 'ear-worm' of those songs whizzing round our heads all night. Today's journey was similar.

Suddenly, Bev was completely overcome with tiredness. It seemed to rush upon her without warning. She has driven hundreds and hundreds of miles at a time and never felt anything like it. If she hadn't been close to the Reading services she would have had to put the hazard lights on and sit on the hard shoulder. She decided it must be the relief that I had finally gone, the stress of the last weeks lifting from her. It was true, she suddenly felt more relaxed and calm than she had for about a month. She knew I would be fine, she'd hear from me sometime tomorrow. Everything is fine, all that worrying is for nothing. Forget it and move on.

She pulled in at the services, told the kids to try to play quietly, as she really needed to nap. She laid her head back on the headrest and she was gone. She jerked awake as if she had fallen from the kerb at the side of the road. She looked at the clock, thinking she had been sleeping for hours. She had been out for the count for less than fifteen minutes and in that waking moment and heat of the car, had completely forgotten where she was.

She took the children for a burger and bought herself a big Coke. She's really bad with caffeine and knew she'd be in for a headache later but she just wanted stay awake and to get home now. She said that she wanted to smell my pillow, play with the kids, and walk the dog. They had a really nice drive home. The M4 was clear and they sat in the outside lane cruising along almost the entire way into Wales. Nice, easy, early afternoon traffic, sunshine and music and children chatting and laughing and sleeping.

Elvy came to see her that evening. Bev told her how she'd been. Elvy said she wasn't surprised with everything that had been going on. She said I would be fine with her when I get back. "He'll be thinking about that bloody mountain, not whether you're moping about him, that's men for you." That's our Elvy, always shoots from the hip.

The next day I called home. I phoned from Anchorage. "It's great to be back in the States again. We're all going shopping tomorrow," on and on I went, chirpy and happy, laughing and excited. Bev thought, 'He's done the right thing.' She said that she felt better straight away. I told her that the team seemed OK. We hadn't chatted a great deal on the plane between the movies, sleeping and reading.

Bev's new office in camp was huge, with a bank of windows looking out across the hills. She had it all to herself. She even had a fridge to keep her drinks cool. She had to keep the blinds down in the afternoon because it was so hot. She said it was like being a tomato in a greenhouse.

It was bliss there. All streamlined systems, good pace of work and everyone polite and about 500 metres from the house.

At the end of her first full day of my being away, she let the children play a game on the computer. They soon got bored and ran off to the park. She was in the kitchen starting the supper when a movement caught her attention through the wall hatch. There was a scrolling message on the screen-saver. 'Smoke me a kipper, I'll be back for breakfast – Good Luck in your new job sweetheart! – See you soon, lots of love Daddy xxxxxxx.' She thought it was very sweet and she left it on. 'Red Dwarf' fans will understand the kipper bit.

* * *

I had phoned Bev earlier to say we were settled in a Bed and Breakfast called Earth Tours and that it was popular with climbers. I was even lucky with the timing that the children came in the house for a cold drink and I got to chat with both Gemma and Rhys and everyone was very happy.

The team had arrived in the States and did the usual stopover in Washington then flew on to Anchorage. We were all glad to get off the planes. I thought that the airport and city seemed much the same as any other but I remember the stuffed polar bear in the terminal building. I thought what a lot of damage we've done. I left the airport feeling quite disgusted and very sorry for the bear. I knew it was part of the U.S. culture but for all my trips there, I have never got used to it. Hunting and fishing to aid legitimately feeding and clothing oneself is one thing but I can't reconcile in my mind the idea of displaying a trophy corpse. We were picked up by a guide called Tom Waite and taken to the Bed and Breakfast.

The Earth Tours B and B, which was run by the mother of Feng Shui and mood music, was simple and had a pleasant atmosphere although I couldn't describe it as homely. Margrite welcomed us all. She was very tall, elegant, middle-aged with blonde, wavy hair and an ever-present smile. She hugged us all and chatted as we got settled in. She described it as a retreat for the soul as much as anything else.

Margrite Van-Lakke was a warm, open and extremely demonstrative woman. She was not at all self-conscious about expressing her feelings towards people. She is of Dutch origin and speaks many languages. She is exuberant and welcoming. The team were a little taken aback by the strength of her personality at first but soon became used to her ways and made ourselves at home very quickly. Being, not just stoic Brits but soldiers too, we didn't reciprocate although we did like her manner.

We stayed here for a couple of days re-checking and sorting our supplies and gear. Some of us went off to shop for more rations and spent some time spilling our copious amounts of equipment out across Margrite's back yard and porch. We finally got ourselves sorted, packed and got ready to set off for Talkeetna.

I called home again, excited and looking forward to the mountain and the kayaking. We were off to Talkeetna for an overnight stop the next morning and then onto the mountain the following day. All being well, she shouldn't hear from me now for about twenty-six days. "We should be back in about twenty four days if it goes really well; at least I hope so because after Talkeetna we're only taking food for twenty-four days." I told her that I loved her and I was missing her. She said it meant a great deal coming from someone who romance didn't flow copiously from. (Not back then anyway).

I reassured her that everything would be O.K. We said no more about it. She felt wonderfully secure again for a brief time and very comforted by the way our conversation went. It lifted her mood tremendously, like she didn't have to pretend everything was great all the time, it was.

We left Earth Tours around 23:00hrs and arrived at our destination around 02:00 hrs. We counted our arrival in Talkeetna as Day 1.

Talkeetna is a very small town that the climbers invade every year. A guy called Tom, who I understood to be a guide of sorts for the kayaking stage after the mountain, drove us there. It was a very long drive and we all slept on and off on the way. Talkeetna is close to Denali and is the base of the Ranger Station for the mountain range. From here the team would fly up in Doug Geeting's air taxi to a glacier at the base of the mountain and then we are officially on the exped.

When we arrived my first impression of it visually was of a slightly tatty, one-horse town with dusty side streets and a busted up tar-mac main street. It was very transient looking with all the touristy shops. As usual, the impression of the aesthetic was over-ridden by the people. Here they were warm, friendly and welcoming.

* * *

Bev started to get to know the other girls a little better on our patch. She had always been pretty much a loner but she was enjoying the company. They all began to gel really well. Elvy came in from next door to see her one evening and Bev told her that in spite of everything, she still had a nagging feeling about the team. If it had been a gang like Zeb Spring, Mac Mackay, Tim Davies, Nick Harding, Chris Short and Sandy Sanderson and other old hands he used to knock around with, she wouldn't have even bothered driving me to the airport. She would have stayed in bed and told me not to spend too much or wake her up when I get back! Well, maybe not quite but she wouldn't have been like this.

They were all colleagues from the past, not exactly grizzled mountaineers, but very good ones. Sandy had been my mentor and probably wouldn't do Denali with me in person but would have guided me in every other way.

Two days later, the telephone rang at home. It was around 21:00hrs. There was an echo on the line and a faint crackle. Bev knew straight away it was from the States and something had happened. The American accented operator on the line asked her if she would accept a collect call from Martin. She said, "Yes."

"Hello, Mart, what's wrong?"

"It's not Martin. He told me to say I was so that you would accept the charge. I'm Luke Mills." Said an unfamiliar voice on the echoing line.

"I had a problem on the mountain and Martin had to bring me back down." The strange voice went on.

"Martin's not here, he asked me to phone you and say that everything is fine and he'll speak to you in a few weeks."

"Where is he now?" She asked.

"Oh, he's gone back up to meet the rest of the expedition."

She asked about Luke's problem and he told her he had an infection in his lips and they were swelling and getting worse, all a result of the temperature. She told him that she hoped he would be better soon and that she was sorry that he was going to miss out on the exped.

"That's alright," he said. "Never again, I'm glad to be down." She was so shocked that she didn't know what to say. She wished him luck and said "Goodbye." As she put the phone down a rush of questions came on her. "Crikey, who is Martin with; I think he's making his way back on his own?" Elvy looked at her. "For God's sake Beverley, look at the state of you, you're going to make yourself bad at this rate!" Bev was asking questions she knew Elvy couldn't answer.

"What's so bad that someone volunteers for a mountain like that comes down in the first couple of days and never wants to go back?" "What is the rest of the team like now they are on the mountain?" and again, "Martin isn't climbing back up on his own is he?" Elvy rolled her eyes and told her to stop it.

A few days later she went into my Unit's office to collect my mail. My Master at Arms, Captain Billy Holmes was in there. Bev had never spoken with him before. She said "Hello," and went straight across to my pigeonhole and picked up a few envelopes. She dumped a couple of circulars in the bin and a signal inviting candidates for a skiing trip. She obviously thought I was on enough of a jolly already. She told Billy how I was doing or rather how she thought I was doing and that everyone seemed to be enjoying themselves. "That's not what I heard" He replied. "I checked and the weather is treacherous over there at the moment." Bev gathered up the mail said "Nice to meet you, good-bye." She was thinking quite uncharitable thoughts about Billy and his judgement as she settled back into her own office and got back to work. As they say, 'Don't shoot the messenger'. She got on with her life and turned her attention to the next big events, Gemma's 11th birthday and her school trip to France.

The weather was gorgeous, Bev enjoyed her job, had new friends, I would be home for the school holidays, when we would spend a week or so on the boat. Her worries diminished, Gemma prepared for her school trip and played with her friends. Rhys climbed trees, skinned his knees and built secret dens and they all took long walks with Sam the golden labrador. She felt at last that we had a good summer ahead.

Tom drove us to our accommodation, for the next couple of nights. It was luxury such as we never dreamed of in such a remote hamlet, (almost). We arrived at Tom's place, a partially finished building and taken to the unfinished roof-space where the gable ends were missing. Here we unrolled our sleep mats and sleeping bags and spent a dreadful night with a swarm of mosquitoes that were in residence. I got up feeling worse than when I went to bed. As the day wore on the team split up and we went about our tasks. Some went to top up rations, Carl and Conrad went to the Ranger Station to book in and I got trashed by a migraine.

I had no idea what sparked it off but I hadn't had one for about two years. I wasn't prone to them then so I have no idea what the trigger was. I had only had about three or four all my life. Bev said she felt really sorry for me when she heard about it as she goes down in the same way I do but I don't feel sick. She can't see, she throws up and if she had a choice between a gun and painkillers she'd probably choose the gun because it's quicker.

I spent the best part of the day trying to sleep it off and by mid-afternoon it had eased and was gone completely by dinner time, so I managed a good night's rest before we left for the air-taxi the following day, refreshed, replenished and raring to go. The extra rest had done me a lot of good.

Eventually, the day had come. We packed up our gear, left our belfry and carried it all to the air taxi, which seemed to be a very long mile away. We had rucksacks, rations and all the other equipment we needed. We had already trimmed down what we could. The gear was very heavy and like Johnny, I am used to carrying a lot of weight for a long period but I felt every pound that day. At least when we were up on the mountain we could organise ourselves and we could eat some of the weight and drag it on sledges.

We arrived at the small airfield that had small aircraft dotted about with people looking pretty busy, in and out of the hangers and around the planes.

The team went to get the bags weighed and then picked up the sledges and snowshoes that are available at the little airport. We waited around to get a place on one of the taxis. Some of the guys sat and had a smoke, they all chatted away and seemed mildly excited and keen to get going, we all were. It was a nice atmosphere amongst us.

When we finally got going it was in dribs and drabs with the equipment. I waited for a place with a couple of the team; we were the second to last of the team to get a plane. I sat up front to the right of the pilot, Doug Geeting and two of the others sat in the back. I couldn't see a great deal, as in front of me was a great bank of instruments and I had to crane my neck up to see properly.

After we took off in the little plane with the gear stowed in its potbelly, I took in what I could of the scenery. We were moving over undulating forest and winding rivers as we climbed towards the mountains. The pilot was constantly talking to other pilots on what looked like an air-taxi motorway. We came to a snow-covered saddle in the foothills and from then on everything below us was black and white. We had arrived in the mountains.

It was 3rd June and we flew in to the glacier at 7,000ft on Denali and unloaded our stuff. The team members that had arrived earlier met us and they all helped with the equipment. They had already sorted out a place for the tents and were ready to meet 'Base Camp Annie'.

Annie (Duquette) is a hardy, energetic woman who spent the whole climbing season living in a tent at Base Camp greeting people on the mountain, relaying weather reports and other information to climbers and Rangers alike. She worked and lived at Base Camp each season for over 10 years managing the airways and being everything from a messenger, relaying safety information and weather reports to being a confidante and councillor.

We met up with her and she took down our names. She gave us a few reminders about the mountain. This wasn't a patronising – 'this is dangerous' chat but more in the vein of conservation and ethics. Litter and human waste has become a problem on mountains worldwide. She also told us that the mountaineers could tune into her frequency for the weather up-dates.

Following our talk with Annie we headed to our tents and got ready to settle down for our first night on the mountain. I was surprised to see how busy the Base Camp was.

There were teams all fresh with clean and pristine gear, focused on sorting out their equipment and getting their admin. done, concentrating on the weeks ahead. Then there were the teams on their way off the mountain waiting for their air taxis back to Talkeetna, looking bedraggled with haggard but happy expressions, all sun and wind-burned. These were talking and laughing and much noisier in general, all pleased that they'd had a crack at the mountain or had been very lucky and made the summit. All of them happily at Base Camp and closer to a real, normal, hot meal, a long shower or even better followed by a soak in the bath, getting rid of the scary laundry and putting on fluffy, clean socks etc. A real bed, a real toilet, walking around without having to jam your boots on, turning on a tap and seeing water come out to make a coffee. In the meantime we made a cache of gear and settled down for our ration supper and bed, (sleeping bag on a thermarest mat on the ice) but it was great.

Thursday 14 June - Day 2

The next day at around 14:00hrs, we left the Camp and dropped down out of the fork onto the Kahiltna Glacier and worked our way up to the next Camp at 7,200ft. There is a ridge there that is now named after

Annie in gratitude of her extraordinary commitment and contribution over the years.

The first part of this section had been a pain, as the sledges tried to pick up speed as we descended and it was hard work for some. There was a lot of falling over. It took us a little time to get used to the equipment and the weight but I thought they had all done pretty well. We were carrying and dragging loads of between 80-100lbs each, (36kg-45.5kg). There were quite a few crevasses but it wasn't too bad. The route was clearly marked and the view was spectacular. (Probably a description I may use a lot, but it is spectacular.) We just needed to get our 'mountain legs' on. We had arrived at Camp 2 about 15:30 and called it a day there. It was a nice steady start for the first day of ascent. Decamping and walking and setting up again. It was another routine we had to get into the rhythm of quickly and we needed time to acclimatise to the altitude and temperature and get our bodies used to a different set of muscles working.

Our whole physiology was going to go through acute changes with the factors already mentioned plus diet, sleep patterns and the environment in general with lack of air pressure as we got higher. Fatigue from this point was only going to get worse so we had to go steady. Also, everyone acclimatises differently and at different rates. We just had to keep a careful eye on each other and ourselves.

We settled in with our tents, sorted out supper and slept, got up, kitted up, breakfasted, sorted kit and off again.

Friday 5th June - Day 3 Camp 2 (7,200ft)

It was now Friday morning, our second full day on the mountain. I checked the conditions and the snow pack by digging out a block section and looking at the way the snow layers were consolidated. It had been snowing all morning and we were ready to move on at 13:00hrs and hit 'Ski Hill' ahead of us.

It all looked good but boots wouldn't do on their own now and so I said, "Right guys, you'd better put your crampons on here." I sat and put my own on and was watching some of the guys struggling and a couple of others just staring back at me. The realisation came to me then that they didn't know how to put them on. They couldn't have forgotten, not

87

already. I knew if they had been to Ballachulish, there was no way they would have come away from a winter course not knowing how to fit their crampons onto their boots.

I went to Conrad with my concern. "Conrad, do you know that these guys don't know how to put their crampons on?" I asked.

Conrad said "Don't worry if we have a problem with them, we can back out at the Ranger Camp." There was an unhappy discussion about their abilities, which meant that Johnny had to be brought into the discussion too. I wasn't happy at all with the situation. At first I thought I'd been made out to be a mug. I didn't expect to be running through winter basics but we decided that between us, with the terrain, the time and the ratios per rope leader we could give the training on the way up. We would have to put time aside at the end of each day to consolidate skills, regardless of how much the guys wanted to retire to their tents after supper. Johnny and I suddenly had a lot of extra work to do.

I got on with it, not very happily and along with Johnny put the extra time into showing the guys how to use their gear, as agreed. We were still a long way off from the Ranger Camp at 14,200ft. I also found I had to teach them cutting steps, arresting falls and moving over steep ground. I was perfectly OK with doing the training, it was basic, everyday work to me and there was nothing wrong with the guys learning and practicing on the job either. Between us, Johnny and I felt we had covered everything that we could find lacking but were astonished by their lack of knowledge and had commented about it to each other and Conrad on several occasions. Johnny was no happier than I was that we were training these particular skills on the actual expedition but we were here now and Johnny didn't have much of a say either.

We felt though that between us we had spent as much time as we could spare going over everything and that the team appeared to be using the equipment quite comfortably. How confident they actually felt themselves was anybody's guess, as now they were on the mountain, it was unlikely that they would be truthful if they had doubts. It wasn't ideal but what could we do, we were already on the hill?

I couldn't get my head around how the ATFA was approved and we had guys who weren't trained. The ATFA is in the forefront of all the adventure training instructors' admin. It's like any skilled tradesman letting himself or his team go on site without a completed risk assessment. It wasn't my problem at the moment...or rather it was, mine and Johnny's

I had a discussion with Steve Brown about how much training they had done and that I thought they had all done at least their basic winter mountaineering course. He told me, no, that wasn't the case and that when he had been to Ballachulish, there had been no snow. I was still under the impression though at that point that the whole team had been there at some stage. Anyway, back to Friday. It had been snowing all morning and we had been snowed in altogether until midday, then we were ready to move around 13:00hrs. The weather was fine at this point and then we hit 'Ski Hill'. I can only describe it as a 'bastard'.

We could see other teams ahead of us plodding their way up and stopping for breaks. As we got into the steep slope ourselves, the novices in the team realised why the other expedition ahead had been so slow.

It was the team's first steep section. With our heads down, we pulled at the sledges and leaned into the hill. It was very hard work and it was there for the rest of the day. Pulling, puffing and blowing and sweating not really wanting to look up and still see everything so far away in front. We could see other teams behind us moving in the same way, struggling their way up, making slow progress. It was a very hard climb but at the end we had Camp 3 at 9,000ft.

I hoped that the extra time that Johnny, Conrad and I were now putting into basic training and practice would bring the guys up to the mark by the Ranger Camp at 14,200ft. If they weren't, Conrad said he could pull the plug on the whole thing. I thought it a prudent and sensible suggestion. We were all coping and if we had to pull out, then at least the guys will have had some excellent experiences and been on a serious mountain and learned a lot in the process. It wouldn't have been a waste. In my job, I could find another opportunity to come back perhaps with a more experienced group and colleagues I knew. Live to climb another day. One doesn't need to make every summit to enjoy the experience or find it fulfilling.

At the top of Ski Hill, we all had a break and a bite to eat. After stopping at the top of Ski Hill for the night, at about 9,000ft we moved on hoping to make the next Camp at about 11,500ft.

Saturday 6th June - Day 4 (9,000ft - 10,300ft).

The weather wasn't good and as the day wore on it deteriorated. Johnny was in the lead but starting to go a little off route. He had his head down following a team of Chinese climbers. I realised that he was still continuing on and not picking up the route again. The weather had turned to a blizzard and it was beginning to get darker. Every step into the snow and ice and pull on the sledge felt like a major exertion to straighten up and step out of again. At that point in the day it feels as though the other leg is not ready to take the burden as it swaps the load to step higher and closer to Camp. It was of course, very cold but no matter what was whipping against our faces and stinging us, we were very hot in our gear and from the prolonged effort. This is something we were all used to whether it was from climbing or some other duty we had been involved with in the past. You just keep your mouth shut and get on with it unless you're in trouble.

The time was getting on and we were not making great progress with the weather as it was. Fatigue causes problems so I called out to stop there. It wasn't really my place, as I was a guest but they were all happy with the judgement. The poor weather soon became a blizzard so we made an emergency camp.

I secured Phil on a long line and sent him around the perimeter of our impromptu camp to check for crevasses. This took a little while and was all clear so I called everyone in and we started to set up camp before the guys started to get too cold waiting. This was quite an operation in these conditions and it turned out to be another new experience for most.

We dug out spaces for each tent and used the 'dug out' now to form little perimeter walls around a metre high (3ft) to help provide extra shelter. The snow was packed back against the walls and a gap left like a small path around each tent. The path was just wide enough to stand in but would help prevent the snow building up too much against the sides of the tent itself as it blew in.

We struggled with getting the tents up quickly in the blizzard but it was great experience for the team to find themselves making safe in these conditions. The site itself wasn't too bad but not brilliant. It was narrow and there was a lot of spindrift and the snow was a little wet and it had become very windy now. I went around each tent to make sure they were secured and battened down properly and we all settled in for the night.

I was partnered in my tent with Phil. He started to cook supper while I sorted other stuff out. Very grateful, I tucked into the hot (or warm) meal and crunched down hard onto the pasta. "What the hell is this?" I ask him.

"Lasagne, why, what's wrong with it?" He asked defensively

"You're supposed to cook it before you put the sauce on." It did end up pretty funny although we were hungry. I hope he has learned to cook since then.

This overnight stop of the 6th June turned into four days, as the blizzard ripped at the mountainside. It was not a leisurely rest for us all either. We had to keep putting on wet gear, which was very cold and going out every couple of hours to push the snow back from the sides of the tents and compact it against the walls of the dug-out areas. The dug outs can only do their job so far in such conditions.

Sunday 7th June - Day 5 (10,200ft) Snowed in

The dump of snow was heavy so we also had to keep digging ourselves out, which was difficult because the snow valances for the tents were buried in the snow and it was difficult not to trip over them and rip them. At one point, Phil did just that. He caught his crampons in the valance and stumbled and ended up sitting on the tent, which did it no good. He was like Edward Scissorhands. The more he moved the worse it got. I really yelled at him at one point for his carelessness but it was more because I had envisaged the potential for damage than any damage actually done. I felt a bit bad about it because he's such a nice guy. Phil was OK and we didn't fall out about it, we just sorted out and hunkered down again.

The tents were robust mountain tents and flexed enough to take the impact. The problem would have been that if the tent ripped open because crampons got caught or the weight was too sudden, we would be a tent down early into the expedition and we would struggle with three men and all the extra kit going into other tents that already held two men. We still had a lot of time on the mountain to acclimatise, get up there and steadily get back down again. I made a few notes about the day in my diary, something I always did especially on expedition.

Monday 8th June - Day 6 (10,200ft) Snowed in

Blizzard continues, complete white-out, weather supposed to improve later today.

As the blizzard went on for so many days and nights most of the team passed the time chatting in the tents, cooking, (not very successfully in our tent, as we were both poor chefs) and reading. Although we got out to see someone else from the team on occasion we all tended to stay in our own tents because the weather was so rough. The main reason we had to come out of the tents so often was to stop them getting buried. It took up quite a bit of time kitting up to go out, sorting the tent and de-kitting the wet stuff again.

That was another issue many people don't appreciate about the hardship. The cold, wet gear has to be taken off and stored in plastic bags in the bell-end of the tent so that the inner tent stays dry and its inhabitants can stay cool or cold instead of freezing. Sometimes the gear was brought into the inner if it was bagged up again to help prevent it freezing too much. This gear is put on each time one goes out of the tent and only exertion and the resulting body heat thaws it out.

Each day, the gear was frozen including the climbing ropes, lines for the paulks, outer shell clothing and metal climbing accessories. Everything was frozen stiff and difficult to handle until it warmed up in the sun.

Tuesday 9th June - Day 7 (10,200ft – back down to 7,000ft)

Weather improved and we thought we were all ready to move up today but not so. Luke (Millsy) Mills had got a mouth ulcer during our little sojourn. This had now become infected and as he already had a slightly protruding lower jaw and of course lip, this was now a frostbite issue with the infection and inflammation.

We discussed what to do. It was decided that as we were so early in the expedition that Phil and I would escort him back to Base Camp and see him off on a flight back to Talkeetna where he could go on back to the Bed and Breakfast at Anchorage. Phil and I would rest at Base Camp for a while then hoof it back up to the rest of the team as soon as we could get there.

We geared up our stuff and set off back down with no problem. After some time we stopped for a break and we were quite peckish so I asked Millsy if he had some 'grits'. He wasn't going to need a load of rations now. He dug around inside his rucksack and slung a plastic bag across into my lap. I nearly jumped up onto my feet when I noticed he had mistakenly launched a bag of semi-frozen shit at me. I called him a sewer rat and flicked the bag back at him but my aim was off and it slapped him in the cheek. All credit to him, he just shrugged it off without a word and got the grits out and passed them over to us.

The trip down had been hard work and because it was undulating there were still hills to negotiate (or fight with, Heartbreak Hill in particular). We were roped together and Millsy through inexperience or feeling unwell kept standing on the rope, which made the going harder.

We finally made Base Camp safely, made the arrangements and I asked Millsy to call Bev for me and let her know I was alright, as I really didn't want her to be worried about me. His flight took off at 21:00hrs and he took off waving at us looking very pleased to be out of it. He really did look as if he hadn't much enjoyed any of it, but then how can one tell what anything is going to be like until it's been tried?

Phil and I sorted our tent out and settled down for a noisy night of broken sleep listening to the noisy 'Yanks' enjoying themselves around us. The trip had taken us 5 hours to go about 1 kilometre. It was going through my mind how long it was going to take us to get back up to the rest of the team in the morning. It certainly wasn't going to be 5 hours.

Wednesday 10 June - Day 8 (Base Camp 7,000ft - Again!)

After the exertion of the previous day and the happy, noisy neighbours Phil and I got up late. It was unintentional because we wanted an early start but we didn't really worry about it. What did disturb me when I woke up properly was that I had been dreaming about Bev a lot. I knew why things had gone awry before we left and it wasn't lack of love between us. I did tend to let things overtake us as a couple and she tended to overreact. We both had some insecurity for no good reason, which was a mystery, as you can't bomb us apart, that's evident after what is now well over 30 years. I found that even in the middle of all this going on the mountain, she invaded my thoughts right now and I missed her. I hoped things would be better when I got back. They usually were as soon as she flung herself at me with every greeting, even after a normal day's work back at home. Still, I woke up that morning wishing I could just convey to her that I missed her. I shook myself out of it and cracked on with the task of the day.

Phil and I were not in the least bit interested in approaching and working our way back up 'Ski Hill' again. Anyway, we finally did it and took a break at the top. I was sitting on my rucksack facing Phil when a small sparrow-like bird, I think it was some kind of linnet, perched on my left shoulder. I froze and slightly looked to my shoulder out of the corner of my eye. The bird was completely un-fazed and was looking around. I looked over to Phil and Phil stared back astonished, not speaking. There was nothing for miles, no trees, just glacier and snow. We couldn't think where it came from. We could only see that it was a greenish colour but because I couldn't turn my head properly without scaring it off, I never got a good look. I carried on eating, slowly and the bird stayed there for around 15 – 20 seconds before flying off. We were both so surprised and amused by it. I thought to myself it was my little guardian, I was completely charmed by the experience.

The trip up 'Ski Hill' had been really hard work. The initial trip had taken 3 days and this time, Phil and I made it in just 6 hours. We arrived back to the rest of the team to a warm and happy welcome from everyone. We were happy to have got back so quickly and set about getting ready for a good, long rest. We were very tired.

Thursday 11th June - Day 9 (10,200ft - Camp 3)

We got up about 09:00hrs only to find white-out conditions again. It wasn't so bad as before, as the wind had dropped a lot so we started to get ready to make for Camp at 11,000ft. We moved up with Tory's tent and two sledges and scrabbled our way up a short but steep hill to 11,000. We found it to be an excellent tent site and it had just been vacated by a Japanese team climbing ahead of us, so it was already trampled flat before the snow came in and gave us more work to do. We had a good break, stuffed ourselves full of food and made a start at making the next Camp up, (no.4).

On the way up we had passed three teams that were on their way down again. All three teams had summited successfully. It lifted our mood further to see how happy and tired they were. There was nothing much eventful going on within the team. After a prolonged break, everybody except Phil and I was rested, we were still fairly tired. The climbing was going OK as everyone was moving well with the kit.

There wasn't a lot to teach them at this point except some were walking with the crampons and ice tools and making sure everyone had practice at arresting a fall before we got to the steep and dodgy parts of the route. We would have that final decision at the Ranger Camp at 14,200ft, so there was still time yet for Conrad to make a judgement.

Friday 12 June - Day 10

We moved up to our cache at approximately 12,800ft. This was beside 'Windy Ridge'. It was a hard day of climbing and quite slow with poor visibility. This was a first time in crampons for some and they got on very well and found a big difference in the security underfoot with them. They just have a different 'step'. Conrad fell into a small crevasse up to his waist, which made everyone a lot more alert but he was fine and we got on with it. The whole trip lasted 6 hours, which is more than enough in those conditions and we didn't want to rush acclimatisation. We didn't want to climb too quickly. Acclimatising can be a slower process for some and we didn't want anyone sick before we'd even made Ranger Camp at 14,200ft, which is where we wanted to make a steady plod to tomorrow.

Saturday 13 June - Day 11

The team ascended (sounds easy doesn't it, like we just floated there or something) to 14,200ft. It was a really tough section. Each rope team was persuaded to take one loaded sledge each and 'long haul' it on a line bit by bit up to the Camp. We did it and it took us 9 hours of slogging up there but it also saved us a re-climb and extra time at the Ranger Camp to acclimatise, get ourselves checked and re-group a little before we moved up to do the next cache. It sounds like it was hard then easy with long breaks but it took three days from our emergency camp. For three days we strained our way up and along the terrain with our heavy rucksacks, pulling our paulks and hoping our snow shoes didn't sink in a soft patch. We crossed snow bridges over crevasses and passed beneath the West Buttress and traversed upwards through 'Windy Corner', which gave us a welcome surprise in not being windy. We finally made the Ranger Camp as the day was drawing to a close on the 13th June.

The Ranger Camp was busy, like Base Camp there were tents all over with groups on their way up and down. The Rangers tents were obviously much larger, more permanent looking and there was a large enough area for helicopters to land. Our first impression as we approached was the cold. It was definitely much colder here. Every time we stepped out of the sun, everything started to freeze. Our clothing would crackle as we moved and our facial hair growth was frosted if we stayed in shadow.

Sunday 14 June - Day 12

This was a 'Day Off' so we stayed at this level and worked all day pretty much, just not 'up'. We got our team camp organised and settled in to acclimatise a bit longer and finalise our summit bid. We checked in with the Rangers and had a briefing about the routes. There had been some discussion about them and I heard second-hand that the guides had suggested our team do the West Buttress route, probably due to the lack of experience in some of the team. I wasn't at the initial meeting with the Rangers in Talkeetna. I know Conrad and Phil went and I understood it to be just formalities, so I wasn't needed apparently.

I did not attend any other meeting at 14,200ft but was puzzled to find out that Conrad had decided to take the West-Rib cut-off route after all. Conrad and Phil as his second-in-command did most of the liaising and passed information on to the rest of us.

Johnny and I worked on trying to make it work with the team. My job, as technical advisor was to try to make sure the team got up there safely, whichever way we went and with what resources we had, which included the experience we had in Johnny and Conrad.

The West Buttress route was certainly simpler and safer but if the team was up to it, then there shouldn't be a problem. I could make any technical belays or cutting in the snow and ice pack with Johnny and

Conrad could help out. Phil was certainly very capable with team management and fit enough so we had certain assets along with able bodies.

We could plod our way slowly and steadily up. As long as the guys were O.K. with the altitude, the only problem I could envisage was that the going would be very slow, as it was for everyone who would be fully kitted up.

The West-Rib cut-off was within the capabilities of the 'qualified' rope leader's to take their small teams through. We are now talking about a high altitude section, which is fatiguing and therefore needs more careful consideration to rests and leadership skills.

I felt that we really needed a few days here to acclimatise and was pleased that we did just that. The Coriolis Effect near the Arctic Circle really does make a difference in the air at lower altitude. It was quite a difference to the Alps or Mount Kenya.

We all had our O_2 sats, (Blood oxygen levels) taken to check fitness to continue or rest further. Mine has always been good and was amused that it had to be taken 3 times because they thought the machine was malfunctioning, they read so high. They had a similar experience with Tory Boy, so our team appeared to be acclimatising very well.

Sunday 14 June - Day 12 cont...

We were to spend another couple of days at 14,200ft and rest, acclimatising to the altitude the whole time. It is something that is different for everyone and there's not really a sure way of knowing until the climbing starts again.

The headache is common enough and is a mild enough symptom although it can be quite a severe headache. Sometimes the headache can be caused simply by fatigue, the strain on the back of the neck and shoulders from the weight and dehydration. We all tried to take care that we looked after ourselves as well as possible on the way, so that we didn't succumb, as it could put a damper on an otherwise good day. There was nothing we could do about the tiredness at the end of a day. It was hard graft in the thin air; nobody was trying to race up a mountain like this. It can't be done, there's just not enough air pressure and therefore oxygen.

So we continued to take a long break except for a trip up to make a cache of gear at 16,200ft tomorrow.

It was still very cold at this camp and we had to prepare just as well if we left the tent as we did during the blizzard. We didn't really go out if we didn't have to. Instead we sorted out our personal kit ready for the next cache and for the summit. We sometimes got to speak with other teams, guides and the Rangers to pass the time if we were outside but not for too long.

The toilet was unforgettable, it was simply a barrier about a meter high so that when squatting one was hidden from the Camp. There was a hole cut through the snow and ice below so that waste just disappeared into a crevasse. The view though was amazing, right out across the other mountains of the Denali Range.

Monday 15 June - Day 13

After a few days at 14,200ft, the whole team went up to 16,200 ft to make the planned cache and prepare our Camp for the summit bid. Most of them were very tired at the end of the 2,000ft trek and struggled with the work, though the terrain was O.K. here. We started out at 12:00hrs and took approximately 4 hours to make the climb. After some time most of the team stopped altogether and rested for the remainder of the session. I broke trail on the final section and set up a bivi/tent ledge with Steve.

Steve Brown and I seemed to be faring better so we cracked on with the preparations and dug out the remainder of the platform until it was big enough to take all the tents. It took us an hour and a half to dig it out. The tent area was prepared and the cache done, so we made our way back down to 14,200ft to rest that night and the next day. I was pleased that we had spent a good amount of time at 16,000ft. Had we all worked on the platform for the tents, it would have been over more quickly and even hours spent higher can make a difference with acclimatisation.

It was very hot work in the cold air and I had a bit of a thumping headache for a while. I kept a check on myself but once I had a few good guzzles of water and a reviving cup of tea, I was right as rain, so I was pleased to confirm to myself that it wasn't any level of AMS. It turned out that everyone had a thumping head, so we steadily made our way back to 14,200ft, which thankfully only took an hour. We slept 3 to a tent now after making the cache. Steve, Phil and I shared a tent and we all slept very well that night.

Tuesday 16 June - Day 14

Tuesday was a rest day again. We made sure we properly rehydrated after yesterday and some still had a mild headache but nothing of concern. I spoke with Joel Geisendorfer, (V.I.P. Ranger as far as we're concerned) and he took us in to see his partner, Liz Green who re-did our O2 sats again just to be sure. It was just a headache, so we all felt much better for knowing and drank more tea.

It was Gemma's birthday soon and we were hoping to make the summit the same day. I came up with the idea of a great present for her. My insulated sleep mat was bright yellow on one side. I got hold of a marker pen and wrote out 'Happy Birthday Gemma' 19 June 1998, Summit to the Sea, Mt McKinley, 20,320ft and got all the team to sign it. Steve Brown took a picture of me holding it. (The mountain was called Mt McKinley then and it was recorded as 20,320ft back then too).

Wednesday 17 June - Day 15

On the morning of 17th June, we set off for the 'Summit Camp' at 16,200ft. When we got there, another team had used the space we dug out for their camp the night before and had stamped a big 'Thank you' with their boots in the snow. We liked it. They were two young American lads, really nice and enthusiastic. They had given us sweets when we had met them previously and been chatting about the days ahead. We liked that too, their names were Jeff Munro and Billy Finley, really nice young lads. One had a problem with a crampon so I did a quick repair to it. Brief little friendships like this help to make for great memories and bring back smiles when these moments are remembered but there is a reason I remembered their names.

We were here now at our last stop before the summit. We all felt better than the last trip to this point. No headaches, no dehydration, well rested and keen. Everyone was now up for the bid to the top. Everyone seemed fit and able but we still relaxed and pottered about for the rest of the day to let our systems settle in.

I think the decision to move the following day must have been made late into the event and based upon everyone's apparent condition. There was a few days good weather forecast so that obviously helped clinch it. At least then if our ascent was to be as slow as I expected it to be on the chosen route, then we would need that weather window and some time to spare.

A very long, hard day ahead tomorrow but we had beat the weather and just a couple of days to the Summer Solstice so we had the best light we were going to get, especially at that latitude, no darkness, just dimming and another day floods in. For now, we appreciated the few days of rest we had had after our gruelling climb to this point. Everything was calm and quiet.

Chapter 7 - Calm before the storm

As events at home are just ticking along we leap ahead. It was Thursday 18th June, the sun forced its heat through the blinds in Bev's new office but relief came from all the doors wedged open in the corridor, which allowed a light breeze to whisper its way into the room from the line of windows she had opened. The windows ran the length of the wall, which gave a wonderful working environment if you were a tropical fruit. She loved her office, it was light, spacious and very neat but the blinds had to be dropped before mid-morning or the heat was just too much of a distraction to work. (Air-conditioning is not standard in most U.K. offices and homes.) There were trees and grass right in her line of sight and lots of sky. The entire atmosphere was less stressful just to sit in.

The breeze was fresh from the desk fan and the desk was cleared for the following morning. Her morning faxes were all typed up and stacked next to the fax ready for the next morning. This was the MoD but we still didn't have email in 1998. Even at home we didn't bother with a 'dial-up' connection. It was slow, very clunky and the phone line couldn't do two things at once, so if someone tried to phone in when we tried to connect to the 'web' as it was then described the connection was lost anyway. We had one phone at home on a small telephone seat/desk unit in our hallway and an extension wire we crudely ran over the door frame, up the stairs, around another door frame and behind the bedroom furniture to a bedside table to another phone. That was it. We didn't have a mobile phone at all. It was all scary technology to us then. So, with emails still a mystery, it was down to lots of paper and phone calls on landlines.

Bev did a few bits and pieces on the computer, which she enjoyed now, as she had Windows 3.1, (which seems like chalk on a pavement now compared to operating systems we are now using) and was not working on a computer that only worked off DOS and didn't even recognise a mouse when she bought one, which she had in her old job. How things move on with phones that can run a business and micro-operating systems that would have taken up entire rooms a few of decades ago.

There was an awful lot of paper in the MoD though: white original to H.Q., pink copy to receiving unit, yellow copy to our file, orange-spotted copy to Valhalla and every size of buff envelope and envelope file choking up the stationery store.

Bev felt she had done a good day's work and had great weather for Gemma's party this weekend. She let her mind drift back to the other occasions we had gone to Ma and Pa's for Gemma's birthday. She gave the room a quick polish and watered the yucca that dominated the smart ante-room table, which had been 'lifted' from some sergeants' or officers' mess somewhere at the entrance to the office. She locked up and skipped down the stairs and cycled to the gate to meet the children who should be making their way to the gate from the school bus.

Whilst walking back to the house together, Gemma casually announced that she needed her E111 (European reciprocal health care) form for her trip to Normandy handed in by the morning. Kids are great for that aren't they? Bev had everything planned to the last detail, presents, party, full fuel tank, someone to feed the cat and no laundry left in the basket. She supposed something had to wait until the last minute.

Bev was suddenly in a mad rush but still wondered how I was doing now. According to the itinerary, I should be up to the 14,200ft Camp by tomorrow, 19th June. With no idea we had already reached summit day, she supposed we were still sleeping, as we hadn't even started our Thursday morning as her Thursday was now getting into evening rush hour, such as it was in Cwrt-y-Gollen village. (Pronounced kort-ee-gothlen) - (Kind of) - (apologies to the Welsh!)

She got back to the house, let the dog out, locked up the bike around the back of the house and bundled the kids in the car. If she hoofed it up the road to Crickhowell Village, she should just make the post office and get a few bits of shopping in before everything closed at 5.00pm. She pulled out of the estate and put her foot down on the accelerator. By the time she was level with the camp entrance about 300 meters from the gate of the married quarters entrance she was easing up to 50 miles per hour and slotted into the flow of traffic. She was barely past the camp gate when she heard the engine rev loudly. She looked straight at the dials on the dash. There were now zero revs at 50 miles per hour and the car was slowing down in the flow.

She thought for a moment the accelerator cable had snapped but there was still pressure in the pedal and the revs were still not registering. Something electrical, it had to be. The rest of the dials were OK as she slapped the hazard warning light switch. She was coasting to a stop and knew she wouldn't make it across the carriageway to the lay-by on the other side of the road.

"Bollocks!" Bev cursed the car. The children groaned and waited for Bev to poke around under the bonnet to see if anything obvious had come loose or broken. She checked the wiring that went into the ignition coil but it was all on tight. We had all been through this so many times in the past with our old VW van that break downs meant the AA (Automobile Association, not the other AA.) almost knew us on first name terms. I'm surprised they renewed our membership year after year. After being picked up by one of the staff who worked for the same department as Bev's, they were dropped off at the guardroom. Bev was so annoyed.

Everything had been set up at Ma and Pa's in Staffordshire for the weekend and the post office would be closed in half an hour. The AA would be with her in around an hour. As luck would have it, a young chap was booking his car into camp at the guardroom and offered her a lift to the village. She thanked him and dragged Rhys along with her who wanted to stay in the guardroom and drink a bottle of pop they had offered him and press the barrier button.

All my colleagues were in the office right across from the very flash, new BMW she was getting into. She felt she needed Rhys to prevent any misconceptions about her getting into the smart car with the young man in designer clothes while her husband is up a mountain. Office gossip is the same everywhere and although I could see her predicament, idle tongues wag away.

Bev got to the post office with ten minutes to spare and sorted Gemma's E111 and was taken back to the guardroom. She drank tea and chatted with the guards who had always been very polite and helpful to us. Rhys and Gemma took it in turns to press the barrier buttons whenever a vehicle passed. The guards asked how I was doing and Bev told them what she knew so far, which wasn't much at this point.

Eventually an AA contractor arrived and took the car to the local garage. It was the ignition coil and for a Volvo, she was looking at around £200. She explained why she needed the car back by tomorrow to get our daughter home for her 11th birthday party in Staffordshire and with Gemma looking so stricken, the man said he would do his best to try and locate a second hand coil. Bev assured him that if he did and she had the car back by Friday lunchtime, she would pay cash. He said he could do it and it will be ready, (the magic of cash-in-hand eh?).

Bev got a lift back home from the mechanic and went straight to Elvy for a good moan. Sam, our dog bundled around in the garden and all the kids went out to play together.

Bev knew Elvy would sit there laughing at her so she would soon have things back in perspective. "I don't believe it, nothing ever goes wrong until Martin's away, and I bet he's not having trouble!" She complained.

"I don't believe your luck, where are you going to find £200?" said Elvy sympathetically.

"I don't know; it may as well be £2000 with all that we've paid out for that bloody boat and this bloody expedition!" Bev whined wearily back at her, let her head fall back against the chair and stared into nothing.

"Have a cup of tea my dear", Elvy offered. "Gary! Make us a cup of tea will ya!" She yelled through to the kitchen where her husband had the sense to retreat to.

Bev felt an involuntary smile creep across her face.

"Poor Gary" She said.

"I'll give him poor Gary, while he's off traipsing around the hills in the sunshine, I'm left here with this little devil, look at him, butter wouldn't melt!" said Elvy in a much vexed tone.

The little devil was the year old son who wakes up several times a night, dials 999 when he plays with the phone and turns the house inside out on a daily basis. The little devil, Danny is the sweetest and most angelic looking child one could meet. He obviously only sprouts his horns and tail when there is no company.

Bev was feeling better so she went home and got on with the evening. She cooked dinner while Gemma and Rhys played in the park then took Sam round with her to meet them when dinner was ready. They strolled back together without a care it seemed, (except me up the mountain and £200 for the car she hoped she could get from the cashpoint without it sticking two fingers up at her).

The next day was great. It was Friday 19th June and it was Gemma's birthday. Gemma opened cards and presents and Rhys excitedly got involved by being allowed to help unwrap. They went off to school as happy as larks knowing they were going away for the weekend. Bev was very upbeat and looking forward to the weekend, although family get-togethers always entail putting up with having to smile through the day with particular relatives who loathe each other, she was keen to see old friends too and enjoy the birthday party with the kids.

The phone was quiet and Bev got on with plenty of typing and faxing and emptied her 'In' tray. Everything was particularly quiet today and she even had to find work to do, so she polished the office, dusted the yucca and watered it...again and watched the clock. She tidied the stationery cupboard and browsed through the stationery catalogue but they didn't need anything. She picked up my mail from my Unit's office and nobody had any news from the expedition. No news is good news! So there she was sitting by the phone and fax all day on a military network, no news.

She popped along the corridor to my office again but it was deserted. She checked the fax in my office to see if anything had come through that I might need and still nothing. I don't know what she expected because the signals go out to all units the same way; she would have got the same on hers unless they were direct dialled. Somehow, she and the military network were missing what was happening on the mountain.

Somehow, nobody called my unit, no signal came in informing anyone what had happened to our expedition half a day before. Bev continued trying to occupy herself at work. She stayed in the office right up to her knock off time, which was an early finish today and there was still no call, no signal, and no communication on the military net at all.

Bev locked up, handed her keys in to her boss, Keith who was manning the office for the rest of the day for her and she cycled home.

To the U.K, it was Friday lunchtime. On Denali it was not even 04:00hrs but still, the press here had found good reason to gather and start disseminating information about our expedition.

The sun had been shining all day again, and the garage called to say the car was ready (Bless their cotton socks!) The car was done for £100 cash and everything was loaded up by the time the school bus pulled in. Bev's boss, Keith had given her the afternoon off to help her get away, knowing what the traffic was like on the M50, M5 and M6 on a Friday, (nothing has changed). She stayed at home that afternoon and hadn't had any phone calls then either. Keith hadn't received any news to pass on to her and neither had my office along the corridor, yet the media continued to gather at Talkeetna.

Bev spoke with Elvy and Cindy and told them that I was due at 14,200ft Camp today and that she hadn't heard anything, so that was good. They told her not to worry and enjoy the weekend. Their husbands were still at work and they got no signals or calls during the afternoon. Little did she know what chaos we were in on the mountain and that our circumstances were going to change everything for us at home.

16:00hrs Bev pulled away from the house and turned the corner at the end of the cul-de-sac. Cindy and Helen waved at her. Then Cindy had called her back as Bev had forgotten to leave the keys. Bev had made the decision to leave her house keys with Helen, she had never left the keys before but she felt she should this time. Bev had never been close enough to anyone here before to feel she could do it but she enjoyed having more than a friend or two. "Drive carefully Bev, have a great birthday Gemma! Bye Rhys, be good" They called as everyone waved out of the sunroof. Rhys was always good, so was Gemma, it was Bev that was strict when the kids were young but we found it helped them make friends because everyone found them easy to have round to play. They didn't tear the place up or bully anyone and although nobody ever got more than two words out of Rhys at a time as he was so shy, (no different as an adult) he and Gemma always remembered their manners. That was of course before they hit their teens and early twenties and we did everything wrong, nothing was fair, all their mates were 'allowed', whether they were or not and the independent adults we wanted them to be suddenly began to emerge a lot earlier than we expected. Here now, in 1998, we didn't realise how easy it was and they were.

Gemma begged and very unusually, probably because of the birthday Bev had allowed her to sit in the front seat as the seat belt fitted her now, but with lots of warnings to sit straight and not tuck the shoulder strap under her arm. She knew she shouldn't but so much was less strict back then. They certainly weren't going anywhere fast at that time of day. Bev thought she'd be lucky to make her way through the whole set of gears the way they were going. Rhys wasn't going to object, he had the whole back seat for himself and the dog and it was a really hot day. He pushed Sam's blanket over to one side and dropped the arm-rest in the centre and his arm took possession of it with no argument from Gemma. He had his toy dinosaurs prowling and growling and he was as content as a baby.

They got to the M50 and the traffic ground to its Friday evening halt. It was 17:00hrs on the dashboard clock and the D.J. on the radio announced the 5 O'clock news; "Boooring!" cried Gemma and pushed the cassette tape into the slot. This was the news that Bev's boss heard that afternoon, hearing no more than two British soldiers had fallen on Mt. McKinley in Alaska. He didn't really make the connection at the time. Bev missed it by seconds as the tape paused and found the beginning of its song. They all began to sing along to 'Garth Brooks' without a thought to what the newsreader might be trying to tell them. If Bev had just waited a moment longer before pushing the tape in, she would have turned around and gone straight back home.

By the time they got to the M5/M6 intersection they were singing along to the 'Stranglers' and 'Squeeze' trying to ignore the hours that were passing as they sat in queues. The M5/M6 northbound junction has never changed and we have only ever pulled straight out of it in the middle of the night. Even now with the 'Smart Motorway' it's a choke with the lane slipping off to the big Wednesbury retail park and 3 lanes already on the M6 taking possession of all the available manoeuvring space.

The only near drama they had was North of Birmingham at Stafford after they had stopped for a break at the services and had sat on the grass with their Burger King meals feeding Sam the scraps. The kids thought this was absolutely fantastic. They'd had two bought in junk meals inside a month and tomorrow there'd be party food and sweets, bonus! They were making the most of it before life went back to 'eat the veg first if you don't like it, sweets are for weekends, nag, nag, nag.' Half an hour or so later and a good ten miles away from the service station in the semi-crawling traffic, Bev gasped. "Oh shit, I left Sam at the services!" He perked up his ears at the sound of his name and they all laughed out loud. She couldn't remember putting him in. It woke them all up a bit.

It took them nearly five hours to get home that evening, almost double the time it usually takes and they had sung themselves hoarse with 'Randy Crawford,' 'There's a hole in my bucket' and 'There was an old lady who swallowed a fly'- again.. By the time they reached Stoke -on-Trent, they were in a reverie listening to Joan Sutherland's Lacme, Holst's Jupiter and other favourites. Gemma and Rhys have very clear, pleasant voices, unlike Bev's that could be used to evacuate buildings.

They knew they were in Stoke. The land of pot holes and bumps, roadworks that never catch up and an air of impoverishment to the area and the look of the people. There was an almost fierceness in the look of many, a moroseness. Around the University people were more colourful and cheerful but the industrialness was inescapable. The only other place we have been to where the roads were so consistently bad was East Cowes on the Isle of Wight. Funnily enough, both Stoke and IW are two of the most deprived areas of the UK amongst a few others, especially in education. Such a shame for places with so much potential. Very quickly they were out of the city area and heading towards the Peak District.

They arrived at Longsdon and turned off the A53. The track to the house was in shadow with the remnants of the late evening sun flashing behind them through the heavy foliage. They travelled slowly down the leafy tunnel, smelling the heady fragrances of the wild flowers and the dampness that was creeping in with the cooling air. There were gnats flitting around under the canopy and the tyres crunched over the rough gravel leaving a low dust cloud behind them. The track was about 500 metres long so they bumped along slowly avoiding little dips and bumps along the way.

The track opened out to the old pumping station; large, pre-war and Victorian buildings with high arched windows, mahogany double doors and heavy brassware. Then round the bend to the sight of the workers cottages swathed in a shawl of flowers. There were containers, baskets and pots everywhere bursting with surfinias, petunias, bizzie lizzies and too many others to mention.

Bev noticed a fence in progress on the front lawn; they had been busy. Before she pulled the car up to the garage Ma and Pa were there, coming through the curtains of flowers to greet them with laughs, hugs and smiles. We never got a shabby greeting here when we'd been away for long periods and it's a refreshing sensation after a long drive. After much excitement and chatter the children were eventually put to bed and Bev followed them an hour or so later. She did a quick spider check around the bedrooms, (compulsory here), jumped in the shower and settled down to read a page or two before she gave up and slept deeply for a couple of hours or so before the heat became too much.

Saturday 20th June

The morning was perfect, (in the U.K), the sun had just peeked over the trees at the side of the houses and Bev had no more sleep left in her. It had been a hot and restless night but the morning was pleasantly cool and dew lay across the lawn.

She decided to run around the Deep Hayes Country Park, which is just about five hundred metres from the track entrance. She set off with our dog Sam and trotted down the limestone, hardcore drive. Bev had her inhaler with her just in case. The last time Bev and I ran through the park, she ended up trying to breathe through her hat to calm her breathing, as she had left the inhaler at home. She had developed mild asthma after working in Scotland. The doctor thought it was a combination of the dust from the feed sheds where she worked and the pine tree pollen. After never having any problem, she wasn't impressed at developing it at the age of thirty-two.

The run was great. It was around 06:30hrs and the mist hovered over the pond by about a foot. Ducks and moorhens swam along breaking up the glass surface as the soft sunlight filtered through. There were two or three fishermen dotted around the edge of the pond sitting in the shadow of the trees. The air was clear and she ran well for a change without the restrictions her chest usually put on her.

She thought that I would be proud of her and she wished I were there with her. She looked back at the pond as she reached the top of the gravel steps in the wood. She wondered if that was what Avalon was like. Her mind drifted on to a book she had read some time ago about the Arthurian legend and imagined living through that time, (Probably not nearly as romantic as she was feeling).

She arrived back around 07:15hrs and went straight into the shower. She felt so good, she felt years younger and she felt a good day was ahead of her and was looking forward to putting Gemma's party together. Events in Alaska now have to go back a day or two.

Back in Alaska - Summit Day and Back to Thursday 18th June - Day 16 (16,000ft Summit Camp)

The sun was already sending sparkles of light across the crust of smoothly undulating snow on the slope, as we rose very early and quietly prepared for the day ahead. Each of us checked we had what we needed and began the days climbing.

It was 06:00hrs and my head was clear of the pain of the headache that was par for the course for some at this altitude. Today was summit day, the weather was superb and everyone was raring to go. Spirits were high at the prospect of the summit being just hours away. There was now lots of cheerful chatter and the rope teams got their gear together with a new zeal today. There was clinking and chinking of hardwear, rustling and crackling of textiles, soft whooshing, creaking and sometimes crunching of snow and ice underfoot. Steaming, freezing breath against the blue, blue sky.

The teams set off about an hour later with the concentration they had learned to apply to the task in previous thousands of feet they had behind them now. Conrad's rope team led off in front, followed by Johnny's rope, then mine. We had only been going for a couple of hundred metres when Conrad and Carl had to turn back with Gaz Keep. They came thumping their feet down past us and said something about going back to the 16,000ft Camp. Gaz had realised he had mild altitude sickness and he felt worse immediately as we ascended, even though we all thought we had had enough time here. We couldn't take the risk of Gaz being ill. There was nothing he could do about it. He was just extremely unfortunate and his safest and best treatment was to go back to the tent and rest. It was too much for him to continue and he would have been at risk of severe problems even over just a couple of hundred feet of altitude. It was exactly the right decision. I thought maybe Carl would stay with Gaz and Johnny's team would wait for Conrad, who would join one of our ropes or that Conrad would take someone from Johnny's rope to stay with Gaz. Conrad would sort out what he was going to do.

111

I pick up from some notes that Carl gave us for our research in this chapter and I quote directly from them in places, as they make such interesting reading. The only change is to refer to Carl in the 'third person', as I have been referred to in the 'first person' so far and it makes it less confusing.

At 16,200ft on the day of the summit bid, we set off at 7 in the morning having made breakfast. Carl in front, Gaz and Conrad were at the rear. At about 16,800ft, Gaz felt bad once again with altitude sickness. Conrad decided to take Gaz back to the tents at 16,200ft and leave him there. Carl said to Conrad that he would go down with Gaz and stay with him while Conrad went up with the rest of the team, but Conrad said Gaz would be alright by himself and they would pick him up once we had got to the summit and come back down to 16,200ft that night. As Gaz was going down to the tents, Conrad loaded Carl's rucksack with the rest of the gear from Gaz's rucksack. Carl's rucksack now weighed nearly twice as much as normal (instead of being light for the summit bid.) Conrad carried almost nothing, banking on the fact that they would reach the summit and make it back to 16.200ft before dusk. He had given a provisional turnaround time of about twelve hours.

Conrad returned to where he had left Carl to take Gaz down to 16,200 ft. They then carried on and tried to catch up with the rest of the team. At about 17,000 ft, Carl had a severe headache and felt he should tell Conrad about it. He said to Carl "You will be alright." and they carried on.

I headed my rope team, took the place of lead rope and broke through the crust plunging my cramponed boots down through the soft snow beneath with each laboured step. Lifting my knees almost to a ninety degree angle to break through I still had my own bodyweight and my rucksack bearing down on each leg as I pushed forward breathing hard as I did so. Every few strides there would be a pause to pull in another few lungs-full of air that bore the small amounts of precious oxygen. It was really tough trying to break through to the front from behind, but Johnny's team would take over later in the day to give us a good chance of making our turn-around time.

I called back to ask how everyone was doing over and over during the climb. Everyone said they were O.K. We were all going through the same thing. Lifting legs, dragging the boots through the top of the snow, taking the strain on each leg at a time to hold the weight and push up over and over and over, concentrating on each breath, so we kept on plodding and stopping for breaks. I fully expected a slow ascent, as I wanted Johnny and Conrad fresh enough to take their stints at breaking trail.

All the teams stopped regularly for short rests, some of these were longer than others, as each rope moved at a different speed at different times. The ropes were pretty much in line of sight a lot of the time, but when they weren't, it was still possible to shout to each one and wait for them to come back into sight from the undulations of the mountain. We weren't far apart in terms of real distance but in time it seemed far because of the way we were moving. So a half hour wait, didn't mean a great deal in terms of distance between ropes as the pace was so slow at times.

An extra day at 16,200ft may have given us a little extra speed in moving today but so far there were no more reports from anyone of AMS or even of bad headaches. Carl kept quiet about his headache and the weight of gear he was carrying. It just meant the leading team got very cold sitting on a rock waiting for the following team. Breaking trail is a demanding and exhausting task with lifting the feet higher and breaking through the fresh snow pack like trying to force a path of sorts through water and I was hoping Johnny would be ready to take over soon.

The rest of the team was fatigued to the same extent and thirst raged through us like a virus that wouldn't be shaken off when we got very hot. It was coming up time for a good long rest and some lunch. Steve heated some water as well as can be done at this altitude and made some tepid tea. Even though the water wouldn't boil, the brew was welcome. Johnny's team came into view and then Carl and Conrad. I called back to the teams yet again to see if they were O.K., making a nuisance of myself because there isn't a lot of spare breath to reply with and it breaks the precious rhythm of breathing.

At approximately noon and about 18,000ft everyone met up and had a good, long break for lunch. The team had a photo together with the yellow sleep mat I was taking back for Gemma's birthday. The rope teams were a little spread out amongst the rocks as we rested. Carl said to Conrad that he was feeling pretty rough and complained to him that he was still suffering with his terrible headache and was really tired. He told Carl to make some hot chocolate.

"I can't, I feel really bad." Said Carl. Conrad told him to get on with it. When I saw Carl myself I asked if he was O.K. He seemed a bit morose and said his head was bad. He was lying across a rock to rest and let his headache go off. I told him to make sure to let us know if it didn't go off or got worse. I settled back for lunch with my own rope team.

Carl made the chocolate and gave some to Conrad. It seemed to Carl that everyone else was in good spirits, even if they were all tired, except him. He simply didn't want to be where he was and felt he should have stayed with Gaz and recovered their headaches together. He was really worn out and not enjoying Conrad's company but what could he do. Conrad was his boss here and in the UK. He kept his mouth shut and did as he was told.

We all rested for about one and a half hours and in the meantime, Carl's headache subsided, which was a good sign. The weather was with us so the turn-around time was not making us anxious. If we missed it, it wasn't going to be a huge deal, we had daylight throughout and we would feel better with every step of descent.

The team chatted and basked in the sub arctic sunshine, breathing the clean (if thin) air and taking photographs of each other and the stunning views. Everyone seemed to feel a lot better for the rest and no problems were made apparent when asked if they were ready to move on. It was almost as if to utter a complaint at this stage would jinx our luck. My rope team prepared to move off again.

By the time everyone was on the move, Carl said he was feeling at his peak again, such as it was although he still had some headache and was tired. He said to Conrad then, "If I feel like that again at 19,000, I won't be able to carry on." He was serious, the headache had been excruciating and he was very tired. The pain had made him feel pretty 'washed-out'. I would have fully expected him to sit it out at 19 with anyone else who didn't feel up to the last 1,000 plus feet and make himself comfortable for two or three hours while we made our turn-around. By

19, we would only be about an hour and a bit away from the summit and nobody hangs about up there in the cold and thin air. There would be a few pats on the back, a few 'Thank fucks', a few photos, a few 'Wow's' at the view and straight back down. I wouldn't have liked to split the team anymore but it would have to be done if Carl was feeling that ill again. I would probably need back-up from Johnny and Phil to try to persuade Conrad to leave someone with Carl if needed. The problem was that we didn't really know just how bad he had been because he only reported how bad it was to Conrad.

Conrad reiterated what I had been thinking but didn't mention leaving anyone with him. He said to Carl, "The only thing I can do is leave you at 19 on your own and pick you up on the way back down after we have reached the summit." On this point, nobody was happy with the fact that Gaz had been left at 16,200ft on his own. It is one decision that I think regardless of success or failure I wouldn't have taken. I have never left anyone on their own on any size of hill at any altitude, even sea-level.

Carl and Conrad followed on at the rear, as the two other teams were already on their way. Carl told us after the expedition was over that after about fifteen minutes of getting under way; Conrad himself took a turn for the worse. His speech was slurred and he was asking Carl if he had any spare water. They may not have been bosom buddies, but Carl knew that Conrad was not well and became concerned. Carl offered him some water and Conrad took a few welcome mouthfuls. After a short pause, they headed off again, but within about five minutes, Carl was alarmed to see that Conrad was clearly suffering.

Conrad was moving and speaking as if he was blind drunk, then dropped to his hands and knees and started licking the snow. "You can't go on like this," Said Carl, more than a little worried now. "I'm going to go and catch up with Martin and tell him what's wrong."

"No, I'm fine, I'll be alright, stay here. You don't need to tell Martin anything." Snapped Conrad. He was alarmed at the suggestion Carl might report it and struggled to regain his composure before continuing to 18,900ft where Conrad said he needed another short break.

Carl knew that Conrad didn't want Johnny or I to know what was happening. He knew that we would halt the summit bid between us or leave Carl and Conrad to rest or take them back down a little further and make the summit without them. Carl felt he was in the disobeying a direct order from an officer territory now and Conrad was his boss and life could be hell back at the Regiment if he made the wrong judgement. He was thinking what else could go wrong? If he reported Conrad's condition, he'd never be forgiven. So, they stopped for a break and had been resting for no more than 30 seconds when they heard an urgent shout that they thought was Johnny.

* * *

"How are you doing?" I called back to Phil.

"How are you doing Steve?" I had to call louder to Steve who was number three on the rope and was looking very tired. Steve and I had done a lot of work in previous days, cutting in steps and digging like ten men. I suppose with our background as engineers digging and bridge building was second nature.

I could tell the guys were getting fed up with me calling back to them so often, as the reply was an effort. It interrupts the rhythm of breathing and stepping, which feels almost impossible at this height. We got to the stage where we were resting more frequently now as we waited for the other two rope teams to catch up. We weren't so much moving more quickly than them, it was just bloody hard work and we kept a similar distance between us all the way.

Johnny came through with his team. "You're going to ask me to take over now aren't you mate?" It was more a statement of inevitability than a question from Johnny. "Yes, I am mate" I replied with a big grin and a supporting nod.

"I can't mate, I'm fucked!"

I could see that everyone was struggling to beat the sunset back to our Camp, such as it was at this time of year. I knew well that we'd not make the summit unless I carried on breaking the trail. I wasn't happy or being a martyr about it, I was just resigned to it. It was like a twenty-four hour step aerobics session with a rucksack and heavy boots. The lack of oxygen was telling on all of us. "OK mate, don't worry about it". I was a bit pissed off but not with Johnny, he's a sterling bloke, it was just the position we were in and maybe it was just my physiology in that I was just a bit luckier to have higher O_2 saturation in my blood, like Tory Boy.

We were getting very close and we were just going to have to make it a longer day and completely crash when we get back to the tents at 16.2 with Gaz. At least if he's rested he can make all the brews for us, so that was one consolation. Off we went again at a steady plod.

Conrad and Carl were still bringing up the rear and from my view up front looked to be moving steadily towards Johnny's team. Neither of them looked to be trying to get Johnny's attention nor dropping back. Nigel and Tory didn't notice anything amiss with Carl and Conrad either at the time but they had their heads down treading into Johnny's footsteps on his rope team. The gaps between teams stayed pretty much the same, which was an indication that we were all knackered but still progressing.

Carl, however as I have said was not having a good day. His body ached and had struggled with every step. Since leaving Gaz behind, Conrad loaded a lot of spare gear onto Carl who already had his own. Nobody knew about that and he was suffering in silence. The spare water had been guzzled and his boss had been in and out of 'Cloud Cuckoo Land' for a spell. Carl was in a dilemma and didn't know what to do. Reporting his own boss to two or three other guys from other Regiments was going to get his arse kicked he figured. He kept his mouth zipped.

Conrad had surprisingly little gear but to everyone else he looked like he was carrying a normal bag full. The weight of his pack still would have felt fairly heavy, but nothing to what the rest of the team were carrying and nothing to what we had been carrying every day so far and certainly nothing like what Carl was loaded with. Summit day is usually a lightweight operation to get it over and done with but still with emergency essentials just in case.

Conrad freely admitted to not being very fit but now he was compromising himself with what he was leaving behind and until things went wrong, nobody would know what he had left. It must have been difficult for him to decide what to leave behind, knowing he had made the decision to lighten his load. He just really wanted the team to succeed after the previous expedition he went on failed and so tantalisingly close to the top. He was clearly suffering now. He appeared to be such a nice and charming personality that we all wanted to succeed for him as well as ourselves. He and Carl stopped to rest again.

Carl sat on a rock feeling totally pissed off. He had already wanted to stay behind with Gaz, the summit wasn't that important to him He had been loaded down with all the extra gear, his head ached terribly, he was extremely tired and thirsty and there was Conrad crawling around on his belly licking the snow. He describes Conrad as being totally 'out of it'. He had gained the reputation of being Denali's Captain Ahab chasing his 'white whale' at all costs. It had been a bit of a joke really amongst a few of them but with an undertone of 'actually, I think we all mean it.'

He had worried most of the team at some point with his ambition to get up there and with the kayaking phase that was still to follow all of this but he was reassuring and would overrule arguments, which most of the guys put down to leadership. Anyway, those worries were sporadic and dissipated and they kept the camaraderie going and Conrad was an affable guy for the most part. He just liked things done his way, as happens on all expeditions every leader is different. He had to make sure that there was no mistake who the expedition leader was. He had to keep the momentum and morale going and arguments and explanations had to be plausible.

This way, there was no doubt who was in charge. He had put a lot of effort into getting the expedition out of the U.K., especially with training issues and rope leaders dropping out or not wanting to join. It didn't seem fair to him that the expedition would fold over so small a thing as fitness or a headache that would ease in a few hours.

Carl would not be placated, he could barely face the hours ahead, loaded down and carrying twice his share of the weight on his back. Carl was wishing he was on one of the other ropes, or at least that I or Johnny could see what was going on without him having to try to visibly draw attention to it.

Conrad himself must have been rather alarmed at his own actions when he became lucid and realised what he had done. He would have to try to recover this later and hang on to some respectability. Carl would just have to understand that these things happen with altitude and oxygen deprivation. It was nobody's fault. His respectability wouldn't be in question for altitude sickness. It's what he does when the plan falters that makes a difference. You could almost peel open Conrad head and read all these thoughts that must have been going through his mind.

The summit was now only less than two hours away. I took the trail over to a safer route that was less exposed with rocks below to help break any potential fall. The problem with our position now was that we were too close to the Orient Express for my liking. The advised West Buttress route didn't come this way but this was quite manageable and I'd cut through to plenty of routes in my time, it was pretty much routine. However, I didn't think the guys should be exposed to it in the event of a fall.

I veered off to approach the 'Football Field' from beneath. This would lead us to a cornice, a windswept wave of solid snow that I would be able to make some simple cuts through as I was planning on my approach. This is the type of work I have done on many occasions, as I said. It is a bit more work but the time spent is worth it and it would make a safer and shorter passage to the safer ground and really, it only takes several minutes.

We could have another short break here, I'd cut through and the guys would just step up through to the slope of the 'Football Field'. This is a snowfield, almost a gently rising plateau to the summit. It would be nice terrain to finish off, though of course it was still up-hill. Another rest, another plod, another rest and so it continued, calling back to check on Phil and Steve. 'Still with me, good', I thought, feeling reassured that they were still up to the task. Dragging themselves along in my footprints Phil and Steve brought up the rear all of us feeling utterly depleted. I think we had gone beyond muscular pain and were now spending determination instead.

At last, we reached the cornice, we knew once we were through this the climb on to the summit would be a walk in the park compared to what we had just been through. We took another breather, (we wished). Anyway, we rested and looked around. Luckily, I saw a nice, natural break in the cornice that would be a perfect place and easy to cut through, as nature had partially done the work. Not too much exertion and quite quick too and positioned right where we wanted to go. We just needed a neat little step through and we were on the 'Football Field'.

'Just another short rest before we go on,' I thought. Johnny, Nigel and Tory Boy were still following but had just dropped out of sight as we got to the cornice and would be in view where we rested at any moment. Conrad and Carl were still some way back from us but still within a good distance of Johnny's rope when we last saw them but should arrive pretty soon too. None of us on the other ropes realised the state that Conrad was in now and how he was suffering and of course the knock-on effect this had on Carl who was past being exhausted and couldn't have cared less about being near the summit. All he knew was that he was having a really bad time and he knew the further up we went, the further he would have to walk back down again. This was his last mountain, he swore. All he wanted to do was get off the mountain or at least get as far away from Conrad as he could.

The distance between the ropes had been closing again, as we got higher and even taking it easier now would mean reaching the summit. It was all going great now and we were now an hour and a bit away from the top. The weather was good for the bid and we would make it back before the light dimmed to make deceptive shadows on the snow and trick a fatigued climber into a fall.

It was now about 19:20hrs. It had been a slow day but we still had a lot of daylight, excellent visibility and plenty of it left for the descent after the summit. Ready to move, we'd had a good little break and we were all three up on our feet, Steve had taken his helmet off during the break probably because he was so hot maybe and we waited while everyone got their kit back on and sorted. I stood still until I felt we were ready for the cut through, waiting for Steve and Phil to sort themselves out and I looked up at the solid wave of snow that rolled above us. I made up my mind just where to make the first cut, while Phil and Steve secured their last bits of gear. As I reached around for my other ice axe I said to the other two "OK guys, you'll need your other ice..." the instruction was left in mid-air as I saw Phil sit back as his harness was pulled hard from behind pulling him right off balance.

The horror shot through me in the blink of an eye as I saw what was about to happen "Shit!" was all I had time to say as Phil's face tensed to a shocked grimace and his eyes widened, startled as he toppled and stepped out with his right foot into thin air. Steve wasn't there, he was gone. I immediately twisted round to the front to brace myself and hold their weight. The tension built up on the rope and the snow-pack started to give way beneath my feet. Immediately I threw myself into an ice-axe arrest. The pick had barely bitten into the surface when I felt the tension pulling me on the rope and was plucked from the steep slope in a way I can only describe as like being shot from a catapult and down the face of the mountain.

The pick of the axe was whipping through softened ice and snow. All I could see was the white rush of the ice spraying all around me as the pick tore it away. I held the axe hard into my body, my arms locked into position as I waited for it to start biting into the ice. All I could hear was the rush and roar and scraping that our fall was creating then; 'Bang!' my axe was wrenched from my hands and wrist so quickly, I didn't see it go, it had hit hard ice. My teeth were biting together so hard I thought they would smash. My arm was momentarily deadened from the ice axe being ripped away with the weight of three men on it.

A new sensation I was suddenly aware of was that of the rope somehow being above me at some point and I felt as though I was slowing down. Then the rope came whipping past me and again I was catapulted down. Obviously the other two were tumbling out of control and not arresting with their axes. There was nothing to slow us down.

I was clawing frantically at the surface, embedding my hands as hard as I could at the unstable ice on the near vertical surface. The rope jerked again as the weight of the two men below pulled at me and sped the descent again. We were falling a long, long way.

The fall was lasting so long that I had time to think to myself, "What can I do now?

All I could do now was a desperate act that would either flip me over so I was free-falling up-side down or break both ankles but slow our fall. If I didn't try something, we were dead anyway, no kidding, it was two-miles down from where we were. I desperately felt for contact with the surface again and as my body closed in to meet it I dropped my lower legs to dig my crampon points into the ice.

I was braced ready for the pain as my points bit at the surface. They rattled at the rough surface at first, as I continued plummeting at speed feeling the hard vibration travel through my body. Then it came, within a few long seconds. The crack was clearly audible even above rushing sound that was filling my ears.

The pain shot through my body like a hot and freezing blade. With the full capacity of my lungs, I screamed out with the pain. I knew my boots would hold my ankles in place regardless of the pressure I applied. I continued to dig in now with my mind now in full combat against my pain. All my effort was in digging my toes into roughened ice and hoping I wasn't going to be flipped over if I hit something big. In my mind the worst was to come because I knew I had to do it again with the other foot. I did it and there was the same pain, the scream across the sky and gasping but I heard no crack this time. Don't pass out, please don't pass out. I was grasping at the surface, I was panting, gritting my teeth.

Suddenly, a new and terrifying realisation came to me; everything lightened and I was lifting away from the surface of the mountain. With fresh air between me and the mountain, I wasn't going to stop falling. Startled now I whispered "Oh God, No!" I had nothing else to stall the weight of the two men on the rope and myself, nothing. Suddenly and almost before the realisation that I have made contact with anything, I found myself lying almost prone leaning on my right side, somehow we had stopped and it was absolutely miraculous.

We had slid to a halt on a very small, gently sloping, rocky ledge with our lower legs dangling over the edge of what looked like infinity. We were over 'The Valley of Death', at least two and a half miles of space dropped and faded from vision beneath us. A wrong move now would send us to our deaths never to be recovered. I couldn't believe we had landed and not died.

The rope had become entangled in rocks. It looks like a lot of rope when gathered in loosely. I looked over to my left and saw Phil sitting next to me, slumped and hunched over with his legs also over the edge. He was looking shocked and dazed, of course he was. He probably had no idea how he was still alive, the same as me. His head was bleeding but not too badly and he was trying to pull the metres of rope away that had landed around his head and shoulders. "Are you OK Phil?" I shouted shakily.

"Y-Yeah, I think so!" stammered Phil. We looked for Steve. We didn't see him immediately but heard a whimpering and whining sound from just below to the left of Phil.

I tried to put some weight on my feet, but it was impossible. Whatever had happened to them, I wasn't going to look. I couldn't work out whether the severe sharpness and agony I felt was hot or cold. I really thought at that point both ankles were broken. They were going to stay strapped up inside the plastic boots and I would just have to deal with it for now. I can't say whether the act slowed us down or not but they did bite in and stayed for a while before I lost contact with the mountainside. They hurt a lot but not like they did when I first pushed them into the ice. I guess I was being fed a great deal of adrenaline by now and I was in some mild shock myself, as was Phil.

I crawled over to Steve by following the line of rope and clambering over Phil who was still trying to get rid of the damned metres and metres of it bundled around him. Steve was only about 10ft - 15ft away. He was clearly conscious and I couldn't work out what he was doing bent over. He didn't answer when I called to him. I crawled across and I grabbed at him and dragged him close enough to see what was wrong with him. To my horror, Steve was on all fours with his head dangling downward, swaying and trying to clamber to his feet right on the edge of the precipice. He had his back to thousands and thousands of feet of sheer drop below him and he was trying to untie himself from the rope. I remember thinking, 'Oh, my God, he's going to kill himself!' I sat leaning back as far as I could and hurriedly hauled the slack of the rope in to try and snatch it from Steve's hands and get them away from the harness.

I was using all my strength to try and pull Steve away from the edge. I could get no traction on the ice with my knees as my lower legs were out of action and the pain as I leaned back against my ankles was snatching at my breath. Steve was still trying to untie. I was yelling at him not to and still trying to pull him in but I couldn't. I was now really frightened in a different way. I couldn't get control of him. I felt as though I were flying Steve, semi-conscious, like a giant, very heavy kite, as he staggered and swayed against the edge of what would be another unrecoverable body on the mountain if he untied and unclipped. In an effort, I didn't think I had left. I yanked Steve towards me and tried to take control finally.

Steve was bleeding profusely from a head wound. I tried to secure him, but he was fighting me off violently. He was obviously badly concussed and not at all compos mentis. I used his section of rope and tied him off in a more secure position to the rocks but was only able to drag myself around or crawl, so was having trouble keeping him tied on.

The pain I was in now the adrenaline had filtered away was making everything very difficult to say the least. Steve had obviously decided in the depths of his now addled brain that he was going to untie and unclip himself at all costs and run off the edge of the mountain and he seemed desperate in his attempts to succeed. He had clearly not had chance to strap his helmet back on as I stood looking up at the cornice and had somehow gone over. We later think that as he stood back up too quickly in the thinness of the air that he had fainted. It's the only explanation he had for it later and it is perfectly plausible. The other suggestion was that as he stood up to adjust the last of his gear, he took a peek over the edge of the steep slope while he waited for me to do the cutting and had simply slipped. We just don't know. Nobody was moving around at the time, I was just standing in front of the cornice, Phil stood quietly behind me and Steve just disappeared.

Phil was now fairly coherent and not too badly injured. He was mildly concussed and had numerous lacerations and bruises but it was very luckily superficial, he was obviously shaken and would need some suturing on his head wound. We were all shaken and I was very grateful that Phil wasn't too fazed by the fall to help. I needed all the help I could get with Steve, and Phil wouldn't be ready for that just yet. He needed a little recovery time. The safest thing for all of us was that he sat quietly and waited for help while I hoped Steve would stay settled until Johnny got to us.

Chapter 9 - End-Ex.

Johnny, Nigel and Ian, (Tory Boy) must have seen the fall occur. They were all initially frightened at what may have happened to their team mates, as we whistled past at some distance to the right of them.

Johnny yelled back to Conrad and Carl who had just stopped to rest briefly some way behind but were still in earshot at about 18,900ft. Conrad and Carl heard clearly something had happened but couldn't tell whose voice it was. As I said earlier, they thought it was Johnny. "There's been a fall."

Johnny immediately started to make a route down and across to his stricken friends with what haste he could summon after the exhausting climb. The sparseness of the oxygen he was trying to feed his body with compounding his efforts to reach us. He very carefully picked his way over to us.

Back on the ledge we had just found a spot to rest amongst the rocky surface when we heard a shout; we thought it sounded like Johnny calling to Conrad that there had been a fall. We knew they were close, as we could hear part of what was called out.

Carl and Conrad heard the shouts and as the message hit home. After everything, it was incredulous. Conrad threw down his ice axe, fell to his knees and said "Well, that's fucked the summit bid up then!"

He was exasperated, suffering from hypoxia and now his white whale had got away for a second time. He was in and out of confusion, but started to make his way across to the ledge with Carl. 'End-Ex' (expedition over). Carl was shocked by Conrad's reaction, but kept his mouth shut again all the same. Conrad was just bewildering Carl now, thinking that they didn't know exactly who had fallen or how bad the fall had been. They didn't even know if everyone was alive. Carl was pretty disgusted at this point.

They got up and went to look for the fallen climbers. Conrad appeared to Carl to be in the blackest mood. He looked furious and disgusted himself. He had to just get on with the new scenario now and make the best of his decisions. All that work wasted.

As they rounded a large boulder, they saw Johnny had anchored Nigel and Tory to a rock over to the right. A good precautionary move. Further to the right was Johnny busy treating the casualties and chatting to them. As they got closer, they saw that Steve was in a very bad way, Phil was injured and I couldn't move much, I was shuffling around on my knees and we were all a bit bloodied. Phil and I did not bleed too much and Steve's bleeding had also almost stopped to a light seeping into the dressing, thanks to the cold we were unlikely to bleed too much anyway. It was all a bit of a mess, but we were all alive. Conrad could now see that afterall it was pretty bad and not just a tumble.

Carl got one of the medical kits out of his rucksack and started to try and help the others sort Steve out. Even if they weren't injured, there would be nobody from this team standing on the summit of Denali. With no camp for shelter and the sun descending slowly towards the peaks, the others would, at best have to make their way back to the 16,200ft Camp we had left early that morning. They could bring warm gear and food back to hunker down and wait for rescue if they couldn't get the injured back to the tents or down to 14,200ft. Even in the height of summer in good weather, Denali is not a mountain to become benighted on without some shelter. As soon as the sun moves away from the surface, the cold returns instantaneously.

Steve was trying to rip off his clothes while Johnny and I battled to put them back on again. There wasn't a moments respite to it. We couldn't work out where he got the energy from, we were all so knackered. Thankfully, Johnny had traversed his way across and went straight to work on the casualties instead of trying any other task so it was a great help. He told me to sit down and then took over the unenviable task of trying to control the tormented creature that poor Steve had now become.

Luckily Steve passed out a few times, which allowed us to get him wrapped up. Whatever was going on within his mind had him trapped there. Phil and I did what we could to help as Johnny's welcome presence eased some of the pressure that was on us but we couldn't do too much to be honest. Steve was in and out of consciousness for the rest of what remained of the day. Nigel and Tory Boy helped by getting kit sorted out and trying to stabilise everything but they were a little bewildered by what had happened too and followed everything they were told but there was not a great deal they could do. We were on a ledge with no camp, half our gear missing, three injured and everyone knackered.

As Conrad and Carl arrived, the ledge was already busy. Things were quite bad, but not impossible and the rocky ledge was quite small and sloping. The ice very hard and made it impossible material for digging in a snow hole or little ice trench. The drop off the edge was an incredible, sheer 8,000ft with further depth beyond that.

It was just amazing luck that all three of us had survived the fall and were now conscious, but I thought the casualties meant there would be no moving off the ledge tonight. Conrad checked on the condition of the guys.

I said to Conrad, "Get on the radio and call for help!" I went on to explain that they should radio down for a casivac, (casualty evacuation), as there was no way I'd be walking off and it wasn't safe for Steve to make his way down in his state if he comes round a bit more and Phil has mild concussion and could get better or worse. Johnny was on top of the casualties and he, quite rightly wanted us off the mountain.

Our new problem was that the radios were dead. No problem, I thought. I knew it was on the agenda to sort out the spares at the Ranger Station in Talkeetna and they are always kept close to the body for warmth, so they will work in extreme conditions. "It's no good, they're dead." Said Conrad, he turned and stepped away to carry on his tasks. I was slightly taken aback at this as he didn't look for the spare batteries or even attempt to check them. I had asked for the spare batteries to be sorted out at the Ranger Station, they can't be dead, they're new, and we haven't even used them yet. Surely they would have been kept warm.

I didn't want to voice what I thought, but I felt he was lying; they had been left behind to save on that precious weight. I was angry at not being able to take more control. He didn't try them because he didn't have them.

I realised that they would have to try and make their own way down to organise something. With no way of communicating with the Rangers at 14,200ft Camp, the situation suddenly became a lot more serious. Was I mad or was I the only one here who had any idea what shit we were in now? Probably a good thing, as I didn't want the guys in further stress or panic or arguments starting to break out. This needed to be calm and thought out and the situation with the casualties, the weather and the terrain very, very carefully considered. Johnny was working in his specialist area; I was now hoping to get some headway in mine.

We needed to concentrate all our efforts on Steve. I observed Johnny working away and trying to quietly reason and argue with Conrad over something. Johnny and I looked at each other from time to time and I recognised the expression on his face. He obviously knew too, we were right in the shit. Clearly Conrad knew but we were all keeping ourselves in check and letting him think this through. It was clearly a tough deal for him and the more he thought of splitting the team, the more decisions he would have to make. It would just multiply the problems.

I guessed Conrad had no bivi bag with him as he was sitting, hugging his knees and staring off into space. "Why don't you get your bivi bag out?" I asked.

"I'm fine." Replied Conrad. I knew then for sure that he had left that behind too. I wanted to empathise for him and his situation but I couldn't understand why he had left his gear, even if it was heavy. I was pretty annoyed with him now. He could now easily become another liability to the team not a resource we could utilise to improve our situation. He wasn't going to lose face with us by admitting the gear was too heavy. It was damned heavy, even today at half the weight it was heavy but we would have worked something out. We'd have just taken the piss out of him, good-heartedly, that's expected. I would also expect that Conrad was wishing that he had either brought the batteries or at least taken up the offer of hiring a mobile phone from the Ranger Station back in Talkeetna. The Rangers give us every opportunity to help ourselves. Boy, I was annoyed now but what purpose could it possibly serve to start a row in this situation, almost like kicking a man when he was down.

Sleep was a luxury that few managed for more than a few moments at a time. Steve's need to escape whatever bonds he thought he was trapped in were as strong as ever. He was constantly whimpering loudly and writhing around trying to fight off everyone who was trying to help him, as they fought to keep him clothed and trying to reassure him.

Johnny waited until Steve fell into a restless sleep and took the opportunity to dress his head wound properly, trying to put his warm hat over the dressing to keep it in place. Steve would have none of it. Johnny's painstaking efforts were ripped away in another writhing and whining motion. All the guys took it in turns to try to look after Steve. He was in bad shape and they would have to discuss what best to do in the morning. What a night we had ahead.

In the meantime, Conrad took the decision to send Johnny to take the rest of the team down to the 14,200ft Camp and raise the alarm. The fall had occurred just over an hour earlier and it was best to move now while there was still good to fair visibility. Here Conrad met with strong resistance from Johnny at last.

Johnny and I had been over-ruled already on a couple of points but this was different. Johnny was angry and put up strong opposition and the discussion became heated between them. They began to argue more fiercely. Conrad said that Johnny should go and that he, as the expedition leader was in charge of how to task the team members. Johnny was not having rank pulled on him and argued that he was the only qualified medic on the team; he wanted to stay and tend to Steve instead of taking him down in his poor and still dangerous condition.

The row went on, Johnny felt that Steve would live for the time being, but he needs help, it was that serious. Johnny thought he was the best one to assess and judge whether Steve could be taken down at a later stage, it was so soon after the fall; Johnny held the qualifications and had a lot of experience on the ground of Arctic conditions. In the end Conrad barked at him saying, 'I'm in charge, do as I say!' Johnny went to gather up the rest of the team reluctantly, taking Phil and the others with him leaving Conrad, Carl, Steve and I on the ledge. Everyone stayed silent except for the odd mumble here and there when someone really needed to speak. He had the rank pulled on Johnny after all. I wished him luck and said 'Cheerio'. They left at 20:30 hours, Thursday 18 June. I was sorry to see him go.

I had lost some confidence in Conrad too, as the situation was not so much being managed as cobbled together even with advice from I and Johnny. I felt as if all I was giving were 'opinions' not 'advice' from the way most of my contributions were received on the expedition. I had been treated with respect but plenty of what I and Johnny had to say was paid lip-service.

As it turned out, sending Johnny to the Rangers at 14,200ft was not a bad decision afterall because he was strong, capable, reliable and experienced. What it left us with on the ledge was one man who had a good level of expertise and a lot of experience but was 'hobbled'. We also had a strung out expedition leader who now demonstrated a lack of experience even if his intentions were good and nobody else with any experience of any part of our situation. The rest of them were injured, exhausted or out of their depth with what had happened or was about to happen. The person they felt they had to listen to was the expedition leader and their boss. This is where they needed some confident and positive leadership.

At least that would be one minor casualty off the mountain and Johnny knew he had a good chance of making it. Tired though he was, he would be capable of making the trip and would have the strength to hold Phil on a short rope all the way down. Phil was also able to work for himself to a good degree, in spite of his concussion. Phil was a steady bloke, very capable and measured and far too diplomatic and nice to enter a row, I was very sorry when he left too. The two others, Ian (Tory Boy) and Nigel just went along and did as they were told, like good soldiers, they got on with the job, worked hard, put up with a lot of shit, found humour wherever they could and kept their mouths shut. I think they were happy not to be involved in the discussions. They were a nice team, I liked them. We had the potential to do this with the personalities and strengths of character in these lads.

We had found the weak link and we were angry and disappointed but couldn't help feeling bad for him at the same time because he came across as such a nice bloke but Conrad had lost the expedition before it started by not getting the training done that should have been second nature before we had even left the UK.

The problem I think Johnny, Phil and I and of course Carl had in our own minds was that now, in this situation, we had probably realised earlier that the weak link was the boss but had conflict of rank and leadership. Loyalty in a long-served soldier is virtually a duty and in-grained. This isn't Civvy Street where you just risk a written warning for telling the boss, 'You're messing up bit by bit so we're taking over.'

Anyway, that was most of the team now away from the ledge and headed back to a far safer spot.

Johnny made his way back down warning Phil, Tory Boy and Nigel to stay in his footprints. It was pointless worrying about his heated exchange with Conrad. It was out of his hands but he hoped that Conrad was up to looking after Steve. Conrad had been looking pretty rough, without having to monitor and care for a man that was a danger to himself and the team until his concussion cleared, if it didn't kill him first.

Phil still had slight concussion and his ankle was unstable, he had also been shaken by the fall, as we all had so was further depleted by his previous shock. He fell a few times, but had managed to ice axe arrest effectively. He was a very well behaved casualty. He was clearly exhausted but managed to keep up the effort, being a Royal Marine, he was physically capable of the trip and mentally plodding through the incentive to keep going. The fall line in front of him was a good 3,000ft and he had to put any little faith he had left into his crampon points, trusting them to bite in and hold each step. He'd had good reason to have his confidence knocked in the last 24 hours but he learned to trust his gear again in spite of the frightening terrain he was travelling over.

Johnny had become concerned about losing light, he wanted a clear view and time was pushing on. Flat light, as it's called on white ground makes obstacles and hazards very difficult to see, as any skier knows when they hit a mogul and are dumped. They began warily to make their way down the 'Orient Express'. As Phil was new to mountaineering so, his faith in his equipment was virtually blind now. This was his first very serious descent. He was being short-roped all the way by Johnny so he wouldn't drop more than a couple of feet, but it had been a rather bad day! Phil had just fallen 300ft, just stopped short of a 2-mile drop to his death and here he was, with head and ankle injuries still at the top end of one of the world's most hazardous mountains. He'd get a few beers out of this story.

It was now Friday 19th June - Day 17.

They followed Johnny closely and by half past midnight, they arrived at the 16,200ft Camp that they had left in such high spirits only that morning. Johnny was a Parachute Regiment Sergeant, so had good leadership experience and he was winter qualified, so the others listened to him with seriousness. Nigel and Tory had been left at the 16,200ft Camp to rest with Gaz; they would be safe there. They now had plenty to pass the time with now there was a tale to tell and they would be making the steady walk back down to 14,200ft without the others after a good rest and a brew.

What they found at 16,200ft was that there was no Gaz. What we didn't know was that Gaz had felt quite a bit better and already decided to leave and had soloed back to the 14,200ft camp to get treatment. He had been treated in the medical tent with Diamox and oxygen and put on an I.V. until he was much better and discharged at midnight of the 18th just half an hour before his friends had arrived back at 16,200ft Summit Camp where they had left him. Conrad would be in for a bit of a wrist slap from the Rangers for allowing Gaz to be left alone.

Usually full of cheerful and chaffing banter with the team, there was no mistake that nobody was going to try anything foolhardy. Now, Johnny continued to make his way down with Phil towards 14,200ft Camp. He didn't want to leave Phil with the others at 16,200ft, he needed medical aid too. The slope of the Orient Express was not nearly as bad here, they had made it through some of the bad parts but they weren't down yet. Once off the glacial slope, there were plenty of crevasses waiting for a falling climber. The ice is like polished glass and hard as concrete. It is very steep and very deadly. Treacherous is an appropriate description because so many think they can make it down and some of them have died. If Denali is not a mountain for the faint hearted then this section would get anyone's heart thumping hard with every little slip and recovery.

They had only been going a very short while when the sound of clattering gear could be heard. At 00:40 hrs Johnny looked up towards the West Rib above them to see two climbers with all their gear sliding down very fast towards him and then continuing past. There were no screams or shouts of fear and Johnny's first thought was that they were sledding or glissading their way down. It was hard to tell as the orange-outfitted climbers whizzed past him. He quickly realised this was no glissading attempt at a short cut and he was worried for them. They came to a stop and Johnny waited and observed them for a few moments to make sure.

"You guys having a party down there?" yelled Johnny,

"Not quite!" Came the American accented reply.

"Are you OK?" asked Johnny,

"Yeah!" called the shaken voice "But my partner's got a problem!"

Johnny and Phil immediately went down and across to the two climbers to see if they could help. They knew them; the British team had met the two American's on their way up. They were new friends, even if it was a brief friendship like kids have in the school holidays when they go to the beach. They were the ones who had used the 16,200ft Summit Camp the night Steve and I had finished digging it out and had left a big 'Thank you!' stamped into the snow to the team before they left. The two Americans that had dished out sweets to the team and departed with lots of friendly exchanges of good luck. The guy whose crampon I had repaired was the one that was now in very bad shape. He was Jeff Munroe, aged only 25 years and his friend, now trying to help him was Billy Finley, aged only 24 years, both from Anchorage. They had been climbing partners for a long time and wanted to tick Denali off their list.

As Johnny checked on Jeff to see what he could do, Phil gave his gloves to Billy, who then lapsed into shock, (no surprise given what had just happened). Johnny's assessment of Jeff was that he was in a terrible state. His breathing was very poor and there was foam about his mouth, a clear symptom of pulmonary oedema. Jeff had sustained a severe head injury and couldn't be moved without a litter. Johnny thought that Steve had been in a bad way but this young man really was at death's door.

Johnny instructed Billy so that there would be no mistake at the seriousness of the injury and their position, warning him that he must keep his friend awake. Johnny secured everything, using what gear was available and made sure that the two friends were tied on. Billy was in a rough state but the task of keeping an eye on his friend would also keep him going too.

Billy had made the summit at 22.07hrs, then met up again with Jeff and decided to pick their way down to Orient Express. They had been making good progress until they found themselves on solid ice. The going got trickier until Billy over balanced and fell forwards. They were unable to arrest the fall. They were the second group Johnny had been with that day that were lucky to have lived through such a severe fall. Johnny now had to make sure that everyone survived the aftermath. He had a lot of lives in his hands now and the pressure was on, it was already getting on for 01:00hrs. He had been on the go since 06:30 the previous morning and he still had hours of work in front of him, to which he gave no thought what-so-ever.

He had to get going and couldn't afford the extra time with Phil moving with him. Phil completely understood and agreed. Phil felt very unwell but not catastrophically ill. He was lucid and stable and able to function on his own to some extent. As long as Johnny got back sometime, later would do fine. This poor young soul in front of him could do with an extra pair of hands to help keep him going until the medical team arrived.

Phil was left to help Billy keep Jeff as conscious as possible and try and stop them all from slipping farther down the glacial terrain. The snow was unstable on the slope and every now and then, it would crumble under them. Phil dug new shelves out to hold them several times, but if they started to fall again, Phil would not be able to help. There would be no way of him holding the weight of two other men as well as himself. It had already been proven with my team. They were basically trying to hold themselves onto soft, unconsolidated snow, which was dusted over an enormous, steep, wet ice-cube that would likely kill them if they slipped any further.

Phil shivered and felt his teeth clattering together. He could see for himself, without Johnny's qualifications, how sick Jeff was. He desperately needed the Rangers' skills and equipment and quick. He couldn't stay on the mountain much longer and live. Jeff's breathing pattern and sound was very bad.

Johnny faced into the direction of the camp and walked as hard as he could. Phil blew his whistle in the vain hope that the Ian (Tory) and Nigel would hear it at the tents at 16,200ft. They were tired, would be wrapped in their sleeping bags, and wouldn't hear anything but the wind and snow rattling at the tent and their own breathing. Their thoughts though, must have been running wild at what was happening around them, they slept only fitfully but anyway, they were just too far away to hear anything like a whistle on the mountain.

Seven men were relying on Johnny to make it to camp, and fast. Johnny didn't let them down; he did 'P Company' (Parachute Regiment basic training) for a living and spent plenty of seasons in Norway. He was pretty much at home in the snow, but as they say, 'This is not a drill.' The terrain was as hazardous as it gets and the camp was a good distance away. There was still a lot ahead that could go wrong in his haste. He knew there were deadly seracs and crevasses, so he was thoughtful about his route. The light was dimmed and not ready to lighten to day just yet even here, a whisper away from Summer Solstice in time and the Arctic Circle in distance.

Phil had to lay with Jeff and keep a keen eye on him. Phil had his own head injury that wasn't being too good to him at the moment, his head felt groggy and fuzzy and it ached badly, but Jeff was in an ever more serious condition. Phil woke him each time he fell asleep and kept watch over Billy too who was quite understandably very distressed at the accident and suffering from the effects of shock and exposure himself. Phil knew he had a dying man with him and such a young one. It felt tragic already.

Here, as on the ledge 3,000ft above them the cold crept in and went to work on trying to claim a few more victims.

Johnny reached the 14,200ft Ranger Camp, not allowing himself to slow down with the relief of reaching it in one piece; he dashed straight for the medical tent and plunged through the entrance.

As the four men had left the ledge earlier and started their way to the 16,200ft Camp, they were only about 25 metres into their trip when

Conrad shouted after them. "Hey, have you guys got a radio?" Carl and I were open mouthed in shock. Carl was worried and silent, as he knew this was an on-going problem now, but I didn't, it was all new to me. "Conrad, they're our own guys," I said.

"Oh, yes," replied Conrad and then carried on about his business. I kept an eye out for Conrad, hoping it was just a lapse and the altitude wasn't getting too much of a grip. I had no idea how bad he had already been. I looked at Carl but he kept his moody expression and didn't say anything.

The light diminished only slightly on this night just coming into Summer Solstice. But it still cast deep, cold shadows. Carl tried desperately to scrape small amounts of snow together on the windswept ledge and place the mounds in a line to form a small wall. Almost as soon as he rammed the snow in place, the wind went to work shaving away at its surface. Undeterred, Carl continued to plod on like an old workhorse; exhausted, dehydrated and bitterly cold the wall grew slowly as Carl grew more depleted. He felt it was better than just sitting there.

Finally, there was nothing to be done. The icy ledge had too little snow to offer as building material, the wind was too strong to allow it to be built to any height and Carl's body was screaming at him that it was time to stop, he had nothing left.

The wall was barely 2ft high and had taken such a tremendous effort to put in place. He hoped it would provide some barrier against the knife edged winds whipping over his companions. He had tried desperately to dig a small scrape, knowing it would be hopeless to try and dig a snow hole on the ledge. It was solid. He took turns during the night to take care of Steve and slept when he could for short periods. As bad as this was, it was better than tramping up the mountain carrying all that kit and wondering what the hell to do about Conrad.

As the hours passed, Steve was showing no sign of improvement and was a worry to everyone, still noisily trying to throw himself around and not allowing anyone to dress his head. I struggled to help hold Steve as several attempts were made to patch him up, but nobody could do anything for him when he was conscious and there was little the others could do when he slept. It was taking all our energy just to make Steve keep his jacket on and we were already so very tired and fighting for breath. He was certainly the worse case that I had experienced in my career.

I got to the stage where I thought we would all be better off, including Steve, if he was knocked unconscious. I admitted that I was tempted but Steve was too delirious and I was afraid that if I socked Steve, that he wouldn't wake up again. It turned out that Conrad had the same thing in mind, worrying that Steve was going to become a liability to the guys trying to help him, they were after all perched on a very small area that sloped away towards the edge, something could easily go wrong. He also decided against it, as he was afraid that a blow in his condition would be likely to kill him.

The night passed very slowly and Steve became quiet and seemed to rest a little easier. The team had settled into our bivi bags to try and get what rest we could, each taking our turn to look after Steve.

Conrad again sat staring out into nothingness, without his bivi bag hugging his knees, and rocking himself back and forth. He was the expedition leader; the decisions ahead of him were unenviable, but were ultimately his. As they say, the right way isn't always the easy way. He could have done things the hard way and been out of trouble now. What he had to try and do was improve a bad situation.

I was highly qualified and had my years of experience behind me including my mountain first aid experience that had been called upon on numerous occasions in the past. Johnny was very well trained and experienced in survival techniques, he was also the appointed medic in the team. Conrad himself had not only been on expeditions before; he had been on this very mountain before. With all of that, we had the resources to come up with something between us. We also had fit and able bodies with us that weren't going to fold on him in the face of their dilemma no matter how exhausted they were. He was also aware by now that Carl and I suspected or knew that he was suffering with the altitude and that was nobody's fault but he should have told us and maybe Carl was at the point where he wanted to tell me but still felt that he couldn't.

It was alarming to realise that he was having lapses into confusion, slurring and having hallucinations. He would need to get down himself before long, before he got any worse and worse is all that it will get.

As the leader, he had to try and hold it together, he didn't want to go walking off the ledge thinking it was the entrance to Mc Donald's and he was going to fetch us all a Big Mac for our trouble. What went through Conrad's mind that night was probably a series of thoughts that nobody else will probably ever know; he had a great deal on his shoulders right now. As sleep tried to break through and ease us, the cold tore us back to consciousness again. It had been a very long night.

As Friday the 19th June arrived with us we had more difficulties ahead. With the morning came the decision-making. It wasn't pleasant for anyone. I still couldn't stand and Steve, although more strong and coherent, was withdrawn and not at all well. He seemed to lapse in and out of the real world and back to delirium.

At one stage he was sitting next to me staring at my injured legs, for all the world looking calm and compos mentis, as if he were carefully deliberating about something then he suddenly shot forward and grabbed one of my injured ankles twisting it around as hard as he could. I screamed out and lurched in agony with my whole body jerking and juddering. When I managed to draw breath again, I saw hands pulling Steve back. I could feel that wave of shock start to take me, with the nausea and light-headedness, my whole body and legs juddered but it passed as the heat and cold of the pain performed its long, slow, deep incision. It took several minutes for the very severe pain to slowly withdraw to a powerful throbbing. I still felt the nausea and the dull pain and shots of sharpness as they pulsed on for a long time.

The idea of knocking Steve out now was more tempting than ever before. I was furious, but had to remind myself that Steve just didn't know what he was doing. We had got on really well on the way up and remained friends after everything was over. As the hours went on I felt sick and distracted with the pain and tried to relax and let it pass. Eventually it turned into a heavy ache with occasional stabs if I kept in certain positions and so I stayed as still as possible.

Carl was utterly exhausted from his efforts with Steve during the night and trying to build a small snow wall, which took more hours of effort on and off during the day and got whipped away and in less time than it took to scrape it together. We were all hoping that Johnny had raised the alarm during the night, but there was no sign of any aircraft coming up to take a look. I was wondering what the delay was. We had the weather with us for now. I was hoping nothing had gone wrong for Johnny and the others.

Today was also Gemma's birthday, I looked out across the mountain and the sky and felt very disappointed not just that I was away from her again but that I hadn't even made the summit. I really missed my children. They were still the ages where they leapt at me and hugged and kissed me and climbed all over me when I had been away.

I thought a lot of time had passed, sufficient time for Johnny to have reached the camp and something to be organised. We were expecting a ground rescue to be under way any time now. We would have heard helicopters by now or heard the drone of a fixed wing aircraft if that wasn't viable. It must have gone through somebody's mind by now that perhaps some kind of complication had occurred and a rescue was not coming at the moment. It was going through my mind I know that and I couldn't distract myself from it for some time.

Conrad became anxious to get off the mountain and take Steve with him. Although Steve was more aware of what had happened, he still had the after effects of a bad concussion and his behaviour was erratic at times, but he was looking better and seemed brighter as time went on. Carl and I thought that he looked in better condition than Conrad did now and we felt better for him. In fact, Steve had improved so much in such a short time; he was almost his old self again. Conrad got ready to move and Carl and I helped to set Steve up for the trip down.

I had my reservations about the trip down and questioned Conrad directly now. "Are you sure you're alright to do this?" I asked.

"I'm fine." Said Conrad, confident and convincing as ever. Conrad suggested cutting the rope in half, leaving a half for me in case I wanted to try to climb down later. This confused me at first, thinking that half a rope is not enough in those conditions for two men.

"You don't cut a rope in half, Conrad." I said with an inflection that sounded almost like a question. Again, I wondered if Conrad's judgement was all it should have been.

I told Conrad that I was going nowhere with the state of my ankles and half a rope wasn't any good to anyone. If he wanted to make himself and anyone with him secure on steep ground, he would need the whole rope. It was going to be hard enough going as it was. He was tired and Steve may have been on his feet but he was still an unpredictable casualty and could still relapse.

I reminded Conrad that he would have to make his way down in plenty of 'pitches', (within the length of the rope), and that if he were going to be belaying Steve all the way, then he would need a full rope length. It may have been a bit patronising to a trained mountain leader but I just didn't feel comfortable with the whole thing. Conrad reassured me that he would be back later with a rescue team. Conrad then went to speak with Carl out of my earshot.

Carl told me later that Conrad told him that he would need his help to get Steve down and asked Carl if he was ready to go. After what he'd been through with Conrad the day before, he didn't want to go anywhere with him. Carl had to think quickly if he was to avoid the trip with Conrad. "What about Martin?" asked Carl.

"He knows what to do, he can look after himself!" Said Conrad, he gestured towards me, as I was preparing to baton down the hatches of my bivi sack, so I didn't hear the exchange.

Carl said "I'll stay and make the brews."

Conrad asked him "Do you know what you are doing by staying?"

"Yeah, I'll stay; I'm too knackered to go down anyway." Carl replied. And so he was and he'd made up his mind that he wasn't going anywhere with Conrad again and this was his chance to be parted from him.

Carl had given up the spare water to Conrad the day before and carried the gear of two men as well as all the work he had done on the ledge. He had been working like ten men and he knew he was in no fit state to try and make a descent; he'd probably kill himself on the way down. Descents are very hazardous and he had the sense to see this in his condition. He thought he would probably end up stumbling and sending the three of them down the Orient Express and that would be the end of it. He was so dehydrated from the maul of carrying the extra load and himself the day before and he still also felt unwell from the dehydration and altitude. Carl knew that if Johnny had gone down the night before and Conrad was on his way now that a rescue would be on its way within a few hours anyway. They would probably be tucked up in tents and sleeping bags by tonight. What was the point of going through more hell in the company of Conrad when he could sit it out with me?

Nothing much was surprising Carl now where Conrad was concerned. He thought we would be rescued sometime the following day. None of us had slept at all during the early hours that we had all tried to sleep; fatigue and cold were dominant here.

Carl was a man of so few words; it was sometimes difficult to drag a conversation out of him. He also had a steady and mature character and that was what was needed if we had a day or so to wait and the weather didn't get better. I hoped quietly to myself that he had enough stamina left to fight the cold in his deteriorated condition, but that was something that wasn't under his control. Everyone's thermostat is slightly different.

Everything was set; Conrad left with Steve. The original ten-man team was now widespread. Millsy had gone down to the 7,000ft Base Camp and had missed all the 'fun'. Three (we thought) were in tents now at 16,200ft Summit or Balcony Camp and out of danger, Nigel, Ian (Tory) and Gaz (who was actually at 14,200ft) probably wondering if all mountain expeditions were as bizarre as this one. Johnny and Phil had hopefully reached the Rangers at 14,200ft without incident, (They hadn't), and Conrad and Steve were in the precarious position of trying to make their own way down to 14,200ft via the Orient Express.

In the hours ahead, we would both need to be kept awake in defence of the deadly cold that would snatch our lives in our sleep. We needed to be aware and as alert as possible.

Carl thought that Conrad wanted to get Steve down because he wanted to get down himself. His behaviour the day before, crawling and licking the snow had been a worry and embarrassing for Carl to witness. He had also been asking his own guys for batteries.

As I hadn't witnessed any of the previous behaviour, I wasn't so concerned but I knew that Conrad had been making errors and not communicating as much as I would have on an exped. The batteries being left behind was bad enough but the row with Johnny had been badly handled and I was wishing I had been more forceful earlier but that was in hindsight, I didn't know everything that had been going on. .

Several years earlier I had been on the Haute Route with a colleague and good friend from my days at the PT School and later in the British Mountain Training Centre in Norway, Tim Davis and A.N. Other from 22 Regt. S.A.S. The route is a high level Alpine tour of ski-mountaineering from Chamonix, France to Zermatt, Switzerland, which takes about ten days if you really push it. It is excellent mixed skills ski-mountaineering and stamina training. Tim was a belting skier and had plenty of mountaineering experience too. I don't know how far into the route we were but Tim suddenly stopped dead and was astonished by what he saw. "Here look at him, what's he up to then?" My other companion and I stopped, looked puzzled and looked to where Tim was pointing. There was nothing there. Tim pointed again, excited and amused with a big grin across his face. Tim could see a man, completely stark naked running across the snow not far away.

"There's nothing there mate." We replied to Tim with a bit of a snigger. Of course, it was a bit of mild altitude sickness. Either Tim kept his mouth shut about anything else weird he saw that day or he quickly recovered. It certainly provided us with some entertainment and goes to prove it can happen to anyone. Anyway, that was just the same as I had witnessed with Conrad over the batteries. He was making a descent to better air, so I knew he'd be just fine anyway so I shrugged it off. I just hoped he could manage Steve and I was only 50/50 about that. Steve was strong and had good endurance as long as he didn't relapse.

Conrad's comments about leaving me to fend for myself with a suspected broken ankle and the urgency to get Steve down now he was recovering confirmed in Carl's mind that Conrad just wanted to get off the mountain. He resigned himself to keeping quiet, as he felt he wasn't an expert and at the end of the day it was only his opinion, there had been enough conflict regarding the decisions and opinions in the last twelve hours.

Witnessing the effects of hypoxia for the first time had left Carl feeling unsettled with Conrad. He knew a little about the confusion caused to the mind with increasing altitude from his lecture back at Canterbury, especially as an instant later Conrad would seem normal again. It was like witnessing somebody's bad and confusing dream.

Steve did need attention and Johnny was gone, at the time I had more confidence in Johnny but I still thought Conrad to be a qualified winter rope leader and would therefore be capable of the task ahead. We were unlikely to survive a very long wait on the tiny slab if the team didn't get back with help. It was so exposed; there was no hope of a scrape into the surface, let alone a snow hole.

Steve had been dressed up as well as possible and Carl strapped on his helmet for him and sometime between 16:00 and 17:00 they left. We had watched them go, neither of us convinced about splitting the team further. I had told Conrad that I didn't favour the idea but if he felt he was up to it and if the weather catches up with us as predicted, we could all be in more trouble. At this time though just as they were ready to go, it was not a good time to try to reiterate any doubts and neither of us, Carl and I, were voicing our dark thoughts. I had already given Conrad my opinion and had been ignored again. I hoped they would be O.K. and thought that after this shake-up, there was no doubt that they would be extra careful so I tried not to worry for them but I did. In many ways, looking from other angles many of Conrad's decisions seemed to be fine and some of it was luck. I was torn between lost confidence in him and loyalty to the exped leader and nice guy.

Carl moved back next to me and we set about trying to make the best of what we had, which wasn't a lot. Our gear had been swept away in the fall and we just got on with it. We battened down the hatches and were left to our own thoughts. The air was so thin that we needed our breath to breathe; we couldn't waste it on chat. I was really fed up about the axe I had lost.

Carl was very relieved that he didn't have to go down with them; he could rest now and regain some strength. Conrad had given us his assurance that he would be back with help as soon as he had got Steve down safely. To be honest, it did reassure us to some degree even though paradoxically I didn't believe it. I had just lost some confidence feeling the team broken up like this. It was against all my training and experience but this was one exceptional circumstance after another. I'd never even heard of another expedition going like this one was.

I had thought it a strange decision for him to leave, as I thought rescue couldn't be that far away now. I was only there as a guest, they didn't have to listen to my advice but I was entitled to give it when I thought I should and I now wondered if I was just wanted there to lead a rope because a rope leader was required for the ATFA and keep my mouth shut. I had already argued several points on the expedition and thought to bring a halt to the whole thing if it turned foolhardy but, the final decision was Conrad 's and I now had little option with my injury.

This conflict went on in my head. Was I passing the buck or was I really being ignored? Yes, I had confirmation with comments from Phil and Johnny that we were all being ignored at different times sometimes on the same point or on different ones. It's not that we were shut out altogether from decision-making it was that Conrad had an agenda and he wasn't going to be diverted from it. He'd give a little here and there but everything had pretty much been on his say so. Everyone else on the team had concurred on this point. We wanted to be seen to support him but it didn't always go that way and that must have rankled with him while he had all this responsibility and in such a tight timeframe.

Somehow, we still had Gemma's birthday gift, the yellow, foam sleep-mat with her birthday message scrawled all over it. I had turned it sideways so that at least Carl and I could lay our torsos on it. It really would make a great souvenir now, as it was helping to save our lives.

The wind was picking up and the temperature was dropping, though I could barely imagine how far it was going to go in mid-summer. I was discounting the El Niňo effect, which was about to whip up and bite us in the arse.

Chapter 10 - Roger Robinson

Roger Robinson sat up, dazed and confused for a brief moment as Johnny burst through the tent flap and blurted out the terrible occurrences. Roger had to listen hard to the heavily built Scotsman panting to get his breath and speaking in a Glaswegian accent. Scott Darsney, bleary-eyed started to make notes immediately to sort out what had happened. It was now 02:20hrs Friday 19th June. It was six hours from the first fall with Steve, Phil and I and nearly two hours from the second with Jeff and Billy. Johnny had made an incredible effort and made excellent time getting to the Ranger Camp.

Roger was head Mountaineering Ranger of his team's rotation. He had been in bed barely two hours after a run of rescues as well as dealing with all the problems in Camp with climbers having altitude sickness and hypoxia. He is a slim, almost gaunt-looking man with a large, handsome moustache and fair hair. He has kind, blue eyes and a friendly expression. Roger has been a climber since his school days and a Ranger since 1980.

He has a lot of experience to call upon but this was a bad time. The weather hadn't been good this season with the tail end of El Niño whipping across Alaska and the worst had happened. There had been little rest for any of the crew with the events of previous days and the rescues had long walk-ins to reach the casualties. Roger and his team were on their three-week rotation and they were having a real bad time.

His team of four volunteers had carried out three rescues in two days. That's a huge amount of effort in those conditions. Even after a few hours of deep sleep one would wake up still aching and hurting from the efforts of the previous day. Six years previously, he had to receive a kidney, donated by his brother. Climbing and rescue work now required a much greater effort. This was due to the medication he needs to counteract rejection of the organ. His stamina and fitness, in spite of a medical restraint, is incredible.

Denali claimed the lives of three people in the previous ten days all on the West Buttress. A Canadian climber had fallen; also a volunteer

Mountaineering Ranger and good friend of Roger's who had climbed down to help the Canadian had fallen into a crevasse his body was never found. Later a guide who unclipped himself from his rope to help a client with his gear had a fatal fall. Roger had assisted in locating the guide and recovery efforts of the body.

Recovery from such efforts takes time even a few days. Sleep was a state that their bodies and minds were demanding but Roger and his crew were to be denied it yet again.

They listened to the grim tidings Johnny had for them and Roger prioritised the needs of the two teams of stricken climbers. The British team was in a more stable position physically and medically, although they would have to be swift to beat the reported weather that was inbound.

The American, Jeff Munroe needed urgent medical attention, he was in the most danger at the present time. It was also not possible to reach the British team at the time and of course at that time they thought they were going to have four men on the ledge, as Johnny didn't know Conrad and Steve were going to be on their way down. If the weather held up they should be OK for the time being.

Roger Robinson had spent decades of his life in the midst of climbing and climbers. His climbing days began in the Willamette Valley, Oregon when he was a teenager. Now at 44 years of age, he found himself working his nineteenth season on Denali. Due to its severity, the mountaineering season is only open from May to July maybe very early August each year.

The rest of the patrol group, Joel Geisendorfer, Pete Athans and his wife, Liz Green, were set into action yet again. They ran around the Camp waking people up to find guides that were available to help. Things had to move quickly. The Americans were not known to be moving and to their knowledge, not conscious either. An hour and a half later, one half of the team (The Fast Team), set off at a good pace, the slower team made its way up to 16,000ft with the oxygen litter and other rescue equipment.

When the fast team eventually reached the two Americans, Billy Finley and Jeff Munroe, the situation looked poor. Phil was O.K.

considering, he was incredibly cold, still fairly concussed and extremely worried for Jeff. He had lain on Jeff for most of four long hours to keep him from freezing to death before help arrived. Billy was battered and bruised and looking dazed, but he was conscious and of course he was desperately worried for his good friend.

Scott Darsney and Pete Athans were in the fast team. Scott, an emergency medical provider, quickly assessed the two men. Both men were suffering with hypothermia. Jeff Munroe was in a terrible state. He was unconscious and his breathing was laboured, noisy and erratic. He clearly needed to be hospitalised fast for his head injuries, which looked to be a closed, compression type fracture and very dangerous. The team packed the guys out with more sleep mats and sleeping bags to buy some time against the incredible cold. The rawest and most bitterly cold days in the UK that grind the nation to a halt are nothing compared to the temperature here, even midsummer. So many basic functions we take for granted cost effort and energy and so much more time.

Scott radioed through to Anchorage hospital for advice. He was having trouble with the conditions himself. As he tried to administer medication, the freezing air compounded him. Vials cracked open as their contents froze so quickly as soon as the vials were exposed to the open atmosphere and the needles had to be held between his teeth to help prevent them freezing in the few seconds that they were exposed. The slow team, moving as swiftly as they were able with all their kit finally arrived an hour later, which included the oxygen cylinders so desperately needed and the litters to transport casualties so the lowering process could begin.

3ft long stakes were driven into the snow and tied with webbing to provide an anchor for the 900ft of rope. A descending device was fitted to the rope and the litter was clipped on. Two men litter attendants were clipped to each litter to guide them down and stop them from running away. Jeff was lowered first and Billy was second. The slope was steep enough so that the rope could only be paid out very slowly. The two attendants struggled to keep their balance and hold the heavy litter that was constantly trying to break away over the snow and ice, not just with the weight and gradient but the instability of the snow pack. With crevasses ahead and the litter trying to snatch them off their feet it was a hazardous trial for them all. Over and over the task of driving in the stakes and trudging slowly down, bracing against the weight and trying to remain balanced continued slowly and carefully.

The snow was very deep, the temperature around minus 20 degrees and the air carrying far too little oxygen for the task. Two pairs of legs plunged deep into the snow straining against the litter and its cargo teetering on the edge of life. Legs were lifted high again, with thigh muscles screaming and plunging down again to the next laboured step. Every stumble had a domino effect and the message to 'Stop!' would cry back through the radio to the belayer to hold fast the rope. At the end of the 900ft haul, the whole system was dismantled and repeated over and over until finally, both Jeff and Billy were safely back at the Ranger Camp. It was a very long and exhausting operation.

They had done remarkably well in the conditions, given that some of the team were already exhausted from the outset from previous work. The last of the team plodded back into the Camp at a snail's pace, their stamina proving a great credit to them.

It took eight hours to move about a mile, which helps to illustrate just how tough the conditions were there and an incredible amount of manpower to bring them down. The teams had given every last scrap of themselves to do it. Utterly exhausted, the rescue was over. Rangers, guides and volunteers collapsed with relief and exhaustion.

For Roger and the others, the work was far from over. Working frantically in the medical tent several physicians and others medically trained volunteered to join in the fight to save Jeff. Michael Dong had been a combat medic in the past; Dr. Dudley Weider, Dr. David Moon and Dr. Phil Spraling all worked in earnest on the man fading before their eyes in what can be mildly described as very challenging conditions.

With a compression injury it can sometimes only take the slightest increase in pressure against the brain and it's all over but if there is no sufficient blood supply to the area then there is no oxygen either. It was very tricky.

Roger was despondent. He thought at the time that Jeff would not make it through until morning, a concern shared by all present and Jeff was so young. There had been so many falls on the Orient Express. Billy and Jeff had made it to 19,000ft together. If Jeff lived, he would be only the third to survive the long fall on the notorious chute at that time.

They needed a helicopter and right now. The promised weather had closed in on the mountain and the Chinooks of the U.S. Army's High Altitude Rescue Team gave up trying to find a way through the cloud, as it was so low and so thick. Temperatures plummeted further and wind was increasing. The distinctive deep, rhythmic thudding of the air that is the signature of Chinooks now began to fade from the Camp, Roger reflected on how much death he had seen lately, he turned his thoughts to Jim Hood.

Jim was a long way from home. He lives in Alpine, Wyoming. This summer though, he's a mountain rescue pilot. His little helicopter, a skeletal SA-315B Lama of 1960's French design, was his partner in Denali. Flying helicopters to fight fires in the Rockies, Jim was persuaded by Evergreen Helicopters to take on a three-month contract, flying the Lama for the National Park Service in Denali. Evergreen have several aviation interests in the U.S.A and also have a base in the U.K.

Jim looks like a man from the old Marlboro ads. He is tall with a hint of a smile in his eyes. His hair is thick and dark and he has a big, dark 'Tom Selleck' moustache. He even wears cowboy boots and hat. Steady and self confident he is adept at telling it like it is, but so far from taking himself seriously, he shows the best that humanity can offer in his compassion and self-effacing attitude. Today though, the hint of cheerful mischief in his eyes is eclipsed by the concern mirrored by the Rangers. He knows in himself, that he would be flying on the mountain in the hours to come.

Jim had been sitting in his truck listening to the depressing events at the 14,200ft Camp. He felt, as he watched the dull shades of the clouds moving overhead, that there was a tragedy unfolding slowly above him on the mountain.

When the call finally came, as he knew it would he was ready. His pick-up crunched through the puddled potholes and gravelly streets of Talkeetna to go and get kitted up. His Lama, kept in perfect condition by the tenacious mechanic, Ray Touzeau, was about to be put through its paces more rigorously than it ever had been.

The Lama was designed at a time when machinery was more basic and the Lama had never failed to do what was asked of it within its capacity. It didn't need to fail now!

Jim eventually got through Talkeetna for the next round to begin. With a hoard of experience behind him he knew the risks well. He had already landed near the summit at 19,600ft of Denali on four previous occasions, a record for the Americas.

The Lama was capable of making it to incredible altitude and holds the record for it at 40,000ft. The problems he faced on Denali were vastly different to those he faced in the Rockies. At 14,000ft one could still suffer frostbite to the digits, but here in Alaska, one can lose consciousness inside half an hour if not acclimatised. The problem he faced was that of altitude for himself. He was based at Talkeetna, which sits at just 400ft above sea-level. He wasn't acclimatised for the area he would be working in. What took most climbers one or two weeks to reach and acclimatise to he would take less than sixty minutes. He took two cylinders of oxygen, which would last him ninety minutes and loaded them into the Lama. He also had the back-up of a fuel and oxygen cache at the 7,000ft Base Camp.

He climbed towards the 14,200ft Camp where the landing is no piece of cake but this was no ordinary flight up the mountain. The visibility was so poor that he had to circle the entire base of the huge mountain as he tried to climb and critically, he could see nothing beneath him because the clouds were so thick. There is always a 'will I, won't I make it?' factor to the place. Each landing is made on the assumption that he might have to pull up again at the last moment. The air is sufficiently thin (low pressure), at the Ranger Camp to affect the efficiency of the rotors to grab it. It makes taking off again and lifting higher that much more tricky.

Jay Hudson flying his Cessna over-head relayed the conditions to Jim. The cloud was too dense for Jim to continue and he had no choice but to turn back. As he began to make his retreat, Don, another colleague radioed that he could see a clear area through the broken cloud beyond the South Buttress. The weather was moving in from the South and the South

Buttress was acting as a barrier to it for the time being. Jim knew he needed oxygen above 12,000 ft, but needed to climb to 17,000 ft to seek the clear weather over the Buttress. He was ready to chance it.

The Lama climbed its way up and Jim found that the weather was clear as he crossed the buttress. He was also very light headed as a result and dropped the Lama into a dive to reach the richer air below and clear his head. He skimmed over the clouds with their protruding peaks and descended to the Camp at 14,200 ft.

There are strict rules regarding flying conditions and Jim had to stretch them with an amazing flexibility to drop to the Camp. He couldn't land unless he could see the ground. All he could see was the cliff face as he went down. Well, it's a solid surface but it's vertical and not a horizontal plateau. He eased his way lower and lower, following the cliff down. It was a matter of perspective but an incredibly dangerous risk for him. He knew he was probably the only way out for the guys trapped at 19 and for Jeff who was borrowing time like no other.

The Lama finally reached the Camp area and Jim touched down safely to the relief of everyone. The medics were there with Jeff all ready to be loaded. The Lama stayed at the 14,200 ft Camp just long enough to whip Jeff Munroe off the mountain. This was no simple flight down the 'hill' either. The weather was 'socked in' as Jim describes it. It was worsening and the visibility prevented Jim from taking a direct route. He couldn't fly back to Talkeetna. He had to fly around to Kantishna, which is barely NNE of the mountain about 33 miles (53km) as the crow flies but still deep within Denali National Park boundaries and granted a concession permit by the National Park Service to operate an airfield within it. Once safely there, Jim found a U.S. Army Pave Hawk helicopter waiting for him. Jeff was barely stabilised, in a coma but with so many people working on him for all those hours and the rapid evacuation to hospital, at least he had an outside chance of survival.

Once Jeff had been carefully transferred, he was whisked away to the care of Alaska Regional Hospital in Anchorage, which if able to take a direct route, (which it wasn't) was still about 163 miles away but there was a crash team ready and waiting to receive him.

The hospital is situated on the slightly North-Eastern outskirts of Anchorage and is, like most hospitals surrounded by car parks. This one however, to the North and West of the perimeter of the car parks has air strips and hangars that can comfortably accommodate about 300 or so fixed wing aircraft. Once an aeroplane or helicopter has landed and taxied near to the hospital building, a casualty can be whisked out of the aircraft and wheeled straight into the hospital. It gives an indication of the vast area that Anchorage is part of and the remoteness of the areas that it has to serve.

The communication between all the services working at different levels on and off the mountain was key to the co-ordination of logistics. It wasn't just people that needed to be flown up and down the mountain, medical supplies were running low very quickly. It wasn't just a case that they were being used up but the temperature was exacerbating medication use as the vials were splitting as the medication kept freezing when it was needed and fuel had to be re-supplied. Fuel is also heavy. Everything has a problem attached to it that has to be accounted for. Everyone working here has to be steps and steps ahead.

The Ranger Station at Talkeetna was a very busy place too during this period with the radio comms going back and forth and supplies and people coming and going and the media wanting the latest information. It was tightly controlled to prevent it becoming a mad-house.

The forty-eight hour stretch on top of all those strenuous days previously, had taken its toll on everyone in the 14,200ft Camp. The operation to get Jeff, Billy and Phil down to the Camp had taken not just eight hours to perform; it took eleven people those eight hours, eighty-eight man hours to get three men down a distance of one mile.

Absolutely dead-beat Roger, Scott and the others sighed with relief that it was all over. They were about to open a bottle of champagne that had been given to them when one of the climbers in Camp, Steve Hanson, came running up to them. He came to tell them that he had just seen two climbers fall down the Orient Express, to the exact spot they had just executed the painfully laborious rescue of Jeff, Billy and Phil up at 15,800ft.

The exasperation was enough to bring tears of despair. Their energy so depleted by now and another rescue inside half an hour of evacuating Jeff. Scott and Roger saw no movement as they found the point on the glacier where the casualties were. They watched and thought they must both be dead. Scott went back into the medical tent and collapsed into a deep sleep, for what could they do for them now anyway. The sleep didn't last long.

Chapter 11 - The Orient Express

Conrad held Steve on his rope and led him away from Carl and I and the ledge that he had been vehemently trying to throw himself from. Conrad felt nothing was getting accomplished sitting on a ledge that was barely larger than a picnic table, with a gradient towards the edge to boot. The surface was scoured by the wind and so hard they couldn't dig any kind of recess or shelter.

Steve was better and more lucid, but Conrad thought he was only going to get worse if he stayed. He was sure in his mind that he had done the right thing. The heated debates with Johnny and I hadn't helped his situation. He was expedition leader and the decisions were ultimately his to make, he had to stand by that. Steve was a liability to everyone if he didn't remain stable and Conrad knew that he didn't want to become a casualty himself through hypoxia and hypothermia, it would just add to the problems. He had already had to leave Gaz in the tent at 16,200ft.

He had tried to persuade Carl to come with them; he thought he would need his help in getting Steve down. He decided I was well enough qualified and experienced to last out by myself even with my injury, especially since a rescue team would be on its way to me before too long anyway. At least this way there would only be two men for the rescue team to worry about. He was as sure with his decision as others had doubted it. It didn't matter, he decided it was the best move and everyone in the team who doubted would concede and agree when they made it down when Steve was safely tucked up in a hospital bed and a ground team met with Carl and I, as planned.

It was hard going for Conrad and Steve. The Orient Express spread wide before them, swept downward on a steep slope. It was around fifty degrees in places. The only thing one could do on a fall here is pick up speed and probably take flight from the surface altogether. It fell away beneath them, a deathly slide of over 4,000ft. It was a drop that rarely took prisoners and those it did take would need to be taken off in all haste. Almost all who fell here had died.

Conrad decided to make his way down in front of Steve. Conrad was feeling washed out and dizzy in his hypoxic state, he had been suffering since leaving for the summit the previous day. Normal, safe practice would have been to short rope Steve from above, he would then be able to hold him tight on the rope and lower him to prevent Steve from falling in the event of a stumble or collapse. Failing that, they would have worked their way down in pitches, belaying and lowering Steve ahead, waiting until the rope length was reached and then Steve would secure the rope to stop Conrad falling too far below him. The first method would have been better.

Steve was on his feet and walking and seemed to understand what Conrad was shouting to him, so they walked down, the rope tied between them. The effort and concentration of each footfall was wearing them down. Steve listened to the familiar voice of the Captain and put his faith in each step behind him. Suddenly and predictably Steve fell and slid, crashing into Conrad and nearly sending him down the face, which is the problem of Conrad being below the casualty.

They continued on. They were also very lucky that they had been spotted by Michael Dong at 14,200ft, as two tiny specks moving painstakingly slowly down the deadly chute. Roger had prayed that they would make it down in one piece and left them to it.

The descent was harrowing and took reserves of strength that Conrad didn't know he had left. Each step was made with trepidation, each breath thin and empty. Each push of his diaphragm to force his lungs wide was too much effort for what he got from the dry air, starved of oxygen and stealing the precious vapour from him. Steve heard him mumbling and cursing, groaning and panting. Steve could do nothing but try not to skid his crampons over the surface and fall again but his knees and thighs were weakened too.

Conrad was moving at a relatively good pace, but Steve was slow and poorly coordinated. He shouted down to Conrad to stop. Conrad was walking too quickly for him and the rope was pulling him off balance. He fell and somehow had the wherewithal to try out and succeed in executing his first real-life ice-axe arrest. It slowed him but didn't prevent him from bumping into Conrad again. Conrad cursed and they gathered themselves up and got back into the descent again.

Down they clambered through deep pockets of snow; it was heartbreaking to think that they had to lift their legs out of them for the next step. Exposed expanses of convex, blue ice, deep and polished, scoured by the wind waited as it had for centuries for its next victim. The light dusting of purest white powder didn't soften the appearance or calm the pounding hearts of the two men daintily treading and grinding their crampons onto the surface, praying for purchase.

Not wanting to think how they had crossed over it, not wanting to think at all, they plunged into snow again, which now they were grateful for. The wind raced faster with each hour that passed, pushing them around to knock them off balance. They stopped to rest constantly, it was getting colder and Steve fell again and again, each time trying to arrest and careering into Conrad below. The falling and getting up was a huge effort each time. Still, Conrad did not change the order and continued on below Steve instead of above him.

Conrad's patience with Steve crashing into him time and again had just about worn through and he was shouting and cursing at Steve but knowing that he was out of his mind with exhaustion too. The wind almost drowning out every word and buffeting them continuously made it all so nearly impossible.

Again they struggled to their feet, gasping all the time. The rope was gathered up and they set off again. It's pointless to think of warm duvets, soft beds and hot, nourishing meals. They would have given anything for a mouthful of stale, room temperature water now.

Steve was in very poor shape by now, but was managing to take the deep steps as they descended. Conrad was still suffering with the effects of hypoxia and struggling to make up belay after belay to hold his companion but with Steve above, it was woefully ineffective.

The descent went on and on. The exertion, concentration into each footfall and laboured breathing to pull in the oxygen, was as bad as it could have been. It was exhausting; it was a mauling effort that needed all the pent up despair and aggression that could be summoned. Was this really happening to them? Were they really clambering their way down the most notorious and dangerous descent on the Continent?

Depleted, cold and still struggling to fight concussion and hypoxia. At around 17,300ft they struggled their way down towards the Camp at 16,200ft below them where they thought they could hear the shouts of their team mates that had been left safely in their tents. At last, they were going to make it. They just needed to get to 16,200ft then they could help get Steve to 14,200ft.

Conrad was still moving more strongly than Steve was. The rope between them tightened yet again and again Steve fell. At 23:00hrs on 19 June Steve fell again, but this time as he fell, he slid feet first slamming hard into Conrad. Conrad felt Steve's crampon points bury themselves into his thigh. This time their luck ran out. Conrad could not hold Steve; he yelled out and lost his footing, pulling Steve along with him. They were going down with no way to arrest; Steve tumbled and bounced over the ice. The fall was long, fast and seemed to last forever. Conrad was able to count the seconds that he was airborne, then, he would land hard, skid rapidly over the solid, polished surface and be airborne again.

Down and down they fell, past their companions at the tented site at 16,200ft and on down battering against the surface and bouncing hard over it, the Orient Express hungrily trying to consume more victims. They tumbled over and over as they raced down. At some point in the fall Conrad hit a cluster of rocks at such a velocity he felt his leg shatter and he screamed out in agony. Pain and shock grabbing him hard, he fell on. The pain rattled through him over and over as he fell. Eventually the falling stopped. They had tumbled and been freefalling for over 1,500ft landing at the 15,800 ft level.

According to one source at the Ranger Camp at 14,200ft, Roger had been spotting Conrad and Steve trying to make the descent through the telescope and saw the fall but that doesn't tie in with the official report that states only that 'Ranger staff' at 14,200' also witnessed the fall, where plans were developed for their evacuation.'

They had landed at almost the same point that the two unfortunate American climbers, Billy and Jeff had just been rescued from. Steve came to, after a few minutes of unconsciousness and heard Conrad screaming. Conrad had somehow managed to lose his jacket and both his outer and inner gloves. Steve was wrapped up in the rope and it bound him so tightly it was cutting into him. He spent some time freeing himself, fumbling for his knife to cut the rope, and then stumbled over to take a look at Conrad. He was crying out in pain. Steve took off his own jacket and wrapped it around Conrad. He put his gloves inside the jacket and told Conrad he could see the 14,200ft Ranger Camp from where they were. He was going to get help. Conrad told him he should stay and not leave him there alone...(the irony!). Steve argued that they had no radio to call for help and nobody knew where they were or that they had fallen. Conrad yelled at him to stay, but Steve ignored him and was already stumbling away in the direction of the Camp.

The temperature had plummeted as the day wore on and the winds were getting higher. The tail end of El Niño storm had arrived and was going to sting the area badly. Steve could just make out the Ranger Camp at 14,200ft below him and headed straight down the fall line of the mountain, unaware of what was hidden from his view. A safe route had been marked out by the Rangers just a short while earlier during the rescue of Jeff, Billy and Phil but Steve had somehow not noticed it. It would have taken him round to the 16,200ft Camp and down into the 14,200ft Camp.

He did not know that the horrific scene had been witnessed from the Ranger Camp. They declared at the Camp that they must be dead. Surely, nobody could withstand such a battering fall, and for such a long, long way. All eyes were on them now. After some time they saw one of the tiny figures in the distance moving. It was Steve. Was he delirious, concussed or coherent? He was something of all three states. Not knowing that their fall had just been witnessed at the Camp, Steve was determined to get help for Conrad in as much haste as his befuddled mind and trashed body would allow him. The other thing he didn't know was that they had landed right at the spot where the two Americans and Phil had stopped and were rescued from.

Steve continued missing the bamboo route marking stakes and heading in a direct line for the Camp was an action that was to cost him very dearly. He figured that if he could get to Camp quickly, there would still be people around to rescue Conrad, even though the Rangers would have left to bring Carl and I down.

He didn't know that the rescue was postponed to bring in the critically sick American, Jeff, who at only 24 years old was at death's door either as they had no batteries for a radio, they could not communicate with anyone. He thought nobody knew they were there. He thought he was everyone's only hope now and went bravely on.

His fingers felt solid and sore with the incredible cold. He knew he couldn't do anything for Conrad at that stage. He had made sure Conrad was wrapped up tight in his jacket with his hood over his head, he felt sure he was doing the right thing now. He had lost his mountain glasses somewhere on the way down. The dull light reflecting from the snow was hurting his eyes and the wind speed was making them stream with painful, freezing tears.

He stumbled, on looking up from time to time to make sure he was still heading in the right direction, trying to focus on the blur of the Camp in the distance and trying not to think of the biting cold. Without his jacket he was bitterly cold.

He strode out as well as his heavy legs would go, then he suddenly stepped down. With a gasp and a rush of fear, he fell straight down into what he thought was a crevasse at first, being buffeted on solid ice on the way. He slammed to a stop not knowing what had happened. He had just fallen off a 20ft ice cliff and tumbled on down a steep slope where he had become buried in debris. Still numbed from the impact he tried to work out whether he was hurt or not. He came to the conclusion he wasn't. "How many more times am I going to fall down this fucking mountain?" he said to himself.

Back at the Ranger Camp the startled screaming and shouting of warnings had ceased and were replaced by a shocked and sad silence at seeing the lone climber fall to his death down the side of a huge bergshrund, (a huge chunk of ice that cracks free of the mountain rock face, ice face or glacier) making as described a cliff.

Chapter 12 – Birthday

Just before 07:30am, Saturday 20th June she heard the phone ringing. Bev thought to herself that it was a bit early that she dismissed it. She could hear Ma and Pa's muffled voices from the bedroom where she had just started to dress. Ma then came running up the stairs and burst into the bedroom.

"Don't panic, Martin's had an accident!" She said with panic in her own voice.

"What's happened?" Bev asked as she struggled to pull on her underwear and head out of the bedroom door.

"Alan's just phoned and said that two of them have fallen on the mountain!"

Bev was really confused now to add to the panic she felt in her stomach and chest. She continued to pull her clothes on as she descended the stairs.

Alan was an old family friend from Derby of Ma and Pa's who only sees us once in a blue moon. 'How the hell did he know anything about Martin falling?' She thought as she was dressing on her way along the hall to the sitting room. Ma explained that he had been up very early and had been watching the satellite channels. It had been on CNN and was on Ceefax, the old text channel. Pa had taken the call. Alan asked him if he was alright. "Yes, why?" asked Pa, naturally puzzled.

"Have you got 'Sky News' on?"

"No, we were in bed, why, what's on?" Asked Pa.

"I'm not going to say any more now, switch on yer telly and phone me back." Pa switched it on the telly, turned to Sky News and there it was. "Fuckin' hell fire!" said Pa. He felt that if someone had hit him with a sledgehammer it wouldn't have hurt as much. It was at that point Ma had come running up the stairs. Really annoyingly, Bev had to stand and listen to the entire repeated exchange before they had finally told her that I had been named as one of the climbers.

Pa and Ma felt the same as Bev did when it hit home, that they wanted to do something but couldn't.

Bev picked up the remote control and switched it to Ceefax, as the news channels had moved onto other stories and couldn't find anything and there it was:

'Two British soldiers fell 1,500ft on Alaska's highest peak. Sgt Martin Spooner had broken a leg, ankle, and Steve Brown who had suffered head injuries.'

Bev felt sick and anxious. She knew what Ma and Pa didn't and that altitude and temperature were going to be major factors here and why they were. There was no internet as we know it now and the house didn't have a computer anyway. She wanted to know the weather forecast and who was there, what was being done, where, when, what, why?

Information was what she wanted now. She raced around for Cindy's number, whispering curses and mumbling to herself in frustration. She had left it on the dash in the car, but couldn't find it now. She didn't have time to fiddle about under the seats and ran back to the house to call directory enquiries. Cindy must have been hovering by the phone.

"Cindy?"

"Thank God!" Cindy exclaimed as she answered. "We didn't know how to reach you; we got a phone call at 2.00am this morning because you weren't answering your phone. We explained that you'd gone home to Martin's mum and dad's for the weekend. For some reason, they don't have Ma and Pa's number or address. (They'd have found it alright if he was AWOL Bev thought to herself.) I'll put you on to Andy and he'll explain everything, please don't worry."

Andy, Martin's friend and work colleague came on the line and explained that they only knew that I had fallen 300ft and had injured both legs and that a rescue was being organised. He didn't know what my current condition was, what equipment I had, nothing. She fired question after question at Andy but he had been given nothing, he didn't know. He also had no answer as to why there was no information on the military net before this, when the news agencies already had the story for so long . He said he couldn't understand why they didn't all know before she left for Staffordshire.

Bev asked so many questions. Who was with me? Is he a trained climber? Can he help me if I go into shock? What gear have we got?

What's the weather like? Poor Andy said again and again that he didn't know anything but he said he was sure that I would be fine. Bev spoke with Cindy again and asked if she could get the keys and find her address book. Bev would have a lot of phone calls to make. Cindy said "It's so weird after what you had said about not wanting Martin to do this trip and leaving your keys this time when you wouldn't before. Oh God, and that joke about the insurance. It will be OK Martin's one of the best and he's as tough as an old boot."

She did as Bev asked and was back on the phone inside ten minutes and was soon reeling off names and phone numbers for her. Cindy said everyone was wishing us well and to phone her with any news night or day. Bev felt a comfort that Cindy was there and wondered immediately whether she would be better off back home where she could be on the military phone line day and night. Bev nearly left, she really wanted to. She suddenly felt cut-off and trapped at my parents. She wanted to be around people who would understand what was happening and know what questions would be asked and how to answer them. She couldn't go; my parents would want to know everything as it happened too.

Bev wondered what to do next, and then remembered the birthday party. There was a brief discussion on that and they decided that it could still go ahead. There would be plenty of people to help. She thought she should phone family but she decided to phone the adjutant at Arbourfield, my HQ. His name was Andy Johnston and they began the first of countless telephone calls back and forth. That was Bev's control throughout. She kept the phone, she owned it and every call and made notes, then re-wrote them, underlined names and roles.

Bev wanted a flight out but couldn't have one because the Training Accident Investigation Team would be taking the RAF flight out and there were no places left on board. She knew she wouldn't be allowed anywhere near the rescue operation whether things were good or bad but this is a circumstance where she would normally have been 'indulged'. She tried to explain that she is strong enough to cope with the truth and that was what she wanted all the way through. That was made clear, even though she knew nobody from the Army was coming to sit with her and break the news if it was bad, she knew it was going to be the phone. She wanted it, the candour, the instantaneous delivery of news from each event but she suddenly felt very weak, a bit faint and clammy and very isolated.

Bev had to switch her mind to doing anything she could to gather then pass information. She telephoned the BBC news desk and complained about the news article giving the names of the soldiers and asked how they had found out and if they knew anything else. She hadn't intended to complain at all but if they could find out fast, why couldn't she? She wanted to understand and have claim to the process.

Bev wanted to be there and it maddened her that nobody in the military would give her a reason why she couldn't get an indulgence flight. Surely with an investigation team in-bound, they had decided on a flight and let's face it, just how many British Servicemen/women need to fly to Anchorage on a regular basis? Zero. She knew she was being fobbed off, and was sure there'd be a few seats spare. She was suppressing fury and frustration. The story had already come through an American news agency and others and that by the time breakfast news was on all channels would have the story. He's mine not theirs she thought, but she was soon to find out that she was very wrong. I was theirs. Bev was held off at arm's length until the military had control of every bit of information, in and out. It wasn't as if this was a security issue. They had to turn this into a positive story.

BBC News desk hastily apologised and explained that they had not known that I had not been informed and wished us all well. The impotence of every action she carried out suffocated her. Control of anything had been taken away from her.

The family and all our close friends were informed and given Ma and Pa's number so that they could call in for news. So began the 'perfect' day Bev had foreseen for them.

Preparations for Gemma's party went ahead with everyone trying to make everything look and feel normal. Bev can't remember anything about it except the cake and singing 'Happy Birthday'. Faces appeared in front of her all day and voices talked at her but she had no memory after of who was there and what was said. She stuck a smile on her face and played with the children a little. Micky came with his children and spent as much time as he could with Bev but he had to leave for work that evening. My brother has always been close to me but he didn't stay there. We wouldn't have expected him to be, he has a family and he was home looking after them. He was checking in several times a day, like everyone else, hoping to hear something positive.

Pa sat for some time watching all the children running around and playing on the big lawn at the front. Occasionally he came in to see what was on the television. He couldn't watch and wait, so he went for a walk around the old pumping station buildings then wandered back into his shed behind the house. He didn't really do anything but it was his way of coping. Ma kept herself busy, she only sat down to watch the latest bulletin or come and wait for Bev to relay the next phone message. Ma topped up glasses and plates all day, made copious amounts of tea and washed up every half an hour. She looked tired. Bev was so absorbed in what she was doing that she barely saw the children but there was lots of squealing, shouting and laughter from them outside. The adults waited and they hoped that things would get better if the rescuers could get to us quickly.

As the day wore on they began to feel more despondent. They were also more confused with what they were seeing on the television. The Ceefax pages now said that instead of Martin Spooner and Steve Brown being injured after falling 300 ft, it now said that the fall had been 1,500 ft and his companion now was Carl Bougard. Pa, although hopeful thought I had gone. He had no feeling that I was still there.

The news got worse as the day wore on. They didn't realise that Carl was now on the ledge with me after the 300 ft fall and that Steve had gone with Conrad and tumbled down the Orient Express. My friend Zeb phoned and said he was in-bound and wanted directions. Bev wasn't sure about him coming, as Ma and Pa had enough to worry about without a guest to look after. Ma said it was fine but he'd have to sleep on the sofa if he didn't mind.

Gemma seemed to have a successful party with cousins and friends and Bev saw a good friend she had made in a previous posting in Ripon, who now lived in Leek, Sharon. Sharon had brought her sons to the party, who had previously gone to school with Gemma in Ripon, so that was a nice reunion for them all and Gemma was thrilled to see them again. They all played on the huge lawn. Anything Bev did towards the party and games was lost to her distracted state. She spoke in hushed tones with Sharon and the television stayed on all day, switching from one news channel to another.

Bev was very pleased to have Sharon there. As another military wife, she understood the 'distance' Bev was feeling and the system that was in play. The phone rang and they all waited for Bev to answer, listen and relay. There was nothing significant. Sharon bit her lip, scowled and shook her head again and held Bev's hand again.

It had been in other ways a lovely day. The weather had been superb. Children ran in and out all day breathless, asking for more drinks and running around with cake and nibbles. Bev didn't do the big organised games on the lawn that she usually did. She couldn't get her head around organising them. She didn't play outside with them much this time.

The children didn't mind but Gemma wasn't easily fooled. Every now and then she'd hover around by the sitting room door and listen. Bev knew she wasn't stupid, Gemma knew it was serious and we were controlling the information. What Gemma was utterly shielded from was that it was life threatening. Gemma also seemed a bit annoyed that she was kept at bay. She has always been a bit of a fast cat and even at eleven years old she knew that this was really big for us and she started to take charge and usher Rhys about protectively out of earshot. He knew something had gone wrong but he was still six and was easier to shield up to a point. He had been standing in the doorway at one point looking at everybody standing in front of the television when a new news bulletin came on. He couldn't see past us but he knew we were all very glum. He stepped away quietly, knowing that he should be elsewhere.

Bev told them the truth head on, as far as she felt she could. I had fallen a long way and hurt myself. I was stuck where I was because the rescue team couldn't get to me because the weather was so bad at the moment. I was staying where I was to rest and make sure I didn't hurt myself anymore and so that the rescuers would know where to find me. Fairly accurate with a couple of omissions.

Rhys on the other hand understood it very simply, he knew I was stuck and the rescuers couldn't get me yet because it was snowing hard. I had broken my ankle and he wanted to draw pictures on my cast when I came home. Well, he was six and a half. He still slept with Bayer-Bayer, (he couldn't say bunny bunny as a toddler and the name stuck) his fluffy rabbit and Paddington Bear. He also wanted to know if I was going to have those 'arm-sticks' or a wheel-chair.

In truth, Bev knew it was cold and high, she didn't expect anything but she had that worst of all gifts from Pandora's Box. She had hope and it force-fed her frustration and she felt it was ready to betray her, so she felt it with suspicion. She felt trapped where she was but daren't leave the phone for several hours of motorway travel. Nobody in the family had a mobile phone in 1998. She really wanted to go back to Wales.

The party wound down, everyone left and Gemma had a lovely day, except that she didn't know why daddy wasn't down from the mountain yet? Would he be down in the morning? Bev said she expected so. Gemma instructed that if Bev spoke to me on the telephone, she was to tell me what she had for her birthday and that Gemma would show me when I got back. Bev was grinding her teeth as she smiled. Gemma went off to play with her brother upstairs on the beds and her birthday presents, her long hair still wet from the shower laying down the back of her nightie.

Zeb arrived early in the evening. The sun was still shining and the weather warm and the flowers that smothered the front of the house were fragrant but nobody appreciated it. As his large frame came through the doorway, he met Pa. The first thing he said was a huge comfort to Ma and Pa. "Don't worry, he'll be alright. I helped train him when we were in Norway he knows what he's doing. He'll survive, I know Martin."

He came in and Bev introduced him properly to everyone. He went on to explain that the first thing I would do is secure myself and dig in. Once he was settled, Bev disappeared into the kitchen with Ma to get the Jack Daniels. Bev couldn't eat or drink all day, not even a glass of water but she belted down a big gulp of bourbon and poured herself another glass before Ma took a glass into Zeb. Pa told Bev later that Zeb got on the phone. He didn't know who he was speaking to but he was really giving them some hammer about the information they were getting.

To be honest, the news agencies still seemed to be far quicker and more in-depth with their information than the Army. I suppose the news agencies have a faster network. He had an air of confidence about him that put them all at ease for a while. He made one phone call after another and talked a lot about what I would be doing and what the Rangers would be doing. The fact that he had been to Denali himself helped a lot too.

Chris Short was another friend who had been with us in Norway and had been to Denali, so his advice was really helpful too. When Chris phoned he spent time talking Bev through what the operations would be there and just to be talking to someone who knew anything at all made her feel better, though no more empowered. It all built a clearer picture for them. Bev was really touched that they were trying to help and very touched and surprised by how many people were wishing us well.

Ma and Pa began to feel that I had survived after all. They went to bed feeling there was still a chance but still fearful that their boy wasn't coming home. Pa cat-napped during the night and Ma like-wise, Bev couldn't sleep and each attempt ended up in fitful fidgeting and feelings of panic. Ma and Pa held on to each other all night both thankful that they had each other to get through it. Pa described it as a 48 hour long night and they were glad when the sun came up early.

Bev watched for the news all night as Zeb tapped away at the remote control and brought up weather reports on the television text stations.

He came up with a telephone number and spoke to someone at the other end explaining who he was and what information he was after. He waited and then spoke to somebody else and then passed the phone to me.

The softly-spoken, gentle voice at the other end introduced himself as John Philpot the duty forecaster at R.A.F. High Wycombe in Buckinghamshire. Bev said she was sorry to trouble him so late.

He said very nicely, "Oh no, not at all. I hope I can give you some good news."

He then gave her a running commentary on what he was doing and they waited for his screens to give him the required information.

He simply reported it back but gently and with a hint of regret he told Bev the weather forecast over Denali for the next 48 hour period. He told her that the weather was very bad at the moment but showing a slow improvement over the next 48 hours. He couldn't say to what degree but he said it could still change and that there was a possibility that the cloud will break sometime tomorrow and that a weather window could still appear sometime the following day. If it breaks then there could be visibility at 10,000ft. He can obtain 6-hourly reports for Alaska but nothing was going to change dramatically as far as the weather was concerned.

He wished us all the very best of luck and hoped we would all be back together fit and well soon. She shakily thanked him. Before they hung up, he invited her to call again anytime if she felt she needed to. It was her weakest moment of the entire weekend. Maybe it was John's sympathetic and gentle delivery of information, like a soft hand resting on hers to try to comfort her but with none to give. It was the closest she came to being able to release the tears that were choking her since she first found out. She has always remembered John and how he spoke to her. She is always reminded of it when we travel the M40 and see signs for High Wycombe.

She thought that I was going to be in terrible trouble in that bitter storm and she couldn't reach me.

Bev went upstairs leaving Zeb in front of the television. Bev watched the light changing through the bedroom window and was relieved that by 03:00hrs on Sunday morning she could just see across the grounds outside as she leaned her head against the glass. Summer Solstice. She got on to the bed but felt even more restless as she tried to sleep. She was so tired but sleep would not take her away even for a few moments. She got up again about 45 minutes later to good light and she watched the pheasants and crows on the front lawn. She now knew that the news overnight stays pretty much the same and it changes at around 06:00 with new bulletins. She waited another 2 hours doing nothing except feeling anxious and restless and going between the little sitting room, the kitchen and the bedroom.

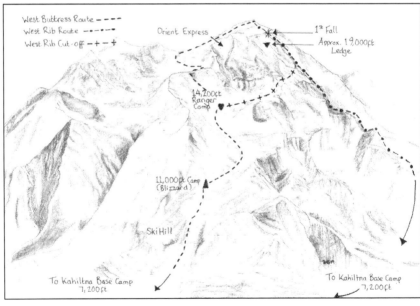

West Buttress Route — — —
West Rib Route —·—·—
West Rib Cut-off —+—+

Orient Express

1ˢᵗ Fall

Approx. 19,000ft
Ledge

14,200ft
Ranger
Camp

11,000ft Camp
(Blizzard)

Ski Hill

To Kahiltna Base Camp
7,200ft

To Kahiltna Base Camp
7,200ft

Phil with Carl in the background checking supplies for the mountain

Phil on the left, Steve, (El Gato) and Johnny waving at the back (Photos Steve Brown)

171

Plodding up and a short break, (Steve, me and Phil)

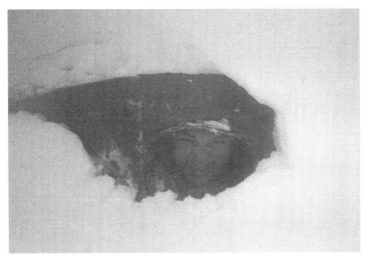

Johnny pops his head out of his tent during the blizzard (Photos Steve Brown)

The mat that helped to keep Carl and I alive (Photo Steve Brown)

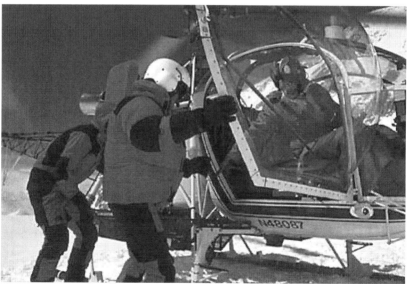

Loading the Lama (Photo: Scott Darsney 1998)

Carl, (L), me, (Ctr) and Steve, (R) in Alaska regional Hospital (Photo M. v Lakke)

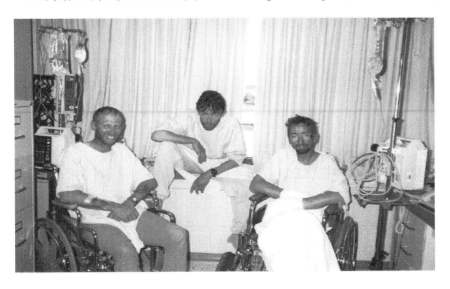

Roger Robinson, Head Ranger and all round really nice guy (Photo J. Dyson 1998)

Jay Hudson, the Cessna pilot who was spotting for the ranger camp

Jim Hood, Lama Pilot, thoroughly good egg and good old-fashioned hero

(Photos J. Dyson 1998)

175

Carl's frostbite injuries

Steve's frostbite injuries

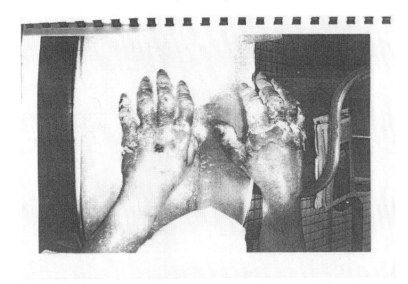

Grateful thanks to both for the photos

Chapter 13 - El Gato

Steve continued his descent after his fall from the cliff and scrambling his way out of the avalanche debris. He had literally been going about 30 seconds when the Rangers saw him heading for a crevasse. By the time he was out of the avalanche debris he was really fed up. He stomped his way towards Camp. He could barely see by now and was so weak; he was working on willpower and bad temper alone. His body refusing to cooperate with him was not being tolerated as he forged ahead. The Rangers were in awe of the tiny figure of the 'dead' man that struggled free of the base of the bergshrund and stormed down towards them. Everyone was watching now.

This time the screaming was frantic from the Camp. This guy deserved to live after what he had been through. It was too much to bear. Steve, oblivious to the screamed orders to "Sit down, Stop, Stay where you are!" plodded on, staggering now ready to collapse as he drew closer to the Camp. The Rangers, guides and climbers watched, yelled and waved their arms.

Steve couldn't hear a thing and the glare of the snow was burning his eyes, he could barely pick out the Camp now as he approached, his eyes were painful. The Rangers and guides could only hold their breath and look away as he approached the huge, gaping maw. The crevasse could be seen so clearly from where they were. The shouting was frantic, but unheard. Roger watched the whole terrible event unfolding before his eyes, each step closer and closer to the deadly fissure, then a startled movement and the distant figure was gone into the depths of the mountain face.

It was totally beyond belief for the Rangers, guides and other climbers still in Camp, and it left some of them a quite shaken and understandably upset.

It was totally beyond belief for Steve that he had fallen again. This time it was serious, (as if the previous falls hadn't been). His resolve was virtually threadbare by now and he looked about him quizzically. No, he wasn't hurt this time either, but he felt as though he had been unconscious for some small amount of time, he didn't know if it had been for a long few minutes or just seconds. He was fantastically cold, he could hardly move.

He got the impression that everything was very dark blue around him and that he was deeper in this crevasse than the last one. He realised that he was in real trouble this time as he looked at his hands. They looked like they belonged to a mummy; they were the wrong colour and the joints felt swollen. He began to have serious doubts about being able to climb out. He couldn't feel his feet and if he fell now he was a 'goner' and for good this time. Amazingly, he wandered around inside the crevasse looking at the walls; it was a miracle that he didn't fall further down as the fissure was at least 25ft to 30ft where he was and he wouldn't have been able to get out of that by himself if he dropped more.

He walked a few shaky paces along the floor then saw a further drop in front of him. To his alarm, he realised he was standing on an ice bridge and not the floor of the crevasse. He walked backwards away from the edge. He found a spot in the wall that he would pick away at and test himself out to see if he could get any purchase on it.

There was a lot of snow in the crevasse that almost seemed to fill it but it was so loose that he could not clamber over it to get out. He tackled it like a spider trying to scramble out of a slippery bath, but the ice flaked away or he slipped off each time he tried. In the end, the only thing he could do was try and bridge his way up.

It felt as though he was in there a long time but in reality it was about half an hour. He stood in a narrow section and pressed his back against one wall and walked his feet up the other wall. It wasn't as deep as it seemed at first. He pressed away with his arms, back and legs and raised himself away from the bottom. It was working. Very slowly and methodically, he squeezed his way up the walls. He managed to flip himself over, pop his head over top and into daylight again. He scrambled over the edge and sat, slumped and exhausted on the snow.

He admits that his memory of the falls and crevasse is vague and muddled due to hypoxia and concussion, so he can't remember much about how long he was in there, only that it seemed to go on forever.

At the Ranger Camp he was a celebrity already, dubbed 'El Gato' meaning 'The Cat' by the team there for demonstrating so profoundly that he had nine lives. Steve was completely spent and couldn't even stand, which the rescue team were now very thankful for. The ascending rescuers managed to yell loud enough for him to hear as they approached and ordered him to stay put.

Roger set the system going once again, like an old VW Beetle badly in need of a service he carried on regardless of the punishment he took.

19 June - Day 17 (19,200 feet)

Carl and I were alone now. There would be no immediate rescue I knew that. I figured the earliest we could expect any sign of activity on our behalf, would be at least another couple of hours and that would be in the Camp. That time frame depended on whether Johnny got straight to the Ranger Camp last night and then another thirty six hours on the outside to get us off the mountain altogether. We just had to get through the night.

The cold that was to creep over us like a sinister shade waiting to wrap us in its deathly cloak as we slept was an enemy we all had in mind as time began to pass. It was like a stinging, sharpness, burning on any exposed piece of flesh and could creep into our layers and suck away at our being.

Maybe, if some supplies could be dropped to us, we could afford to hang around for a good while after that, if a ground team was on its way up. There was also the realisation that a helicopter would have a good deal of trouble getting that high. Water and a tent would have been nice, even if we didn't have food. There seemed to be an awful lot riding on 'if'.

Carl was not too well now; he was still trashed from mauling the extra load and giving his water away the day before. He seemed to have deteriorated somewhat from earlier. Dragging lungful after lungful of empty air into his chest, he settled himself down next to me. His muscles were depleted, his dehydration and the altitude compounded his headache and he felt he wouldn't have been capable of going down with Conrad and Steve and he didn't want to. It is one thing to make it to the summit (or not in this case), but it is another to make the descent without killing

179

oneself, due to hypoxia, exhaustion and dehydration. Carl could have been a liability to them in his condition and he didn't want to send them all flying down the Orient Express, because he couldn't stay on his feet and mentally he needed a break from Conrad, they just weren't getting on. He thought he could recharge himself a little and be company for me. This wasn't to be, because he didn't seem to pick up at all and I was becoming concerned at this point.

The sun had lifted the temperature, but not enough for us to feel the benefit of it, the wind saw to that. We still felt as cold as ever, but at least we weren't going to get colder for the time being. Carl was suffering with his dehydration and more tired than he had ever felt. He didn't feel very rested from his poor night's sleep and he was disillusioned with Conrad. To sum it up, he was pretty fed up with mountaineering altogether. He struggled into his bivi bag and prepared himself for the wait.

It was getting on for 16:00hrs, there was no way of telling what part of the day we were going through by the sky, not until the sun disappeared behind the peaks and dusk appeared hours later, just to hint at darkness for a while, then brightening into dawn.

I was feeling perplexed at Conrad's attitude, but who was I to point the finger. I wasn't so affected by the altitude, so didn't have the battle between reality and trips to hypoxyland the way that Conrad did. Conrad knew what he was doing and the more progress they made on the descent, the better they would feel as the oxygen became richer and fed their starved brains and muscles. Steve really needed help and Conrad obviously gave that the priority, it's just that I would have waited for a helicopter casivac or ground rescue team while the weather was still stable. I really did hope Conrad could pull this off. Afterall, if there was a delay and Steve had got worse on the ledge then I would have been wrong and Steve could have been dead.

Carl had settled down in his bag and would try and rest now. I checked my watch and set the alarm to go off in a couple of hours. I couldn't chance Carl sleeping for too long at a time. His dehydration increased the risk of hypothermia and frostbite. A good, long sleep would be just what he needed, but would also help him shut down and slip into hypothermic unconsciousness. I struggled to make my fingers flex

180

enough to gain the dexterity to press the buttons on the watch. With the time set and another prod to Carl asking him if he was O.K., I squirmed down into my bivi bag to rest myself.

I tried to sleep, but as I relaxed and began to slip into a half-dream state, my arms and legs would jerk and agony would shoot through my ankles making me gasp. My whole body tense against the pain, I waited for it to subside, panting and trying to relax, as each spasm bit me. I tried to turn myself over onto my back, but it was too cold to lay stretched out and be immobile. I would lose what little heat I was trying to hold into my torso. I turned to my other side and hugged myself with my knees drawn up. Even a summer grade sleeping bag would be something. Huddled in a foetal position, I finally fell into a short, fitful sleep. The night hours were still ahead, but at least we weren't going to be plunged into total darkness, which somehow makes worry, imagination and trains of thought more disjointed and stressful.

I awoke with the alarm twenty-five minutes later, feeling stiff and groggy. The cold set my body in place and I pushed against tight muscles and stretched a little. My feet were very cold and I tried to drum my toes inside my boots, momentarily forgetting my ankles. As I flexed them, my ankles gave me a savage reminder that I wasn't permitted to move my feet. I felt that now, one ankle was a heavy, dull pain and the other was sharp, biting and very acute. One of them wasn't broken, I was sure, or maybe a green-stick fracture that would be weight bearing enough for me to operate a little better. I felt also that the wind speed had increased; it was noisier and pushed harder against us. I checked on Carl and any signs of a rescue.

I fumbled for the zip and wriggled it, but it wouldn't come free. It was frozen. I saw that a small clump of ice had formed on the zip pull, which had a melting droplet hanging from it. I sucked at it, realising I then had a tiny water source. It would be enough to wet my mouth from time to time even if there wasn't enough to swallow. I sucked the ice away and fought again with the zip.

I forced the zip down about eight inches and was hit by stinging spindrift in the face. I let my arms fall to my sides. The exertion to hold my arms up and pull at the zip at the same time had tired me and I panted for a few moments. I gathered my concentration again for another attempt. A few inches at a time, resting between each try I pulled open a gap that was wide enough to push my arms and shoulders through. I struggled into a sitting position and with my head dropping down so my chin was on my chest; I shut my eyes to concentrate again on my aching muscles. The sporadic bouts of shivering had left a signature in my back, sides and abdomen. Everything ached from constant tensing and relaxing. I tried not to breathe through my mouth to preserve warmth and moisture, but it was suffocating.

The cold I felt, wasn't due to my coming out of sleep, I would have felt my body kicking in some degree of warmth, as my metabolism worked back to its wakened state. My bag was filling with spindrift and I tried to hold the gap down to stop it. I reached to shake Carl and had to shout to make myself heard above the wind. "Carl, Carl, wake up mucker, are you O.K?" Carl moved inside the bag, "Yeah."

I went on "The wind has picked up, are you keeping warm enough?"

"Yeah, I'm fine"

Carl isn't a talkative guy at the best of times, but I found him easy going and reliable. I hoped he wasn't inclined to keep his mouth shut if he was in real trouble. That's just what he had done with Conrad but I didn't really know Carl that well. I hadn't kipped down with him; he hadn't been on my rope team. I had only a friendly acquaintanceship as part of the larger team up to now. I thought I should keep on at him to make sure. I had already been nagging everyone the night before and checking on them like a mother hen. I knew I was probably starting to get on Carl's nerves.

There was nothing else for it though. I couldn't let Carl sleep for long and needed to keep checking his responses.

I swept in vain at the frozen powder that was blustering into my bag. I was worried that it would melt and soak into my clothing. I knew now that we were running out of time if a rescue didn't come soon. A weather system was beginning to take hold and would soon delay any rescue.

I felt quite weak from the trail breaking the day before. I had given it my all for thirteen hours, to make sure we had a pathway to the summit before our turnaround time. I had suffered some shock from the fall. The fear that came upon me, as I lost contact with the mountain during the fall had drained me too. The pain in my ankles was sucking away at me along with the cold and thirst. Strangely my mind was calm and functioning very clearly and logically, I needed that focus above all else and I clung to it.

I would be fine for another night, I felt strong enough to cope with our current dilemma, but if the rescue were delayed, I would have to think about dropping down to a lower altitude with Carl. I hoped that the better of my ankles would be up to it. It was a last resort for now. My priority was Carl. It gave me a focus, but not as a token subject to keep myself interested but Carl had to be made ready for a long wait if the weather trapped us. Earlier on from our ledge, we could look far below and to the right and see the tiny specks of the 14,200ft Camp but the visibility had gone as the cloud base dropped with the in-coming weather.

I checked my watch repeatedly, waiting for another half hour to pass. I shouted through my bag, "Carl, how are doing mate?" "I'm alright!" Came a muffled reply. He was sounding irritable. I shivered inside the bag turning various possibilities for contingency plans over in my mind. After twenty minutes, I shouted to Carl again. The reply was the same, but he was sounding annoyed now. I couldn't just keep nagging Carl like this, but we had nothing whatsoever to do up there. We couldn't exactly play cards and chat.

The wind was whipping up higher and higher. It pressed against the bivi-bag making the smallest area of loose fabric flap madly. The endless slapping and flapping sound reminded me of clanking halyards that drive sailors mad in dock or a busy anchorage when they are trying to sleep. The snow sounded like the bivi-bag was being pressure hosed. We could barely make ourselves heard to each other. I had to come up with something to keep Carl going, however pointless and inane a task it might seem to be.

I checked my watch again, it was late evening now and I wondered how things were going on below us. Johnny would have made it back at around midnight last night and rounded up some help and they could be up to 17,000ft by morning, if the weather takes a kinder turn. Conrad and Steve should have made it down the Orient Express and be on their way into the 14,200ft Camp. Conrad would then make sure the guys in the tents at 16,200ft would get to the Ranger Camp too. Everyone would be safely tucked up in their sleeping bags by morning and all the Rangers would have to worry about is helping Johnny and a couple of the guys back up to help Carl and I back down. If the guys in the team were well rested enough, they probably won't need any manpower from the Rangers at all until we got back to 14,200ft.

The calculations went on in my head, as I prioritised what needed to be done and what I would be doing if I were doing the rescue. The weather was worrying. I hoped it would blow over in a few hours but it was a real storm now.

I would continue to check on Carl as I had been doing, but if Carl gets too fed up with the nagging; I would pretend that my watch batteries had given up in the cold. I'd set the timer and keep re-setting it for the alarm to keep going off. Carl would never hear it. That way Carl would have a task to perform by having to check his own watch and his mental faculties could be monitored. I worried about hypothermia beginning to grab my companion.

Out of sight, out of my reach and out of my imagination, a series of catastrophes had begun, that would leave me and my comrade marooned long enough for most of the rest of the world to think us dead.

Johnny was ordered by the Rangers to stay in Camp, as he was exhausted from helping the Americans and hadn't got to Camp until 02:00hrs. Conrad and Steve had plummeted down the Orient Express and nearly killed themselves, (several times in Steve's case). This fall of Conrad and Steve's meant that as they were now being rescued instead of us, the weather had time to close in. The weather was set to stay and worsen, which left the novices at 16,200ft to pick their own way down the mountain.

An enormous, tremendously expensive and extensive rescue operation with dozens and dozens of people from all skills areas involving U.S Park Ranger Service, civilians and U.S. military was about to be put into motion. All of which we were utterly unaware of and the world's news agencies would soon gather with astonishing speed to sell their stories to the media groups. Without anyone actually dying up to this point, things couldn't have gone more wrong.

Back on the ledge in our frozen isolation I set my watch alarm and slept again for a while. I woke after another hour of shivering and stabbing pains in my ankle. It was useless to try and sleep properly with the wind roaring and the pain and the cold and fighting for a deep, fulfilling and luxuriant, oxygen-filled breath. I was about to shout to Carl again when dread filled me. My bladder was not going to let me stay in my bag. I hadn't had to think about it before, as I was so dehydrated and had sweated so hard before the fall. I lay there for a moment hoping, with mind over matter, the urgency would go away.

I grasped the zip and went through the laborious process of trying to get myself free of the bag again. After several attempts and lots of puffing and blowing, I sat up in the full force of the weather. The stinging snow sandblasted the parts of my face that were exposed. The wind stole away what little breath I had. I tried to pull my goggles down over my eyes, but they had frozen to my forehead. I pulled at them and felt the pressure of the skin tearing. I left them where they were, at least it was so cold, I couldn't feel any pain and it was highly unlikely that I would bleed much in such a low temperature.

Again, I shook Carl, "What?" he answered almost exasperated.

"How are you doing, matey?" I asked again.

"I'm alright, I was trying to sleep." Came the irritated reply.

I tried to get to my feet to test my ankles, but the pain seared through me again, making me feel sick and dizzy. I put my hands to the ground and let the weight fall back onto my knees. I waited for a moment for the pain and nausea to pass and I shuffled to the edge of the drop in front of me. There was nothing below me but more cloud and swirling snow. I would have had difficulty standing if my ankles were in good condition. The wind was pushing so hard against me as I pulled off the gauntlets I was wearing and carefully tucked them into my clothes so that they didn't blow away and struggled to open my salopettes. I looked back, but decided I didn't want to go anywhere on the ledge. There are no latrines above the Ranger's Camp.

With great relief, I began to empty my disloyal bladder, but it didn't go over the edge. The gusting wind swirled erratically around and had forced some of the urine back all over me, spraying the front of my gortex jacket. It didn't matter which way I tried to face, the wind just blew it everywhere else but where it was aimed. I hung my head in disgust and resignation. I was thankful that being so de-hydrated there wasn't enough to soak me just splash me a bit but I hoped I'd be down before I needed to go again.

I slowly struggled to put my clothing back together and pulled on my inner gloves. My hands looked as if the flesh had been sucked from them and the skin had shrunk onto the bones accentuating the blood vessels and bones. I can only describe it as, the vacuum-packed look. They were also in pain from the short time they were exposed to the cold wind; it was a stinging, freezing pain.

I looked at the gauntlets and smiled to myself. I wasn't going to accept them at first, fearing I might lose them, but my friend, Zeb, who was a veteran of Denali and virtually a part of the family, had insisted I borrow them. I was very grateful now and was sure that I would be more susceptible to frost bite if I had worn my own old, faithful mitts.

I crawled back to my bivi bag and was about to shake Carl again, but decided I should leave him in peace. Carl was getting annoyed with me pestering him. I didn't want to sow the seed of worry in Carl's mind about our predicament. With the weather as it was things were more serious. Carl had no mountaineering experience and if we were in for a long wait, I needed to keep him focused and in good spirits. It had been just over thirty hours since the fall. We were going through our first night alone on the ledge together.

Carl had been through enough for now, he moved around in his bag and his head appeared through the drawstring opening at the top. We were both out from the depths of our chilled cocoons, so we decided to try and light the stove again. We were both very thirsty and our heads pounded from the dehydration and altitude. The disposable lighter was sparking, but still refused to form a flame. Holding it right against the stove, and trying to block the wind with our bodies, the sparks were desperately ineffective. It was exasperating to know we had fuel and the lighter would probably have worked, if only they were a little lower down the mountain or that the wind would ease up. We were just too exposed.

I now had to raise my voice to speak "Not to worry, we'll make do. Just try not to eat the snow it will make things a lot worse. If you must; make sure that you melt it in your mouth first, but only a little bit at a time, alright mucker?" I advised, yelling into Carl's face and barely being heard above the roaring wind around us. I didn't want to have to rely on the ice and snow unless we were desperate. I picked up a tiny lump of ice in the tips of my fingers and gingerly sucked at it. It barely seemed to wet my mouth.

I watched Carl carefully, he was functioning, but he was not very animated and his movements were very stilted. I was still worried because Carl was hypothermic, he was clearly weakening. I thought that we would both probably be by the time we got down, but not to the degree where neither of us could function at all or that is what I hoped at least. However long this was going to take, I couldn't afford to do much more than catnap from now on. We needed to rest as much as we could too to save energy but not sleep.

I checked my watch and looked across the ledge. Suddenly I thought I heard a voice through the wind. Alerted and hopeful I shouted to Carl

"Hey Carl, did you hear that? Listen!" Looking up, but not being able to see anything in the poor visibility, we sat rigid, excited, hopeful and attentive. More like a pair of puppies watching our dinner being made up.

"Yeah, I think so."

I thought it sounded like Johnny. We listened for a while longer. We were not imagining it; we were sure we could hear something. We began to shout back "Johnny, over here!" We stopped and listened again, but heard nothing more. We heard similar sounds, but knew then that it was definitely the wind howling, moaning and whistling over the ice and rocks, Johnny wasn't there, nobody was there.

It was still a little soon to expect a rescue yet, but surely in a few hours we could be hearing something of rescue activity. A kit drop would be an enormous help if they couldn't get us down. We hunkered down into the bivi-bags again. Lying there, on an icy slope the size of a double bed, inside a thin, gortex shell bag with the wind sweeping over us like an in-coming tide, getting more powerful as the hours ticked by, we were left with nothing outside our own thoughts.

I let my mind wander back to the lost gear. I was really disappointed that my rucksack had gone in the fall. I had some cracking gear that was now going to be welded by the ice and snow into the mountain. My Charlet Moser ice tools were from a shop in Chamonix. It seemed so many years ago now but it had been just about four or five. I'd used work gear from the stores on a lot of my ice-climbs so the Charlet Moser tools had barely a scratch when I started the expedition. I only had one now.

My thoughts drifted to a warm and happy place. Chamonix had been so warm and sunny. We'd started our summer leave by driving down from Yorkshire where I was based then to Dover. We got the ferry to Calais and drove down through France and on to Geneva. It was Bev's first glimpse of the Alps. She missed Norway so much; she was excited to see the mountains again. We would be spending a week in Switzerland. Gemma was seven, Rhys not even three. We had a VW Westfalia camper I had bought from my mate Tim Davis and his wife when we lived in Norway. It had an awning we put up on the side. The kids loved it as much as Bev and I. We spent our picturesque week in Switzerland and then moved on to Chamonix and spent another week sight-seeing and rock climbing together, exploring the area on our bikes with Rhys on a baby seat. The following two weeks were the Army Alpine Meet.

I met old friends and colleagues and we planned routes and climbed and climbed route after route. It only rained a couple of times and even in August there were shining, white, fresh dumps of snow on the mountains and red-hot pavements in the town with scarlet geraniums spilling from window boxes everywhere.

Bev played with the kids, did homework with Gemma. Gemma collected slugs on a boulder and tried to keep them corralled in with pebbles. It took an age to wash her hands clean of the slug 'glue'. Rhys's hair got lighter and lighter blonde and he collected anything he could pick up and put in his mouth. We all explored and went on bike rides and walks. When I went up the mountains on one trip Bev went through the Mont Blanc tunnel to Italy just so that she could say she had been. She changed some Francs to Lira, (there was no Euro then.). She bought herself and the children some ice-cream and drove back through the tunnel again to France. The drive, she thought was dull and very smelly from the fumes but she couldn't get over the engineering that had made it. She hardly moved the steering wheel, kilometre after kilometre. It was so warm there in Chamonix, very warm. It was so sunny, so much fun, and so warm. It is so noisy and cold; I was suddenly pulled out of my steady drift into sleep by the pain in my body. I tried not to move my legs but I had to turn over again.

The effort to shout to Carl was nauseating and left me breathless after each sentence. The noise of the wind on the wall of the mountain and the whipping of the snow on the thin fabric of the bags made conversation impossible. All I could do was ask Carl how he was, and all Carl could do was reply.

For all the speculation on what we must have talked about during our ordeal, it must have been a disappointment to the journalists to find out it was no more than could be said in fifteen minutes over the three days and four nights. As much as we would have welcomed a long chat, we just couldn't do it. It would have been great to get to know each other more and help pass the time, or even to express how we were feeling about our predicament. Hopeful or fearful, with barely centimetres between us we were isolated from each other by the dreadfully bitter wind and snow.

The foam sleep mat that we shared was all we had to insulate us from the frozen surface. It was one of the items that would usually not be taken on a summit bid. I had been sleeping on an inflatable, thermal mat, (Thermorest) throughout the trip and took the foam mat as a spare. The intention is always to make summit day a round trip and not to carry anything that wasn't absolutely necessary outside of emergency gear. On the itinerary, the 19th June would find the team at the Ranger Camp, but we had been moving well and the weather, apart from the few days they were snowed in, had been good to us.

I had missed Gemma's birthday before this by being away, but this time it was all the more poignant for me as her gift was playing a contributing role in saving our lives. I remembered again that today, what was left of it, was her birthday. I knew she was having a party in

Staffordshire at my parent's house on Saturday. I hoped they would all have a great day. Bev especially loved doing the parties. I bet she would be in her element tomorrow. She was probably having so much fun with the kids she may not even give me a passing thought until the kids went to bed and she had time to miss me again.

We were already cold and the temperature was still dropping noticeably. I thought I would tell Gemma and Rhys all about my horrendous experience that will become an 'adventure story' for them when I got home. They'd probably not believe half of it, that I had done a 'dad' thing and embellished it for greater drama just for their wide-eyed expressions. I hoped I could take the signed mat with me if nothing else.

We spent our first night alone on the tiny ledge in much the same way that we had spent the day. We slept for short periods when tiredness overwhelmed the cold, then, the cold would fight back and wake us. The pain in my ankle was biting at me all the time. The painkillers I had taken earlier hadn't done a great deal. The good side of the pain was that the stimulus kept me alert, but I would dearly have loved a couple hours stretch of deep, restful sleep. It would be so easy to just go to sleep. That's all there would be to it freezing to death is just a matter of falling asleep I told Bev later, you wouldn't know about it.

Saturday 20th June - Day 18 (19,200 feet)

I checked my watch again and listened to the angry weather. It was Saturday morning, we could realistically hope for a rescue later in the day if the weather dies down. I hoped that the weather front would be moving on. I hoped too that the weather at 14,200ft wasn't as bad as it was here at 19,000ft. Maybe Johnny could have rounded up a couple of the guys to sit out at around 17,000ft until the weather cleared, that way they would only need a few hours, maybe less than half a day, to get to them on the ledge and help us down to 16,000ft even if we couldn't make it to the Rangers at 14,200ft. I calculated what could be done, but it all relied on the weather. The storm was not blowing itself out indeed; it seemed to be getting worse. The wind was pushing so hard against us and temperature was very, very cold, though at the time I thought it was just me suffering with the hypothermia.

I hoped we wouldn't have to trouble the Rangers and guides for manpower. I would be mortified and very embarrassed at the thought of anyone panicking on my behalf. I thought that I was already in for some stick from my pals in the mountaineering world, as well as the guys at work for what had happened. I thought of my old mates like Zeb, Tim, Nick Harding, Chris Short, Sandy Sanderson et.al. They would be laughing their socks off if they knew I'd got myself rescued. I was so isolated that I had no idea what was going on and soon everybody would know and that nobody was laughing.

I surmised that Carl in his state could make it down if someone came along with the gear and helped him warm up. There was nothing we could do for ourselves, as Conrad and Steve had the rope. At least they would be safely down now, I thought.

I had no idea of the chaos the rescue system was having thrown at it below me. I had no idea that the Rangers and guides had a problem with adding Carl and I to their over-stretched agenda because I didn't know about the other falls on the Orient Express. I had no idea that our dilemma was making its way around the world's news. I also had no idea that our friends and families were sick with fear for us and hoping the next phone call would be the right news. Friends we'd lost touch with years ago, were wishing us well, from all over the globe.

As Jeff Munroe had lain near death at 14,200ft and the rest of the Camp curiously await news of the stricken British team, Carl and I can only wait, listen and watch for movement. We also had no idea that at the Ranger Camp they were discussing bringing in log-grabbers to suspend under the helicopter to pick our corpses off the ledge to bring them down. They had to; they can't just leave bodies there if they can be recovered.

The weather was a little kinder the next morning, but we still couldn't feel any warmth from the sun. The wind had dropped just a little but the sky around still looked very angry. I was aware suddenly of a deep thudding in the air, very distant that I couldn't place at first. I suddenly realised, it was a sound I recognised. It was the thudding of a Chinook and my heart leapt. We both listened and soon had enough of a view through the swirling, tumbling clouds to be able to see them manoeuvring below. I realised with some dread, that the Rangers were probably involved with our rescue on some scale.

We watched on and through wisping cloud, saw that the Chinooks were leaving. There was a very small helicopter that came and went too, but we couldn't tell from our far distance what was happening. Carl and I knew then, that there must have been some other incident. Whatever was happening, at least the weather was good enough for helicopters to fly in and out of 14,200ft Camp. That was good news for the time being. I hoped the rescue below, wasn't anything too serious. We thought maybe it was a bit of unimproving AMS at the Camp or someone had fractured a leg or something. It's hard to say in this situation, whether ignorance is bliss or not.

What was actually happening was the evacuation of Jeff and Billy. Jeff sustained the severe head injury we already know about and Billy had chest injuries.

The official report states that after Phil and Johnny had witnessed the fall and rescue teams from the United States National Park Service, (USNPS) arrived to assess, treat and evacuate, Jeff was assessed to be (Glasgow Coma Scale level 4) GCS 4. Anything below 8 is considered severe. By 17:00 hrs, Jeff had developed pulmonary oedema, requiring suction every 15 minutes. The tiny Lama helicopter flown by Jim Hood carried Ranger/medic Eric Martin to the 14,200ft Camp lands at 22:30 hrs to evacuate Jeff. The Lama is flown down to Kantishna with Jeff on board to be transferred to the U.S. National Guard Pavehawk helicopter, which takes off immediately to Alaska Regional hospital in Anchorage, where it arrives to be met by a 'crash ' team at 01:30 on 20th June. Jeff's symptoms at the 14,200ft Camp had ranged from cyanosis, laboured and irregular breathing, weak pulsed tachycardia, fixed pupils and signs of hypovolaemic shock, though he had no external bleeding. He was dosed with varying amounts of oxygen and 4mg of intra-muscular Dexamethazone. He had a 'query' fracture to his left hand and that was splinted. He showed many symptoms of subdural head injury, so he was lucky to still have any symptoms of being alive.   He remained unconscious throughout the entire evacuation and treatment process.

Billy was finally evacuated by Chinook to Alaska Regional Hospital on 21st June.

Both later made good recovery, thanks to the swift actions of Johnny and Phil and the tremendous efforts of the teams involved in the rescue on the mountain and the pilots.

Anyway, back to the ledge and the altitude.

Chapter 14 - Altitude

There are a number of problems with altitude some of which can be very severe. The air contains the same amount of oxygen at high altitude as it does at sea level. The 'thin' air at altitude is actually the effect of the lower air pressure. At 18,000ft, the air pressure is about half the sea-level pressure. This results in the pressure of the oxygen molecules being reduced by the same amount. On Denali, the air is 'thinner' at 19,000ft than at 19,000ft at the equator. This is due to the rotation of the earth causing a flattening effect of the air at the poles.

Reading about the physiology of altitude problems makes alarming reading, but leaves one in awe of the adaptability of the human body.

Climbing to ever increasing heights, the climber first feels the lack of oxygen absorption by deeper and more rapid breathing for the normal expedition tasks that are carried out in the course of the day. Although the heavier and more rapid breathing increases the pressure for the oxygen to diffuse into the bloodstream, it does not reach the same sea-level pressure required by the muscles and organs to provide the normal capacity of output.

The result is loss of appetite, slowing of the digestive system and heart rate and like a car driving up hill in a high gear, the body labours and slows. The condition continues to develop during sleep as the breathing slows and the breaths are more shallow, so the oxygen absorption, in turn lowers further. That is why many climbers wake with headaches and sleep poorly.

This is fairly normal, but can quickly deteriorate into altitude sickness, which really covers a number of conditions. There is no way of telling if a climber who is normally fit and healthy with a good oxygen absorption; will go down with the illness. The climber may have trained and prepared well, but the problem is inherent and not a reflection on his personal administration, though some research suggests that anti-oxidants in the diet may help.

The general term used for early stages of altitude sickness is 'hypoxia', which essentially means low oxygen, a condition that can affect people who are at sea-level with certain medical conditions. Someone who is hypoxic would usually feel a headache, dizziness, periods of confusion, slurred or garbled speech and hallucinations.

Like the more severe illnesses, the first and best treatment is to get down to a lower altitude by a couple of thousand feet and spend some time resting and taking supplemental oxygen. There is medication that is effective against mild altitude sickness and can buy a little more time to acclimatise, but there is often a temptation to press on and climb higher too soon, which only exacerbates the problem and can lead to the more severe illnesses that seem to creep up with frightening speed.

AMS - Acute Mountain Sickness refers to a number of symptoms brought on by ascending too quickly to high altitude. Symptoms show between one and two days after arrival at altitude then appear to go away. Generally it seems to feel like a hangover, but other symptoms are fatigue, nausea, vomiting, headache, light-headedness and loss of appetite. More serious types of AMS can develop into the following.

HAPE - High Altitude Pulmonary Oedema is basically fluid retention of the lungs. Fluid from the blood vessels seeps into the alveoli of the lungs and blocks them, which means that the oxygen can no longer diffuse into the blood and the climber begins a long, drawn-out type of suffocation. The casualty often loses consciousness and red or pink foaming blood can sometimes be seen in the mouth. The victim has to be evacuated to a lower altitude with supplemental oxygen and have the fluid pumped from his lungs. It obviously requires qualified medical care and sadly has resulted in a number of deaths.

HACE - High Altitude Cerebral Oedema is another condition that sometimes goes hand in hand with HAPE. HACE is the retention of fluid in the brain causing it to swell. It often manifests itself as a severe headache that is not alleviated with analgesics or sleep. Sleep tends to make the problem worse unless copious supplies of oxygen can be spared, which of course is never the case. It develops with confusion, the inability to perform simple motor functions like eating or walking and is sometimes accompanied by erratic or violent behaviour. Sometimes though, the apparently exhausted victim collapses into a deep sleep and slips into a coma. It goes unnoticed until his companions try to wake him.

Both HAPE & HACE are extremely dangerous and life threatening if not treated. One study showed that about 2.5 percent of climbers on Denali suffered HAPE or HACE compared to 1.6 percent on Everest. Although there was more AMS on Everest, the rate of ascent was slower.

When revising the chapters on high altitude sickness for this section, I came upon a comment that the climbers who develop these illnesses bring it upon themselves, I thought it a very harsh comment to make, but reading on through the causes, symptoms and the treatment, I can see why the comment is made. However, when running to a strict itinerary, it is easily understood how some people who don't know that they are susceptible can be caught out.

Most climbers would have made themselves aware of the cause and effect of hypoxia and AMS and wouldn't deliberately take the risk to themselves and their team mates. The will to achieve the summit, lapses in judgement due to mild hypoxia and fatigue will mean that it will always occur sometime during the climbing season.

Although a steady ascent and acclimatisation will prevent the sickness in most climbers, there is only a certain height to which the body can adapt. Beyond around 18,000ft the acclimatisation tends to peter out and from then on physical performance begins to deteriorate. It will continue to do so until the descent is made. That is why people who have problems high on the mountains are not physically able to bring themselves down out of trouble, especially if they have spent a number of days there. Continuous lack of oxygen over a long period can prevent a climber from even standing following the huge exertion to climb to the altitude that they are stuck at. It is difficult to comprehend the problems.

Bev started to read books about altitude climbing. By the time she had heard or read the accounts of the Summit to the Sea team and managed to study the chapters on altitude sickness in various books and leaflets without it going completely over her head, she started to have an understanding of it.

I don't think anyone can really know what it is like to try and work and climb through unless they have experienced it. It's not meant to be a condescending statement in any way; some experiences just can't be transferred verbally.

To me, the long-term effects at this stage seem to be poor memory and poor absorption of information. To Bev they are more administration problems and the sympathy that goes along with someone trying hard to bring back something that they are not sure they have forgotten. Sometimes it's funny and we describe them as 'senior moments', other times it is very annoying and causes bickering.

The activity below us seemed to quiet for a time, then a while later, there was more. We hoped it may be something for us, but the weather quickly began to deteriorate again. Watching the goings on below had passed a little time for us, but the cold was far too intense to stay exposed to it. We could hear the wind howling like jets above us and the wisps of cloud rapidly transformed to thick swirls of deepening grey.

We retreated back into our flimsy sacks and closed them to the hostile little world around us. The hours on the ledge merged into one another, as did the days. It finally came to the point where the weather had got so bad on and off and I realised that we were probably out of reach of rescue where we were.

There was a window in the weather and the wind seemed to drop again. I don't even know when this was. The snow and cold were more tolerable. I sat upright and said to Carl, who was mumbling through his bivi-bag. "Come on Carl, we need to make a move." A few more grumbling moans and Carl appeared out of the bag. By now everything was really difficult. Moving at all took such a tremendous effort. We both had bad headaches from the altitude and lack of fluids over such a long period.

I knew by now that if the rest of the team were going to get back up to us, we were going to have to move down and meet them part of the way before the weather turned again. I also realised that there wouldn't be much hope of a helicopter reaching us so high up. I thought that by moving further down it would give my team mates a fighting chance of getting to us without getting too tired.

We struggled to pack up our sparse gear and made ready to move down. Even now before we started we had to keep stopping to rest. I couldn't get my crampons back on as my ankles were far too painful. Whatever happens now, I knew we had to get down. We traversed across from our ledge; I was half hobbling and half crawling. We then came to a slope that had a good ledge at the bottom, it looked pretty secure but the only way to attempt it wasn't going to please Carl, especially as he would have to go first. The only thing wrong here was that I had no crampons on. With Carl on a good ledge below, he could help me brake at the bottom. As we had given Conrad the rope, I had to give Carl a crash course in 'glissading'. It is a quick way of getting down a slope in a controlled slide. One sits on the ice with the legs out in front and using the ice-axe as a brake by leaning into it a climber can control the speed of descent and use the crampons to help stop altogether. I talked him through it and showed him what to do. It is a fairly simple task and the slope wasn't too steep so we weren't going to shoot off the mountainside. I asked, "Are you O.K. with that?"

"Yeah", replied Carl, and off he went. I watched him go and felt that he was making a good job of it considering that the snow was very aerated and the ice-axe didn't do a lot of biting on the way. He went down a bit faster than we both expected but he wasn't hurtling down. Carl landed quite heavily on the ledge but very successfully, as I was still trying to move down behind him. My ankle bit at me as I got myself into position to follow Carl. The snow pack was very soft and I found that I couldn't glissade very well with the pain I was in. I only slid about 10 – 12 ft and made an excruciating landing, as both feet were out in front of me and took the impact of a sudden stop. I made the rest my way down the slope by down climbing. I quickly turned onto my front and using my hands and knees I reached the ledge at long last.

Thinking we had done O.K. I was greeted by, "Fuck that, I'm not doing that again." Carl was clearly shaken by it. I saw that the rest of the slope around the ledge was too sheer. In our condition, we wouldn't make a descent without help. At least we were lower and on a good sized ledge this time. It had more room and didn't slope away so much. It was much safer and stable to be here. There was nowhere else to go now; we still had to wait for rescue. At least we had moved around a little and broken up the waiting time with some activity to get the blood pumping. Hunger was making us alert and clear minded but lack of oxygen making it all so hard to do anything for the time we were active.

We settled in again. I was starting to feel rough after a while but felt that I could hang on until the following day before things started to get serious for me. Carl was not in good condition. We lost track of time here, I don't know how long we spent on this new ledge.

Carl was fairly quiet anyway, but now he had no sense of humour left and was edgy and annoyed, more so than before when I kept nagging him. He was very tired and all he wanted to do was sleep, he was clearly hypothermic now. I knew he didn't have long and it was an alarming thought. His face was greyer and his expression blank.

We watched the activity below and still had no idea that any of this was for us. Then above the roaring of the wind we heard a different tone. We heard a plane, we were sure of it. We looked around and saw the small fixed wing plane come over to us. We both tried to stand and were both shouting.

* * *

Back to Sunday 21st June Summer Solstice and Father's Day (U.K) - Day 19

In Longsdon village in Staffordshire, the house was quiet, except for the sound of the television. It was some time on Sunday afternoon. There was only my cousin and Bev in the room as the next news bulletin came in. Bev knelt in the middle of the floor looking at the screen, knowing what Jane Tranel, who was a spokesperson for the U.S. National Park Service, had said. She told the world very tenderly and sympathetically, very sadly, "It's a long way to fall."

She also confirmed that there had been no radio contact with the two soldiers and that they've had climbers survive three days on the mountain in these conditions but we've already passed the three-day mark and are just praying for a break in the weather.

Bev thought what Jane Tranel had really been saying was, 'We think they're dead, but we'll do what we can anyway.' Bev felt it was so desperately useless to be thousands of miles away. She felt utterly alone and almost wept quietly but even now, her throat swollen, her anxiety gripping her emotions, she couldn't although her heart broke for a moment. Bev then felt my usually stoic and very reserved cousin's hand touch her shoulder to comfort her. She stopped, knowing she was being self-indulgent but didn't care. She had our children with her but she wanted me back too, it wasn't fair.

Bev called Major Johnston at the Princess of Wales Royal Regiment, (PWRR) and asked again for a flight out. Surely now they would let her. He confirmed that she would not get a flight, as at first it was not a 'life-threatening situation' and now that Training Accident Investigation Team gathered and ready to fly out he reaffirmed there would be no spare places on an 'indulgence' (free R.A.F. spare seat flight.)

Her frustration turned to an almost insane anger and she wanted to rip the phone out of the wall and smash it over and over. She was imploding on herself and rammed the emotion down invisibly inside her without a twitch or single grind of the teeth just a slow deep breath, a slight raise of the eyebrows and an almost imperceptible grin of disdain, (a major warning sign to me during an argument). She stood there looking at the phone and gently put the receiver back and went to the bedroom without a word or looking at anybody. Bev sat on the bed staring towards the blank wall in front of her and realised that the Army had total control over me and that she was only in the picture as a matter of courtesy or maybe duty as next of kin. She knew that if she had pushed in the first place that she could have had a flight but merely accepted their word the first time. She felt even more powerless and cheated.

How could we have not been in a life threatening situation at any point since the 1st fall? Bev thought the Army is doing really well with their highly publicised, highly trained soldiers, highly qualified this and that. They barely mentioned the rescuers. She realised she disliked the Army now, didn't trust it but not nearly so much a she came to dislike the newspapers and the Army Media Ops. 'Oh, we fucked up. Let's get a positive slant on this because everyone is watching us.' Whether she was right or wrong in her assumptions and feelings, she suddenly realised she had to get out of there at the first opportunity.

Hours passed again and Zeb had to leave to get back to work. He gave everybody a hug and when he stepped out the door, he looked up at the moon and told Bev, "You know, I bet he's looking at the same moon and wishing he was back here with you." She smiled and thanked him but she thought I wouldn't think like that. I wasn't so sentimental then, or wouldn't have admitted to it. I've grown a lot since then, we both have.

Bev was now alone with nobody who knew the system. She closed the door and went to spend time with Gemma and Rhys as they showered and got ready for bed and played quietly on their beds. Bev brushed Gemma's long hair of the day's tangles. Bev just wanted to bundle them into the car and go home. She chatted to them, folded the clean laundry, tucked shoes under the bed and sat on Gemma's bed to give them the soft version of the updates on me and told them that by the time they wake up I might already be off the mountain.

"You said that last night." They both mumbled in reply.

"Is daddy going to be alright?" Gemma asked directly. Bev shot a glance at Rhys who was watching her. She saw Gemma was looking right into her face for any sign. Bev bailed; she shot forward and hugged Gemma so she wouldn't have to look at her.

"Of course he is, don't be daft. You know he'll be alright." Bev sat on Rhys' bed and hugged him and smiled perkily.

"Play quietly now, I'll be in to switch the light off in half an hour." Bev pulled the door so it was just ajar and hoped she had got away with it. Bev had no idea how she was going to tell them, what she was going to tell them or how to handle them if it came to it. She only knew that if 'it' came, she didn't want it to be here, where she felt out of control of everything.

Chapter 15 - In Extremis - (19,200ft)

Jay Hudson flew above the clouds and broke into brilliant sunshine. The stunning beauty of the peaks of Denali and the surrounding mountains was not a matter for Jay to think about as he approached the summit. He flew past the spot where we, the two stricken soldiers were reported to be. He relayed information back to Jim Hood and the Rangers as he searched for any sign of us. The whole world was waiting for news of whether we were alive or dead. The picture the family got on the television later in the day was exhilarating, frightening and sad. Bev said later, to see me as a tiny detail trying to stand and holding my arms outstretched, made her catch her breath, though at that point she didn't know who it was.

I had to exert myself too much to stand for long and could only get to my knees at first. My ankles were more stable now and not so painful, although the left one was still really quite bad. I could gingerly weight-bear on the right and balance on my left. This was a big improvement. I was able to lift my arms in the correct 'V' position so that my whole body looked like a 'Y' for 'yes' to signal to the aircraft to tell the pilot we needed rescue.

My ankles were feeling shot. The plane was fairly close and very welcome it was too. We saw the pilot in the cockpit and he gave us the 'thumbs up'. I, stating the obvious said, "They've seen us, mate!"

"Thank fuck for that." Came Carl's reply. We were elated. We knew now that something was being set up for us, we were no longer alone. I found that I was waving my arms as the Cessna flew off, dipping both port and starboard wings one after another to wave acknowledgement.

I turned to Carl feeling a little startled. "Shit, I think I gave him the wrong signal!" I almost laughed.

"Eh?" Said Carl, looking justifiably alarmed.

"I think I waved my arms instead of holding them up". I slumped, worn out from the effort of trying to stand and signalling for those long seconds. Carl was dead quiet and far away, he was not just pale but very grey and so cold that he didn't function at all in between any dialogue we managed to have. We were only hours away from being safe now but looking at Carl even that could be too late. He was closing down, even now after seeing the plane.

* * *

At home the family were delighted but Bev sat stone faced and tried to smile. She had spotted it immediately and couldn't understand why the others hadn't seen it. Were they blind? Were they mad? Why are they so bloody happy, can't they see it? She only saw one person move on the television screen. She didn't know who it was and either way it looked bad to her. She waited. She waited hour after hour after hour until more than half the day passed. She paced, and felt suffocated. The image welded into her mind. One tiny silhouette, teetering in the snow and what looked like a completely still body next to it, dead or alive. It was driving her out of her mind. The control was the worst bit. The impulse to run out and keep running far away was welling up inside.

More news came to Bev from Major Johnston on the telephone, she was always pleased to hear from him but it was no news. He said that a Daily Mail correspondent had reported that one of them had been spotted moving. So far that was all he knew. He also asked if anyone from the P.T .Corps knew anything. It dawned on her then that apart from Martin's immediate colleagues in Wales and his friends from the past, nobody from the P.T. Corps had been in touch since the accident occurred.

She thought it odd because either they would be getting information from their many 'Subject Matter Experts, or they would, like the P.W.R.R want up-dates from her when she got news as next-of-kin. There was nothing. She had been calling Cindy, her friend back at the Unit in Wales but really, no immediate hierarchy above Martin's boss, Billy had been in contact. She didn't know what to make of it. Maybe there had been messages that hadn't been passed on. Had Martin done something wrong on the expedition and was the P.T.Corps deliberating some damage limitation strategy to their department? The P.W.R.R. public relations were in over-drive. All their guys were heroes already to some degree but the P.T. Corps was very quiet.

She thought at least some message would have come through from the H.Q. in Arbourfield but she just had a duty adjutant's number to call if she had news to pass to them. Perhaps it may be a small thing but she had been worrying so much, this small and insignificant seeming lack of contact alarmed her suddenly. Was there a reason nobody had been in touch?

'Every man and his dog has been in touch with us. They can't say they don't know where I am now.' She thought. It was the last moment Beverley felt any kind of loyalty towards the Corps out of some kind of misguided loyalty to me. She just wanted to go back to Wales. She decided that she would go back the next day regardless. She was sick of feeling trapped with people around her that had no clue how this was working and dismissed everything she was saying with comments like, 'They wouldn't be like that, they'll tell you first.' 'The newspapers wouldn't make it up.' She was suffocating here. O.K. the press had a job to do. They all had an angle and a style, it's just that she hadn't been prepared to be involved; she was on the back foot with it all.

As far as Bev was concerned at the time, her relationship with the Armed Forces was over, whatever the outcome. It doesn't matter what they've already done for us with career, postings and advantages of being part of it. She was finished. She just wanted me home. Her emotions were all over the place inside her and bolted down with a heavy cast-iron lid. She did not see that I was simply 'at work' for the Army, representing the P.T. Corps, as they had trained me to, whatever the circumstances. That was the reality, when things go wrong, I am not simply 'her Martin', I am a soldier and I belong to the Army too. I'm an investment of a great deal of time, money and nurturing by many people.

"What about the other one?" She asked herself. "I don't know, is he dead?" Questions raced through her in a muddle. 'If it is Martin that is dead, where will I go next in my life if he is not in it anymore?' She was once told that the only security you can make in life is for yourself. She realised that she had deliberately built the last fifteen years of her life to revolve around me. Her thoughts and feelings were beginning to spin out of control, becoming muddled.

It wasn't news that she was watching now, it repeated what she had seen on the television earlier. She hated it now but couldn't help watching as one news programme came on after another, any channel.

She felt trapped in that house, in that parochial village, in the middle of nothing. She desperately wanted to get back to Wales. She just wanted to grab the children, run out and drive a long, long way.

Bev thought about driving to Aviemore in Scotland where Tilly would without question give them refuge from everyone at the Reindeer Centre or their own farm on The Crown Estate of Glenlivet, far, far away, remote, and a hermitage if she wished. Even if she was rude enough to turn up on the doorstep unannounced with two children and a dog, she would be whisked in and given anonymity and solitude and plenty of work to do. She thought that if she went to the Reindeer Centre, she could stroll along the lane to Glenmore Lodge where people would know exactly what she was asking and know exactly how to answer it. She supposed a good chunk of the staff there had probably done Denali at some stage. She gave it some serious thought but then it wasn't going to help anything but her own mind and give the children a very exciting break to go back there again. She would need to get back home in case Martin was coming back soon. She hoped again, despised that feeling of hope as a nasty trick and her frustration continued, tight-lipped.

* * *

I was ready to settle in for the night knowing that we would be fine if only Carl could last out another night with me. The cold was unbelievable now. In all my experience of bad weather and exposed places, I had never known anything as cold as this. I sat up, partially out of my bivi-bag and looked out at the sky. I had ceased to shiver long ago. My body started pulsing in slow heavy thuds, like a single-cylinder engine, which I knew was a bad sign. I did actually feel after each heavy thud of my pulse beating through me that there was some small heat generated from it. After a while, the thudding wore off and I felt warmer again.

I retreated into my bag and curled into a foetal position. Eventually, the cold came back and the shivering returned for short periods and it was incredibly cold. Carl was very quiet now, even more reluctant to respond, drowsy and irritable. I hoped that he would stay awake and not let his life creep away as he disappeared inside himself to sleep The weather was becoming clearer in patches as the night wore on and it got colder still.

The rescue teams were more hopeful now and a rescue was definitely going to be attempted. They had everything, but the weather. It continuously compounded everything. Every new report brought hope or disappointment. Jay had been spotting for everyone and passed the information on and Jim was on his starting blocks again. He had expected with the severity of the winds and temperature over three days and nights that he would be bringing our bodies down. The visibility was still poor to zero but he had to get sorted out with fuel and oxygen for his strategic ascent.

Jim had barely got any down time over the weekend with his aid to rescue Jeff Munroe and the weather beating everyone. His base was in Talkeetna, the Base Camp on Denali is a 40 minute flight away. The 'spotter' Jim was relying on, Jay Hudson was also based in Talkeetna. Jim had a capacity of just 2.5 hours of fuel and two oxygen cylinders with his essential equipment and a ranger to aid the operation. They were dressed in specially insulated suits and they took off for the mountain. Jim decided he needed to take a look at the situation for himself before he could decide just how they were going to get us down. He could pick up more fuel at 7,000ft Base Camp or at 14,200ft

Jim and his Ranger made a hazardous climb up through the clouds and with battering cross winds knocking them about. They got to 10,000ft and put the masks on and switched on the oxygen. At 16,000ft he spoke with Jay in his Cessna making his way around the top of the mountain above them. He radioed down to Jim to confirm we were alive. Jim was elated, you'd have thought it was his own brothers up there and he couldn't believe it could still be a rescue and not a body recovery.

From this information Jim was more determined he was going to make sure he did everything to get us down alive. He knew we had been here all this time with just bivi-bags, no tent, no sleeping bags, no food or water. No food meant no fuel to help keep our bodies warm. I think he was actually as happy to hear that we were alive as we were to see that a rescue was on its way.

Jim climbed higher but by 18,000 ft the thin air finally got to the Lama and it was not gaining any more altitude no matter how hard he pushed. He had to drop back down. The winds wouldn't lift the Lama as they were crossing laterally very hard. They decided that at 14, the Ranger would stay behind and Jim would dump any gear he could to save weight and then go back up alone to make another attempt to reach 19.

This is where there was an incredible stroke of luck that changed everything.

There had been minor breaks in the clouds on and off during the storm and now one was appearing to open again. Jim got a long line attached to the Lama and got a rucksack of supplies loaded to it. It contained food, hot chocolate, tents and sleeping bags but most vitally it had a radio. They all needed comms to work out how bad we were and if we were capable of helping ourselves to help them get us down.

Jim took off the second everything was ready but the highly experienced and steady pilot was momentarily taken by anxiety as he broke through the clouds. With the long line and rucksack swinging and turning beneath him he envisaged not being able to drop it safely. He thought for a moment that if he got it wrong by the smallest fraction with the racing wind that he could knock us off our ledge and kill us himself. He shook the thought away and concentrated on his highly coordinated manoeuvring up the face. He had to make it through the weather, make the drop safely and get back down to 14 before his sparse ration of fuel he had allowed in the weight calculations ran out and he simply dropped out of the sky.

It was truly nail-biting for him and the Rangers. We did not know what he was going through at this point but as the tiny and extremely vulnerably looking helicopter came into view, I just knew then we would be fine, even with a longer wait. At last I had some very confident hope.

Carl was alarming me by his inactivity in every way. He barely even moved his head to speak and he was closing down before my eyes. Rescue was so close, just a few more hours. Carl barely responded, just sat there blank, grey and hardly speaking.

Carl and I watched the small helicopter in the distance trying to wind its way up the mountainside, weaving over the West Buttress and back as it climbed. It was very late but it didn't actually get dark. The sky had cleared for now and it was a deep azure with an aura of deep pink around the bottom, I thought how beautiful it was. I wondered whether the little helicopter was monitoring something that was going on over the other side of the buttress or whether it was using the warm side of the mountain that was still touched by sunlight to help it climb. I've never had much to do with aviation except flights inside or jumping out of them with parachutes.

Then suddenly the little helicopter turned towards us, very slowly climbing up but definitely coming to us. We got ready to move. We could see that there was something hanging from under the helicopter but it was still some distance away and seemed to be working very hard to ascend. I eventually saw it was a rucksack on the end of a very long line.

The helicopter climbed right up above us to the left so close we could see the pilot's face as he struggled to gain more lift. The helicopter moved to the right above us and set the rucksack on the end of its line right in front of us on the ledge with such precision I could hardly believe anyone could achieve it, especially with the wind belting us all.

Jim was worried that I was going to touch the line as he lowered the bag. I knew better, although I had never been rescued myself before, I had lectured enough on the subject of 'earthing' the cable and not electrocuting myself before one can be air-lifted away. I wobbled to my feet and was still able to weight-bear on my right, which felt better again in spite of my over-all weakness now and I could hold myself up more steadily with my weight over my right foot.

I let the rucksack touch the ground and settle for a second to allow the static to dissipate before I reached for the cable to unclip it. With a rotating thumbs up to Jim, I set to work and Jim shot back down the mountainside again without a second's delay. I have to describe it just the way it looked, it just peeled away as if it was falling.

I opened the rucksack and found a radio on top. I sent a message straight away. I now felt more comfortable to have comms. I opened the flask of hot chocolate and we drank it. At this stage I still didn't know how the rescue was going to take place, whether they were sending up a ground crew or a chopper. The Chinooks were not coming up this high, I felt sure. I still thought that maybe a ground rescue would happen if the weather eased.

I called back down the radio joking away in my delight that we could be reached.

"We've got everything, thanks, but where's the beer?" Everyone at the bottom thought that I was hypoxic. Johnny knew it was just me quipping away to keep myself going. Roger told me the plan.

"It's O.K. just send a taxi." My sense of humour did not go down well with the exhausted crew listening to me take everything so lightly. It wasn't a light-hearted situation to me, although I felt I had more time to wait if needed, I was now extremely worried about Carl. I was joking away over and over simply because I was elated and had no idea what they had already been through down there. I hoped later that I had not offended them with my levity.

Carl was in trouble now though, that was plain to see. He was ready to just close down completely and I thought that the joking would tell everyone I was O.K. and not in a panic and that it would help keep Carl a little more alert to hear banter. I also didn't want to alarm Carl about his condition. A man knows at that point that he is ready to die; I was pulled between keeping Carl's spirits up and trying to get the message across that 'We need to come down now!'

Roger couldn't take it. His team had been flat out for days trying to help these guys and their friends. Making a joke of it all was not something he wanted to sit back and tolerate. He handed the mike to Johnny. The banter between us continued for a moment then Johnny brought a stop to it and told me a rescue was on its way and to be ready. I switched back straight away and got my working head back on and Johnny gave me some instructions as to what to do with the gear. I swore back at him jokingly, as I thought Johnny was taking the Mick with the instructions on drill that I already had a working knowledge of and knew like the back of my hand. Johnny acknowledged this and told me what they were going to do next with their plan.

The Americans stood around in bewilderment at the exchanges. British sense of humour is different to American anyway, but the squaddy sense of humour is almost a language unto itself. Luckily, they didn't dismiss my joking and cursing altogether. When I said, 'You'd better get someone here quick before Carl shakes himself off the mountain.' They knew it was a coded message formed as a joke to keep Carl at his ease, but to tell the Rangers 'This is it, I think Carl's going down.'

He was. Carl stared out at me, almost through me, his face ashen and deadpan, his eyes seemed blank and lifeless. "My feet have never been so cold in my life." There was no emotion in his voice and no reaction to the fact that we were about to be taken off the ledge to safety. He was no longer going through the cycles of the great, juddering shivers. Everything seemed to stop with him. He looked calm and still, but not with a peaceful look on his face, he looked haunted. I looked into his eyes and felt a horror shoot through me that he might just get down too late; after all we had just been through.

I couldn't think of any other way to get the message across. The rescue team knew what it was I was trying to say and Jim knew too thank goodness. There was an alarm in the actions of everyone. Johnny was still doing a running commentary on the goings on at the bottom and trying to placate Roger that I wasn't being an asshole. It was just my way of coping with two situations at each end of a radio. Johnny knew if I hadn't been joking, then they would all have real cause to worry for us both. I had insisted that I could last another night if they could only get Carl down. I am still convinced that I could have, but I would have been in a very poor condition to do much for myself.

Jim had to go back down to 7,000ft after the drop because he was so low on fuel. He had to leave the Ranger behind and call on the Army Chinooks that had offered to help. They dropped some fuel barrels for him on the glacier. Jim had no intention of getting caught out by the weather on the glacier for days on end so he decided to fly back to

Talkeetna and get another couple of barrels of fuel which were slung in the external baskets.

Jim heard on the radio that this break in the weather had allowed 14 to open up again. He was on his way but when he finally reached 7, where he intended to make his fuel cache, the weather had dumped itself there and he couldn't make it in. He made his way up in the dim early hours of Summer Solstice with foul weather creeping up on him again. After what felt like an age in that poor light he arrived again at 14.

They decided, I think it was Jim and Roger that as we were military, also that if we had some kind of mobility and were coherent enough to give the correct signal to Jay then we should be able to work our way into screamer suits, (a kind of full-body harness that goes through the legs like a giant nappy.)

Jim had left his long line back at the Base Camp at 7,000ft and only had what he called his 'short haul' line with him which was 100ft long. A short while after arriving at the 14,200ft Camp and deciding on a plan, Jim was off yet again with the 100ft line attached to the Lama. The screamer suits were also attached to the line.

Jim worked his way back up the mountain feeling the Lama struggling away trying to bite the thin air around it. I watched the ascent. I don't know how much of it Carl was seeing. The engine laboured as it reached a point just over our heads, lifting slightly higher with each precious second that passed. It made a screaming noise that made it sound like it was going to conk out. It was quite alarming to see and hear but I tried to ignore it. It was apparent that this was the last chance. I was half expecting a bang, the noise just sounded like the helicopter really didn't like being where it was. The Lama vibrated hard as it lifted slowly higher to the point where the karabiner could touch the ground on the ledge. Jim felt the Lama had nothing left and hoped the thin air wouldn't cause the engine to stall. There was nothing for the rotors to grab and the engine wasn't 'breathing' well. He couldn't get another inch of altitude out of her.

Jim hoped again that I wouldn't make a grab for the line. The cable touched the ground and I picked it up and worked at Screamer Suit clipping Carl onto the line. Everything was as much of an effort as it had ever been, but I worked as fast as my hands would let me. We were both panting away at the effort. In what was a few seconds to me, working as fast as I could felt like minutes to Jim, as he struggled to keep his faithful machine steady overhead. He was being buffeted by the wind and the rotors were struggling to grab the thin air to keep itself up. Jim was more concerned at this stage about dragging us off sideways before we were safely clipped in. We had been told that the helicopter could only take us, and they meant only us, no kit, not even a camera, nothing at all (not that we had one). Jim could feel the little helicopter swaying and juddering, but to me it seemed that it was like a fixed top-rope in the sky, strong and steady. I marvelled at the pilot's skill. I finally stuck my thumb in the air and made the rotating signal. Jim felt it had taken an age for us to suit up. With huge relief, Jim moved away with the cargo he'd wanted to grab for days.

Slowly, with Carl slung across in front of me in a kind of cradled position I held him in close and felt my weight lifting onto my toes. My heels lifted from the ground, but the lifting suddenly paused. Jim was maxed out and couldn't lift us from the ledge. We were too heavy and the Lama had nothing more left to give.

The pulling force on me began to move sideways to the edge. My toes scraped and skipped across the ice and snow then suddenly I was dangling five miles in the air and sweeping away from the mountain. With a pang of regret, what little gear we had stayed there, including my 'old faithful' rucksack in the cold. Gemma's little, yellow mat that had helped to keep us alive fluttered and blew away, somewhere across Denali. It was the only thing I ever really wanted to bring back.

It was like flying and the most exhilarating experience I have ever had. I could see everything, the summit, the whole mountain and what seemed to be the whole world. It was like lifting away from the tip of a postcard of Denali, watching it get a wider perspective and then smaller as we dropped towards the Ranger Camp at 14,200ft and life. It was amazing. WHAT A RIDE! It was a beautiful long and steady descent but there was still another distraction for me.

Carl was alarmingly; horribly quiet and I knew this was the crucial moment for Carl. I had heard terribly harrowing and heart breaking tales of people on the brink of safety, just shutting off and slipping into the arms of death because rescue is there and they give up the fight because they think they can.

"Hang in there mucker, we'll be there soon." Then I looked at the screw gate karabiner in front of me. I thoughtfully twiddled at the screw on the gate. "Hey Carl, what will happen if I undo this?"

"Fuck off Martin, don't you dare." The reply came with such a burst of energy and panic that it elated me to hear it. He would be O.K. this man I shared this unique and increasingly worrying experience with. We had triumphed with all this colossal help against all the odds. We had triumphed over the death that had stalked us for four nights and three days with the help of a huge gang of incredibly selfless and brave people.

There looked to be throngs of people running about as we lowered into the 14,200ft Camp. People seemed to be filming and taking photographs. We touched the ground, euphoric, excited and almost unbelieving that we weren't dreaming it. Carl was grinning from ear to ear and rolled over the ground with me as we wrestled playfully like two little boys in a kind of congratulatory celebration.

It was a short-lived celebration as we were pulled apart by medics who didn't know why I was now stuffing snow down the back of Carl's neck as we played and laughed and wrestled. Carl laid back and thanking God that he was alive and basked in the sublime morning sunlight that kissed the sky and the mountain with new and brilliant hues.

I gave myself over to the medics and still lay joking and ecstatically happy to be down with Carl still alive as Liz Green fitted the oxygen line to my nose. My sense of humour was still going great guns because I was so excited and I felt so awake and alert, it was a struggle for me to lie on the litter and be treated. I did lie there like a good boy eventually but my mind was in overdrive. There was so much air to breathe. We had been slowly suffocating near the top and now I had lungs full of rich air to feast on. So much oxygen even at 14,200ft compared to 19!

I eventually let everyone take over and do what he or she had to. My mind was still racing though and I was already planning what my next move was to be. Above all I had to make sure that Carl was going to be O.K.

The Rangers were excited and extremely happy that the two men were alive. It had been an amazing feat of human resources, tenacity, courage and compassion.

* * *

The telephone rang yet again; Bev had got to the point where she just didn't want to answer it anymore but she did.

"It's O.K.; I'll get it." She said, weary with the stress, dread and that evil she called 'HOPE' that had been sucking away at her spirit since Saturday morning.

"Hello Beverley," It was Major Johnston, a friendly voice that was a feeding line of fragmented information for her, but also the voice that held all that hope and dread for her. She didn't get chance to reply.

"They're down." He said simply.

"Sorry, what did you say?" She asked, as she genuinely didn't catch what he had said completely and didn't dare hope that it was what she thought. "They're down Beverley. They're at 14,000 now. They're O.K."

She could barely whisper the thanks. She turned to Ma and she knew from Bev's reaction that this was the news, but I suppose her face must have been blank with disbelief, because she can remember seeing Ma staring and looking grim. She realised then after a moment that she was waiting for her to speak.

"They're down, they're at 14,000, and they're fine." Bev repeated to her in a robotic way. She turned back to face the telephone to ask if she could go out there to see me. She can't remember what he said or whether it was that phone call that he told her that she couldn't. The reason was that I wasn't in a life-threatening situation, (Yet again.)

Ma hugged, cheered, laughed and cried. Bev joined in the hug but felt very peculiar. She thought that this would be the point where she could finally fold up and let her emotions pour out. They didn't. The tears of relief wouldn't come and she still felt as tight as a drum throughout her body. It was strange to stand there and watch it as if she was outside of her body looking in at it all. She smiled and kind of laughed half-heartedly. She was overwhelmed and didn't think she could

214

cope with the switch in emotions. She felt almost traumatised as everything rushed in on her from the past days.

They went outside to Pa, who was sorting out the log pile. He looked alarmed to see both of them come out to him together. It was as if they had come to the moment he had dreaded. Ma told him that we were down. He almost sank with relief. He laughed and hugged us. He then disappeared into his little shed and broke down. He can't remember how long he was there until calm came upon him again.

Again Bev wanted to run to me but there was nothing she could do. She felt duty-bound and imprisoned. She wanted me back right now. They all had each other. She told the children and at last she genuinely laughed and cried at the same time and felt better, as she watched them jump up and down and laugh and squeal. Gemma, as usual watched our faces carefully to read any signs that anything still wasn't O.K. now. Of course their first question was, "When is he getting back home?" Yet another question Bev couldn't answer.

* * *

Jim flew on down to the Ranger station at Talkeetna that was awash with media. He had had a really dramatic flight and had been the only hope for Carl and I when it came to those last hours. He thought about us two men and what we had been through. He thought about us still waiting at 14,200ft waiting for the Chinooks to get to us later before we can get to hospital and the security of being back together as a team. He thought that we had been through enough and didn't like to think of us being on the mountain any longer than we had to. He had made up his mind. Tiredness was pushed aside once again so that he could put his mind at rest that he had done all he could for the two soldiers who had been through enough. Nobody had thought he did any less. He had bent the rules to fly in atrocious weather conditions over and again when he couldn't even see the ground to land.

There had been the flights up, down and around the mountain to top up with fuel and oxygen and requests to try to summon extra help from the Air National Guard, which were turned down not only due to the severity of the weather but that their flying hours were up. Jim was not happy with them. His tiny, frail-looking Lama against the meaty cargo SAR, (Search and Rescue) beasts that they flew. He risked himself to bring the rucksack to us, more so when he plucked us from the ledge with an almost empty fuel tank. We all owed him a debt we could never repay, but he never gave the work he had already done a thought. He was going to get us off the mountain once and for all.

He got back to the Lama and snaked his way back up to 14,200ft. We were loaded up onto the Lama and given a ride down to Base Camp at 7,000 ft where we were picked up in a plane that was waiting for us and taken in to Talkeetna.

That man had the biggest capacity for compassion and we were complete strangers to him. He will always be what I would class as a hero. Like Roger and his team, he didn't just do what was required or expected, he did absolutely everything he could imagine to save us and get us down. There are many heroes in that team. They didn't have to do anywhere near as much as they did for any of us. They were not under any strict command structure or direct orders, they were just utterly selfless.

What truly overwhelms Bev and I and I'm sure Carl too, is that they thought we were most probably dead but didn't give up even if our outside chance was probably long gone.

Jim may have been done with us but he had one last task that was rankling him. He flew out to the Army Air base where he knew the pilots would be asleep, hovered over their base and switched his siren on for a good, long blast right over the building. Satisfied they had got the message, he flew back. They were under a chain of command with strict remits on flying hours and conditions but it still didn't go down well with the Rangers at the time and especially Jim but there was nothing they could do.

Finally we were safely sitting in a fixed wing plane on our way to Talkeetna when I was suddenly aware that I was hallucinating. On the way out through the mountains I was puzzled to see a group of Native Americans on the mountainside with spears and bows over their shoulders. They had the look of a group just loping down a path after a day's hunting. It was so vivid. They had several feathers hanging down from their hair. They had a deer slung beneath a length of shaved branch like a spar carried between two of them. There were three men in front of the deer and two following behind. The image was really huge and was etched out like a giant charcoal and chalk sketch on the mountain. Completely still, the giants remained as I watched, at least 40ft tall.

I looked at Carl in surprise, and then decided there was something wrong. I looked back but they were still there.

"Hey Carl, can you see that, over there, the Indians!" (Apologies for our ethnic ignorance at that time, no offense intended!)

"Eh!" Replied Carl, wondering what was going on.

"Over there!" I was convinced I could see them marked out in black and white like the mysterious chalk figures on the English hillsides.

"Oh, yeah," replied Carl, not seeing anything and thinking that I had gone off my rocker. It was so real that when I looked back out of the window, they were still there until we moved out of line to be able to see the rocky surface anymore.

To Tim on the Haute Route his naked running man was as real as my hunting party. Mike and I never let Tim forget it, now I knew what it was like myself, absolutely real in my own mind. The oxygen and return of normal air pressures was obviously having a startling effect on my system.

When we arrived at Talkeetna we were transferred to a life flight plane and taken on to Anchorage Regional Hospital. Job Done!

The Rangers could now start to wind down a little and pray that the other expeditions that were still running through all this drama would make it safely back down. At the bottom, Talkeetna was put on the map to the lay people of the world through the media that had poured into the place all wanting to get the most and get it first. The media had already made camp at the hospital.

Chapter 16 -The Hospital

The hospital was an amusing story for Bev at its beginning but not for long. I remembered being looked after by a nurse on the plane who was sitting at the head of the stretchers between the two of us. She monitored Carl and I in turn all the way in. As we arrived and were wheeled out of the plane, I was aware of a lot of people around outside the hospital. Then I realised that there were a lot of reporters and television cameras there.

I thought that The Alaskans were so brilliant at what they do that the reporters were there on a regular basis to see all the rescues come in. I thought they filmed every rescue. I thought something big must have happened to someone and they were waiting to catch a glimpse of somebody really important like some famous person or politician or something. We just didn't have a clue how big this was.

The only one that seemed to puzzle me was a chap who thrust a microphone in my face while I was still strapped to the gurney and outside the hospital buildings. He said he was from the BBC. I couldn't work out what a BBC man was doing all the way out in Anchorage. I don't know if it was the same man but I remember being asked how I was.

"Fine," I said, a little confused, as I thought I was. I almost asked him how he was back but he went on. He then asked what it was like up there. So I replied, "Cold, cold." I didn't know what else he wanted me to say. I couldn't think of what the man might want to know from a stranger and a Brit at that, I wasn't local so why would anyone be interested? I didn't know what I was supposed to say and thought as they wheeled me through the crowd of media and the lightning storm of camera flashes, 'They won't be using a clip of me then.' Carl's experience was just the same. We just had no idea at all. We thought they had mistaken us for somebody else.

Once everyone was in the hospital, we had drinks and more drinks. We were deposited to the E.R. and put on beds side by side and examined. We were wired up to all kinds of medical machinery and then we had our feet examined. I kind of dreaded my scary socks coming off and hoped my feet didn't stink. My feet were very white and blue/grey but that was expected and I was amazed to see my toes were too. I had expected to lose a few, as I still had no feeling in them. My ankles had ballooned right up now that my plastic boots were off and they arranged for me to have X-rays.

Carl's feet were a different story. I could see as they removed his boots and socks that he was in trouble. They were dark grey to black. My heart sank for Carl. I knew Carl was going to lose something of his feet. We were alive but I felt very sorry for him. He didn't even really want to be on the mountain anymore after 16,200ft and now he had this in front of him.

Miraculously, my X-rays were fine, they couldn't find any broken bones but I didn't have any other type of scan on them so they assumed bad sprains and I was discharged a few hours after admission. The loud cracks I heard in them had been the tendons and ligaments being damaged.

I hung around with Carl for a little while but the medical team had work to do on him, so I decided to go visiting and hobbled off to see the other guys. It was then I got a message to say there was a phone call from my wife. I really didn't expect that, how could she know so quickly where I was. I hadn't been in hospital that long, nobody in the Army had time to report anything yet, (I thought). I wondered what she wanted and wondered if something bad had happened at home.

She had telephoned one hospital and was given a number for a different hospital. She was coming apart with her impatience by now and was relieved to be put through to the emergency room. The nurse told her that I had been taken upstairs and she would transfer her. She got through to another nurse who told her she couldn't find me.

"What do you mean, you don't know where he is?" She asked worriedly.

"He's gone visiting, I don't know which room he's in now?" came the reply. Bev was aghast. She thanked the nurse and waited.

The last she heard was that I was just conscious and talking. She expected that I be on a trolley or in a wheel chair with my leg in a cast and bandages wrapped all over the severe frostbite she was expecting. She had been put on hold for a moment, and then another voice came on the line. It was me. I said "Hello" and she replied with some excitement and anxiety in her voice.

"Mart, how are you?"

"I'm fine, how are you?" I said in some confusion.

"Well, I'm OK now that you're down. How are your legs?"

"There's nothing wrong with my legs, what's the matter with you?" I said, sounding irritated now.

I hoped she would get to the point of why she had phoned, as I couldn't understand what was so urgent. I still thought something had happened at home that I needed to hear. She couldn't hide the excitement in her voice. I then said with some confused amusement,

"You'll never guess, my picture's been taken for the local newspaper here."

"Is that a fact?" She said with a little amusement in return.

"Yes, I don't know if anyone has told you yet, but I took a bit of a tumble." I said nonchalantly. I still had absolutely no idea.

"Yes, I had heard, in fact the whole world knows. You've been headline news all weekend, I've had messages from all over." She laughed brightly but it stopped dead there.

I must have sounded irritated, confused and anxious to get away from the phone; I thought she was being sarcastic. She rushed to tell me how they had found out and that they had been waiting all weekend for news. She asked if I had any other injuries, or frostbite. I said I had none and that I was fine. I thought she was exaggerating and I still didn't get it into my head why she had taken the trouble to phone me over nothing. I was only in hospital with a couple of sprains. I've had worse.

I was distracted from the conversation by my desire to see my team mates; I was feeling that Bev was making a bit of a drama out of the whole thing. I wasn't really listening to all she said. Still I didn't take in why she phoned from the U.K. to the hospital as she raced on, trying to keep me on the phone.

I had things to check on and to organise. I didn't know why she was sounding anxious. To Bev I must have sounded so cold and distant that she became upset. I told her to pull herself together, I would call her again when I could, maybe a few days. I said that I had to go because I was still at work, I had to look in on the other guys and that we still had the kayaking phase to sort out, as the expedition wasn't over yet.

I told her again I had to go and told her to give my love to the children and give them a kiss, Bye now, bye, bye I said and hung up before she got chance to say anything else and got more upset. I knew Bev had something on her mind but it couldn't have been important because she seemed to be instantly side-tracked by asking about me and what had happened. We'd sort out whatever it was she really had to talk about later when I had time to talk to her properly. Right now, I still couldn't switch my mind off from where I was and what needed to be done next

Bev couldn't believe what she was hearing. Listening to the manner in which I was speaking, I was obviously still at work in my mind. I didn't realise that Bev wanted just a few moments of me to herself, but the conversation was going nowhere. Before she could protest and ask me to stay on the line a little longer, I said I really had to go. She was unbelieving at what had happened and listened to the buzzing of the line for several moments. She sat on the floor in Ma and Pa's bedroom stunned and very upset, still with the receiver in her hands for a few moments before she carefully put it back and composed herself to go downstairs with a big smile on her face. Her emotions were just a tangled wreck now.

I was suffering with fatigue and dehydration and was just beginning to warm up. I had had x-rays taken of my ankles, which showed no abnormalities. I had 'frost nip' in my fingers and toes, so expected to lose very thick layers of skin from them soon. I had bruises and cuts to my face and hands and bruising all over my body but it was all superficial. Apart from my limp, I appeared unscathed.

I had put the call from Bev out off my mind quickly and I went to see the other members of the team. Carl had frostbite on his toes, Steve had frostbitten hands and a concussion and Conrad had broken his leg in three places. They all had other bruises, abrasions and cuts. Conrad had cuts in his thighs from Steve's crampons and I had a long cut down my shin from my own crampons. I also had an almost perfectly round hole over the knuckle by my little finger where I had been whistling down the mountainside trying to dig my axe into the surface so hard. It had been in contact with the ice as I went down and simply worn away the flesh. It was a small and superficial injury that didn't seem to heal. The cuts to my head were minor too so I was able to go about my business fairly unrestricted.

Back in Staffordshire Bev went into the sitting room and they all asked how I was, she looked at Uncle Brian and said bitterly,

"Well, I don't know what we were all worrying about."

They asked her what she meant so she replied much more brightly to mask what had happened.

"He's fine, he's still at work and has to go and meet up with the others in the hospital. He's busy just now so will call when he gets time."

Ma asked if she had told me that I'd been on the news and in the papers the whole time. Bev replied lightly,

"Oh yes, I told him that but he's really busy, they've got the kayaking to sort out. He sends his love to everyone."

She walked out of the room and went upstairs and sat on the bed staring as she had done so often since this started. Suddenly she raced off downstairs and asked the children if they wanted to go for a drive. They wanted to stay and play. Bev jumped in the car and drove into town and walked amongst all the normality and mundaneness of people shopping. She walked up and down and didn't go into any shops. She just wanted to try to knock her mind into something else, something utterly normal and dull.

Later, when all the preliminary treatment was over, I took Carl up to see Conrad. I was looking forward to seeing him; putting aside all the fractiousness of the pressures we had been under aside and wanted to find out when he was going to be operated on. We could hear someone screaming when we got to the corridor. As we approached his room, we realised it was Conrad. I was quite alarmed at the noise and thought the poor guy was really going through it.

When he saw Carl and I come into the room, he said,

"I see you lot got off the mountain then."

Carl was in a wheel chair and didn't react to what he felt but he was really annoyed by the greeting and wondered why he had bothered going to visit. I was shocked and a little stung by it. We clearly weren't welcome and just turned around without speaking and limped and wheeled out of the room without a word.

One of the nurses later told Carl in jest that Conrad was worse than any baby, knowing how soldiers like to tease each other. It didn't change my mood. I wasn't seeing myself going back to make jokes after that, maybe after he had his surgery and he was no longer in pain, we might have everything back in perspective and get some camaraderie back.

On the mountain things were very different, I could try to find reasons behind Conrad's decisions and attitude and empathise with him up to a point when we were up there but I really didn't expect that though. I thought maybe it was just the pain and that he was so angry at being injured as a result of trying to help us but I was still cross with him about it. I thought perhaps he thought his injuries would have been worth it if we had made it. Not a rational train of thought but we were all in a strange place emotionally.

Carl was unforgiving about it all but then Carl had a lot more to be upset about than I did. I still didn't know then everything that had happened between them from 16,200ft. It wasn't my place to judge what went on in their relationship but I was beginning to see the light, although I would only ever know one side of it.

In spite of the injuries and hardship we had all been through, there had been no apparent bitterness until that point and I didn't want to dwell on it. We were all still suffering now, but in safety and grateful to be back. Conrad's words ate into me. I thought them careless, especially for Carl's sake but I kept the thoughts to myself. I had thought that Conrad's previous behaviour had been due to the pressure put on him by the accident and his hypoxia. Carl knew far more of Conrad's character and behaviour on the mountain, he kept his silence along with me. I just thought that we'd all been through a lot and once we started to get ready for the kayaking stage of the expedition everyone would be the best of friends again.

Bev had wandered up and down the street and bought a bunch of newspapers. She drove back to Longsdon and down the track. She had made up her mind to pack all their gear in the next hour and go straight back to Wales right away but as she rounded the bend on the drive and the houses came into view, so did a lot of cars and a large van with aerials and a small dish on the top. 'What the...' She was puzzled and had no idea who the cars belonged to. She had to stop to try and see where she could park herself now, in spite of all the space we had there. She had only been gone an hour and a half. She parked up and noticed that the people standing around had all turned and were looking at her.

Pa came over and happily told her that some people from the papers were here and wanted to talk to her. There was even someone from the T.V. and Central News. Bev was furious. She walked past the people introducing themselves, saying 'Thank you' to them as they offered their congratulations that I was safe. She walked straight into the sitting room and called Major Johnston to tell him the media had landed. He immediately arranged for a representative from Army Media Ops to go to her. She understood that he was going to be there to help her. She soon learned that she was to be controlled as tightly as the rest of us.

A short while later the police arrived at the house and asked for a list of people that were authorised to enter the site. This was becoming madness. The worst thing for Bev was that it was soon Ma and Pa that were controlling the interviews. It was their house. Reporters were now coming into the house itself and asking to see her. Bev hid upstairs in the bedroom for hours at a time

Ma and Pa gave their telephone number out to everyone and the phone rang and rang. Local papers, radio stations, Bev nearly burst. She flew at Pa when she met him at the bottom of the stairs at one point and told him to get the reporters out. Pa laughed and held her face in his hands and said,

"It doesn't matter now, he's safe." He was right but she couldn't control this.

"Bloody hell, I'm not even back together myself, I'm not ready. Where are Gemma and Rhys?" She whispered, so the reporters wouldn't hear that she was in the hallway.

Pa replied, "They're O.K. they're playing on the front lawn with the reporters." Pa went happily back into the sitting room to continue his interview with the 'nice man and lady from 'The Sun'. Bev was aghast and had lost what little bit of control she thought she had on anything. She ran upstairs and kicked the door closed, hard right up high by the handle, landing her heel perfectly in place with a big crack. She didn't care if the door was damaged, she kind of hoped it was but it wasn't. It must have reverberated through the house.

She slumped on the bed with her hair scrunched up in her fists. She'll never get away now. It was such a novelty for everyone to have reporters and television cameras she could have spat.

I spent a good deal of my time with Carl or back at Earth Tours Bed and Breakfast where I was looked after by the proprietor, Margrite Van Lakke. Margrite took all the telephone calls to vet who was trying to contact the team. She also spent lots of time visiting them in hospital and taking care of any needs she could cater for.

She is a robust, friendly and very deep character who guarded the team zealously against any media. Even close friends of the team didn't get past her defences. She treated the team like royalty and assured Bev not to worry about me, as she would take her place until I came home. This was well meaning on Margrite's part but could have been phrased in a way that made Bev feel less shut out. This made Bev extremely prickly in her current emotional state, especially when Margrite rebuked her for asking if I had gone out and got drunk, knowing I can't drink very well. Bev just wanted to have a little joke and ask Margrite to leave some orange juice and asprin for me for breakfast and say they were from her. Margrite did as Bev asked but failed to see any humour in it. Bev felt pushed out completely, she was suddenly very insecure. She was asked not to call again until he Martin was awake. In my current state, that could be any time, so Bev felt unsure now what to do or whether to wait for me to make the calls.

I had everything that was going on at the hospital to keep me busy and a comfortable place to stay where I was being very well looked after. Bev could only hope that she would be given the opportunity of flying out to see me.

During the first day in hospital, we had loads of photographs taken and we got together as much as possible. The team started to gel again, which was great and those of us that weren't stuck in hospital went out to celebrate. We went to a Mongolian restaurant. It was my first big meal since the mountain. I couldn't eat much at a time, as my stomach had shrunk and I'd lost so much weight. Anyway, we had a great meal, all talking away and laughing. We had a few beers and we ate and ate. I was stuffed by the end of the meal but I was very sorry that I had rice. After the meal, we strolled outside I can't remember where we were going. The abdominal pain hit me. It got worse and worse. In the end it felt like I had such severe cramps that I could no longer stand. I rolled up and lay on my side on the pavement, groaning until the pain subsided. Obviously, I had eaten far too much and the sympathy from the guys was just as I expected, they pulled me to bits, laughing away until I recovered. Gorging following starvation is not recommended.

We were called back to the hospital where we had to attend a press conference. We were herded into a conference room and sat along tables that had been pushed together in a line down one end of the room. There were lots of chairs set up in the room for an 'audience' and there were light stands and microphones set up. This was all new to most of us, if not all.

We were told what was going to happen and what the reporters would probably be asking. There were representatives of the Army Media ops there too. They seemed to be checking what looked like a script to me but I wasn't really interested. The whole thing was a bit too strange for me already. It seemed like a waste of time, as we still had kayaking of the Susitna River to sort out and we didn't have a lot of time left to get it started.

Conrad confirmed it was still going to go ahead and that as soon as he was discharged from his surgery and compulsory hospital stay, he was going to get a waterproof cover for his cast and do the kayaking trip.

Major Gill Prowse was controlling the media at the hospital I understand and had flown out with the Training Accident Investigation Team, (The flight Bev couldn't get on to.) Gill had spoken with Bev at some stage and Bev voiced her concerns that the kayak trip was still going ahead. Gill said she hadn't been aware that Conrad had still planned on completing it and said to her not to worry about it, she was going to put a stop to that straight away. She was going to speak to Conrad. The kayak phase was pulled and the expedition Summit to the Sea was officially over.

A little while later, Carl told both Bev and I in a letter from Anchorage Hospital that Conrad visited him and Steve just the once when they were in hospital, before he went back to the U.K. He also phoned him once while he was in Alaska and that was to find out if the Rangers had spoken to Carl about him. According to Carl, Conrad was panicking now. JD Swed, (Southern District Ranger) had been in based in the Ranger Station in Talkeetna and was the incident commander co-ordinating the operations during the rescues. He had told Carl that Conrad had been phoning the Rangers in Talkeetna to try and get them on his side and back him up. JD told Carl that there was no way in this world that they would back him up on this. The impending report on the expedition was not going to be favourable. Conrad clearly knew he was for the high jump. The Rangers were putting their report together now about the rescues and our team and questioning every decision and action. At this stage I felt I had nothing to worry about, I didn't know what was coming.

JD also asked Carl how experienced we all were at kayaking. Carl told him that he had only been in a kayak a couple of times and done no white water stuff at all. JD said that the mountain may have been a blessing in disguise, because the kayak route that the team were going to do was Grade 5 part of the way, but in some parts went up to Grade 6. JD had just been rafting on the Susitna and it was really difficult, that he had been kayaking for 20 years so he was very experienced and that a rescue in that terrain would have been even more difficult. He was surprised that novices had even contemplated it. For the first time in 2 years, one of the girls, a highly experienced kayaker was actually swimming (term used for being turned out of the kayak) because the rivers were running so fast and they weren't even in flood yet. These are very big rivers with enormous volumes of water tanking down them and with some serious drops to negotiate. JD said the chances of the team surviving that river were minimal. The boulders in the river were as big as the hospital room Carl was in and the water thundered through.

The original press release for the expedition, which I indicated earlier, would be important as Conrad writes of Carl: 'Carl is a highly enthusiastic kayaker and is particularly looking forward to the expedition.' Carl without any hesitation told everyone later that he didn't know why Conrad kept referring to him as the 'kayaker' as he'd only ever been in a kayak twice in his life and had never done any white water. He didn't even know what the water grades were or what they meant in real terms. He kept reiterating this.

So, Conrad's plan of paddling the glacial rivers all the way to the Cook Inlet would have been practically a suicide run. The kayaking phase at this stage still hadn't been ruled out by Conrad or by those of us still fit enough to continue. That is until the T.A.I.T. (investigation team stopped it.) It's just that the research and the preliminary training and qualifications were all wrong. I wouldn't have gone on it myself without someone who had at least level experience to me and I wasn't a Grade 5 kayaker. I had expected someone there on the team was a level 5 and it turned out nobody was.

Of course, I trusted the ATFA and Conrad at the time and didn't suspect the danger. I hadn't researched the river myself; I just read what had been given to me as part of the Summit to the Sea paperwork. I think a 'reccy' visit to it before the trip would have made many of us back out by the time we saw it. Here again, guys don't just go around asking each other if they are qualified. On a trip like that, it is taken for granted that somebody is and that everyone is trained to deal with a reasonable grade of white water, drops, stoppers and rescues, even for novices.

It was incredulous how he hoped to get away with it and it's only because it was stopped and nobody else could get hurt that I smiled at his bare-faced nerve to try and pull it off.

The mountain was enough to control as an expedition but with the water, there was no second chance. It was impossible with our team and now we were all down, we were all talking together and finding things out about each other and our experience and the lack of it, which in several cases was shocking. How did he talk them into it? We still didn't know until much later what lack of qualifications there were in the team but already it was bad enough. I could now see why the Rangers may not be happy with the team.

Whilst in hospital people had to feed Steve. The auxiliaries that fed him were born again Christians and Steve clearly wasn't one so Steve used to get preached to and told to 'Look to God!' This annoyed Steve, although he was grateful for their help. It was a great amusement for Carl who sat in the next bed sniggering to himself with Steve shooting angry glances across at him. The first two weeks that Carl and Steve were in hospital, Steve was out of his head on drugs, so Carl used to say to him that he'd be in the Drug Re-hab Centre across the road if this carried on! They made verbal pot-shots at each other the whole time like a pair of grumpy old pensioners in a residential home.

On most occasions, their auxiliary nurse was a really nice guy called Self Lamont. Twice a day, every day, Carl and Steve used to go for whirlpool treatment to try to stimulate the circulation back into their hands and feet. One particular day Gaz Keep was still there visiting with them. It was Steve's turn to have his hands treated first. While C.C., their therapist was taking dead skin off Steve's fingers with tweezers, he was in so much pain that his face was contorting. Carl said that he was putting on more faces than a gurning competition. Carl and Gaz, true to form with their squaddy humour lost control. Their laughter turned to wheezing and snorting fits of giggles with every new face that the unfortunate Steve pulled as they tried to hold it in. They tried not to look at each other in order to gain some composure, but it was irresistible. As soon as they looked at each other, they would be trying to suppress their squeals of delight at the scene. This was too much for Gaz, who stumbled out of the room to try and stop himself from laughing. It didn't work because the more Carl laughed in the treatment room, the more he could hear Gaz laughing outside in the corridor.

It got to the stage where he was no longer able to stand, Gaz collapsed onto a gurney in the corridor, his laughter echoing the length of the corridor. Carl was so weakened by the hilarity; he was gripping onto the arms of the chair for dear life, because he would have fallen into the whirlpool. Steve, of course was not one ounce impressed by all this, but as the saying goes, and Carl himself humbly admits, 'What goes around, comes around," because in the next couple of days it was to be Carl's turn to suffer as badly as Steve.

Carl had to have morphine on the night that the demarcation line of his frost bite finally broke away and split open; it was behind his toes at the front of his foot. He wept at the pain and even the morphine didn't take it all away. He told me that the pain was beyond belief. He finally had surgery to remove his toes. They needed a lot of work and further surgery later. He had skin grafts taken from his thighs and attached to the front of his now toeless feet. The idea was to allow the healing to continue then sew the flaps of skin over where his toes had been to help the build up of skin there. Carl said that the skin grafts were the most painful part of the surgeries he had in Alaska. He didn't know that there was worse to come in the U.K. The care he had in Anchorage was superb and they kept him informed of everything and were very attentive and friendly.

Steve's hands were so bad that he had most of his fingers removed. There was a little left of some of them and it was hoped to amputate a toe later, trim it down and sew it in place of a thumb to give him more dexterity. Steve later saw a highly skilled and renowned plastic surgeon at St.James's in Leeds called Mr. Kay. Bev and I had met him. By coincidence this was the same surgeon who had performed some minor surgery on Gemma when she was seven years old. Mr Kay was going to take over as Steve's consultant surgeon.

The two men had plenty of visitors at the hospital and had plenty of media attention along with the rest of the team, although Steve didn't want any of it and didn't see the novelty value that the others did at first. He just wanted to be left alone to get on with his life. He already had some pretty dark opinions of what had gone on building up in his mind and the last person he wanted to see was Conrad.

We didn't know why he felt like this about Conrad but it seemed that everyone is gunning for him at the moment. I wondered what the hell he had done that could have been so bad. I was pretty O.K. with him now and he seemed to be the same with me. We were getting on pretty well. I kept out of it and kept my head down. Conrad may have been pretty starry-eyed about his expectations on the trip but I thought he was a good guy in spite of some of his decisions. Some of his attitude I had put down to hypoxia and the pressure of the responsibility he had taken with such a serious expedition and so many novices. Carl and Steve wouldn't have him at any price. They wouldn't discuss it, so for some time it was a mystery where this obvious hostility, (for it wasn't just an indifference or dislike) had seeded itself.

At first, none of us knew why but soon things started to come out of the mist. One of the Training Accident Investigation Team, (TAIT) was a colleague I was friendly with but he worked at Ballachulish. He took me to one side and said he would speak to me back in the U.K. when the initial investigation was over. I was a bit worried that I had done something but then I forgot all about it. Had I not been assertive enough? Conrad would have still gone his own way.

Chapter 17 - Multi-media mayhem

Bev telephoned me again at the Bed and Breakfast, hoping that I would be a little different away from the team. I was more receptive to her this time and spoke excitedly about the media attention and how they think that our surviving was a big deal. I hadn't realised how I had come across to her when I was in the hospital I was ignorant of a lot of situations around me to some extent. My mind-set was so tunnel-visioned while I was still in Alaska.

She said that our survival was a big deal, but I was very dismissive about it and went on to speak about the awe-inspiring skill of the helicopter pilot who brought us down. I spoke about meeting the rescue team but it was all a blur to me and that I couldn't quite take in who everyone was.

Bev said it was good to hear me talking so enthusiastically and she began to relax. I told her about the press conference that had been held at the hospital and when I told them that there had been no heroes up on the ledge, they were audibly disappointed. We had simply tried to survive the conditions. Carl was exhausted and I was injured. We didn't have much choice about staying. Carl had said one thing that I would never forget though and that if he had been on the mountain with anyone but me, he wouldn't have made it. He said that if he ever wrote a book about it he should call it 'Anyone but you'. I was really touched by it. It wasn't a matter of heroics; I simply didn't want him to die.

We had agreed to try and speak with each other everyday and she would ask again for a flight out to see me. She told me that the press was still around and there were cars and cameras everywhere. I laughed when she told me that the furry covers on the microphones fascinated Rhys. Bev told me later that she got the impression that I thought she was exaggerating about the media attention, not just at home but around the world. I said that there had been a lot of attention in Anchorage, but that was understandable. I didn't know why anyone else would be interested.

Bev went on to the subject of a flight out to see me. She explained that in return for an exclusive interview with me, the Daily Mail would set up a return flight to see me plus a few days accommodation. The idea was a hit with me and I asked if it would be possible for the children to come too. Bev promised that she would ask. We said our goodbyes for now and Bev ran downstairs with a new energy.

Bev said she would have hated to fly out there, torturing herself that she might get a cool reception and the whole trip would go badly wrong. A spectre of insecurity had crept in and settled down but for now she pushed it aside.

As she skipped down each stair, she was already planning gifts to take out and what she would wear. She told Ma and Pa that I thought it was a wonderful idea and she was going to speak with the reporter. He was very stoic and said that he would find out from his editor if we could take the children. Bev was on cloud nine. The weariness that had tried to sneak up on her earlier had been out run now by the prospect of us being together in less than 48hrs.

I called Bev back a short while later to say that I would be able to speak with the Daily Mail, but not exclusively, because the Army Media Ops were in control and that I had been told that the story belonged to the Army. Bev spoke again with the reporter and he told her bluntly that they weren't prepared to go ahead in those circumstances. She asked him if he would like to tell her children. She can't remember what else she said but she was determined not to let the reporter see how it made her feel.

Bev went coolly back to the house and picked up the phone, dialled Andy Johnston's number and asked for a flight yet again. He told her that it would not be possible, as I was not in a life-threatening situation. She came away from the phone feeling as if she had been on the tail end of a shabby trick. She knew this wasn't the case and that was the way things went with the press. Being a fan of the satirical Private Eye magazine, she should have known better what to expect, they don't have a column called 'The Streets of Shame' for nothing. But then how could she knock it. She had relied on the news agencies for nearly all of her information so far. She had clung to it like a life raft.

These were people who were trying to sell a story. They weren't going to invest in a goodwill gesture for the sake of a story everyone else was running. She felt bitter that a flight to Alaska and back with a few days Bed and Breakfast was a drop in the ocean as far as the Daily Mail coffers were concerned, or any of the 'nationals' for that matter. It certainly wouldn't have been much of a big deal for the MoD.

How she felt about the Army was a mixture of gratitude at the time that was spent getting her through the weekend although they didn't have much in the way of expert advice. Then there was anger that offers of a flight were not forthcoming when even the Rangers thought I would be dead. The P.T. Corps, my own Corps had been very quiet, not a word from them. She imagined they would be watching and waiting before they would even commit to a pat on the back in a dark corridor. Bev thought that they would be too busy burying their heads in the sand that an expedition they had had a hand in sanctioning had gone so badly wrong. She knew from the depths of herself that she had been right in her reasons to worry before I left.

She was cross at herself for being taken in by the Daily Mail, it hadn't occurred to her that they would get her hopes up then withdraw the offer. She felt like a total idiot, and why hadn't she pushed the Army hard for a flight before? She had just sat back and accepted that she couldn't have one, even though she pestered them. She picked herself up from the floor and went to the kitchen to tell everyone that the Daily Mail flight was off and the Army wouldn't fly her out.

Bev can't remember leaving the house or even driving the car but the next thing she knew she was sitting in the staff room upstairs at Lloyds Bank in Leek trying to hold herself together as she spoke with Jane Gerrard, our extremely tolerant bank manager at the time. Of course they all knew what had happened so Bev had been whisked quietly upstairs out of the way of the eyes and ears of the curious customers. Jane told Bev she would give us a £2,500 limit. Bev told her she had no idea how we would pay it back now we had the boat. She very kindly told Bev not to worry about that now, we would sort something out at a later date.

Bev said she would give it some thought and went home and just wanted to sleep. The weariness that had tried to sneak up on her had now caught and over-taken her, she had lost control of everything. She had barely seen the children all weekend. They played on obliviously. Daddy was safe so we'll go out to play again now. They were right, that was all that should have mattered. She just couldn't let go of the angst that had been her 'control' throughout.

She went up to her room and climbed into bed fully clothed and closed her eyes. Wanting to cry but the tears still wouldn't come and it made her throat ache with the pressure. She just wasn't that angry anymore and tried to concentrate on going to sleep but she was beyond it settling for peace and quiet and wherever that took her thoughts.

Bev had only been there for about ten minutes when she heard the phone ringing again in another room. She put her head under the duvet and curled herself into a foetal position, the way she sleeps most of the time. She tucked her hands under her chin and wished herself away like a small child, eyes squeezed tightly closed making the real world disappear. Ma's footsteps could be heard on the stairs then the door creaked open.

"Bev, there's a lady from Signal radio on the phone. She wants to speak to you."

"For God's sake Ma, can't she phone back later, I want to try and sleep?" She whined.

"But what shall I say, she's waiting on the phone?" replied Ma who was now concerned at what the pleasant lady on the phone would think.

"Tell her to phone back in an hour, please Ma, it's Tuesday afternoon, I haven't slept since Friday." Bev pleaded with her now.

"Alright duck, I'll tell her to call back in an hour then." And she left. Trying to explain to Ma and Pa that they wouldn't care how you spoke as long as they got their article printed or get airtime for their story, it didn't matter a jot. Bev may be guilty of being naive through this but now she didn't care what anyone thought of her.

She sat up on the edge of the bed and rubbed her face, walked around the bed to the window and looked out across the lawn. The new fence was partly built and the children were playing football with the correspondent from The Sun. She had always treated the papers with some contempt saying that one couldn't even rely on the TV guide in them to be accurate but she guessed most were ready to 'whip up a lather'. Most people seemed to want something to sit in a trance with over their coffee. It was often what they decided not to print that was frustrating, with diversions of one kind or another while an important bit of disconcerting legislation slips through.

To be honest, she has no allegiance to any newspaper. She hasn't bought a paper for years now. Her political allegiance doesn't influence her reading either.

She took great interest in observing the reporters below her. They wandered around chatting, Ma brought them mugs of tea on a tray and they admired her flowers and our dog. Everyone admired the dog. Sam is friendly, loveable and has a gentle nature; we intercepted him on the way to the rescue home when an old friend of mine split from his wife. Right now, he was a distraction to them. They paced around waiting for Bev and she watched them from the bedroom. She had made up her mind to leave as soon as she had got back from town, now she was trapped again. The place felt like Stepford to her now. No matter what, she was trapped there.

Bev gave up on trying to sleep and went to the bathroom to wash her face. She looked in the mirror letting the water drip down her clothes, looking and feeling much older and had a line between her brows that looked as if it been set there all weekend. The whites of her eyes were tinged with yellow and bloodshot. Her hair was lank and out of condition. The best that could be said for it was that it was clean. She brushed her fringe back with her wet hand and pushed her face down into the basin of hot water. The shock was pleasant and she held her breath as long as she could feeling she could drift off like this and shook herself back to real time and the real world.

She dried her face and looked in her make-up bag for inspiration. There was plenty of stuff spilling out of the bag but little inspiration came from it. It was not holding much interest for her today. She put on a little moisturiser and mascara. She thought that perhaps she should have put something on to cover her tired complexion or some lipstick maybe. She decided on the lipstick but just couldn't be bothered with her face at all. Her hair got a brush pulled through it and she didn't bother twisting it up in a knot and using the nice clip she had bought days earlier. She would never have stepped out of the house to go to work in this state. Now it has all changed, she felt she had changed.

Her face would be on the nice item of the local and national news tonight and in the national papers tomorrow. Her heart just wasn't in it. If she had been told this time last week her picture was going round the country and across the Atlantic she would have had her hair trimmed, and would have spent an hour on her face and pressing an outfit. She gave herself an empty laugh at the irony.

Looking at herself now, she looked what she was; tired, unenthusiastic with grubby white jeans and a crochet top. She had nothing else with her but her running gear and spare underwear and pyjamas. Everything had to be thrown in the washing machine every night because she hadn't intended to stay long, an over-night stop on Friday, party Saturday and home Saturday night or Sunday morning on the outside. What a way to greet her fifteen minutes of fame but who cares, she really didn't. Being torn between the inevitable interviews because she really wanted to publicly thank the rescuers and Major Johnston and Martin's friends who had been so great or just throw the kit together, walk past everyone, bundle the kids and dog in the car and fuck off back to Wales.

She wasn't pleased by the news story that she took part in. She had a short, prepared statement that she read out that mainly thanked the U.S.N.P.S. Rangers, other rescuers and medical teams that had been involved. It was all cut from the story when it was aired. She had learned her lesson now, in just one day.

Bev, Gemma and Rhys stayed one more night. The reporters had left in the evening sometime, the Media Ops man had gone even later and Bev got everything ready to leave the next day. The phone still didn't stop but she didn't care anymore. She felt nothing except that there was the anticipation of hoping I would come home and that she could escape the atmosphere of the house she now associated with everything she had felt all weekend. They all returned home to Wales on Wednesday. They all said goodbye to Ma, Pa and Bev hugged them tightly before she got in the car. She felt a weight lift from her as she turned left at the main road at the top of the village. It was a massive relief to make that turn onto the A53 and head towards the M6 instead of Buxton and Ashbourne.

They got stuck in the usual M5/M6 junction jam and the journey back was interminable. She wanted me home or she wanted to be in Alaska with me, it didn't matter. Feeling every day apart was causing more damage, she had become very insecure. She wanted to be comforted. She felt the only thing in the world she had control over right now was the car. It didn't matter how long the journey took, at least they were going somewhere and there was no phone. She enjoyed, absolutely Gemma, Rhys and Sam in the back of the car. They were cocooned in their own space and nobody could reach them.

The telephone calls between us after the rescue were far from successful. Sometimes Bev thought I was fine, but not sounding genuinely pleased to hear from her, I had no idea what was wrong with her at the time. She didn't understand that although there was no expedition now, we were still busy here at work and I had to keep visiting Carl and Steve. I didn't just feel duty bound, I wanted to visit them.

Bev was now in a state of confusion and her panic had diverted from one direction to another. On some occasions she panicked and cried, which annoyed me, as I couldn't make sense of any of it and I didn't want to hear it and I would hang up. She couldn't phone me back in case Margrite answered and I had gone out. She would have to wait until she calmed down and speak to me another day and would have to take my calls by reverse charge, as my funds were low.

Bev thought that things had gone drastically wrong between us and she couldn't grasp, why? They weren't what they should be but she was trying to sort it out there and then. She felt she had lost the grip of control over her emotions and she shut herself away, crying into her pillow. I know I was a bit distant but I couldn't comprehend at the time what she had been put through. I couldn't understand why everyone had been worried at all because I still didn't know how public this had been, how big it had been or what a drama it had been. I didn't know what had happened to her and I don't think she understood what had happened to her either.

I told her during one call that I had been thinking about us and that I thought we had better have a serious talk about staying together when I got home. I wasn't used to this level of angst and I told her to think it over and I'd call tomorrow. I put the phone down and hoped this would get her to sort herself out.

Bev sat on the floor by the telephone seat in the hall of our married quarter. She realised that she had fistfuls of her hair. As she pulled her fingers out of the tangle, she had a handful of hair to throw away. She hit herself on the head about five or six times with her hair-filled fists and suppressed a scream through gritted teeth. She pulled her finger nails down the sides of her head and her face and took a deep breath, stood up and went upstairs to take a bath. She would not be able to contact me at all if I hung up or scheduled another call with her.

She had thought that she was low down on the priority list everywhere and with me. It wasn't intentional, it was work I didn't know how badly insecure she had suddenly become. Each time I hung up, she would have to go through the rest of the day and night until I called the next day with whatever emotions were left from the previous call. She swirled around in this vortex. She had gone through that dreadful half a week and I still couldn't comprehend that she had gone through anything at all. I was dismissive because I thought she was just 'playing up' and over reacting.

I didn't know she was still going through any of this at all. She said at the time she felt as though someone had touched her on the shoulder and said "You're mad now!" and she really felt it. This was on the

Thursday of the week after the rescue she submerged herself entirely in the hot water and felt empty but very calm. She retreated to bed and slept for about four hours, the longest she had managed since the news broke.

As the telephone calls continued, she worked at keeping calm and trying to say the right thing. Neither of us had any way of knowing which way the conversation would go. Towards the end of the week, I thought we were going to move on in separate directions. I didn't want all this; I wanted to live my life to the full and didn't want domesticity. Bev felt she had lost me after all, and didn't know how it had happened. She felt she was being selfish, trying to tell me how worried she had been and how grateful she was that I was alright, that I was alive, but she thought it sounded too dramatic for a natural conversation between us and it went awry again. We were pragmatic and would sneer at all the soap opera drama some other people thrived on. This was new to both of us and we weren't handling it well.

I was sick of her anxiety, she was sick of her anxiety. Bev said later that she understood that I wouldn't be myself, but I was hyper-sensitive and sounded far more rational and efficient than she could have been at the time. She said I sounded as if I was working mechanically, both mentally and physically and emotions were to be kept far away from the situation.

Elvy and Cindy had taken turns to come and see her, though she didn't click on to this until much later when she realised that she had one of them with her for most of the day. They were a huge help, particularly because they were in the real world and telling her she would be fine at the end. All she could see at the time was the big black hole from the previous weekend, lurking and waiting for her again.

On Friday morning I made another phone call to Bev. She had a feeling of both excitement and dread each time the phone rang now. I was really pleased to hear her voice this time, I really did want to chat to her, to share my day and I was more relaxed in my manner and I wanted to be home with her and the children. I don't know why, I just woke up that day feeling more myself.

I gave her the news that I was being flown back first thing, (it was evening for me). Bev was over-the-moon. I said we still needed to talk about what had happened between us, as I felt we needed to clear it up. She kept herself in check and said that we would play it by ear, and see how things went from there. She hung up and found she was holding her breath. She was damned if she was going to go through all that, last week and then lose me after I came back alive.

She rushed next door to Elvy, she was delighted and told her that it would be fine once I was home. Elvy knew what was going on and she was sure it was just the grip of the expedition and that I was surrounded completely by the situation out there so the last thing she said I would want is a grizzling wife and that men were all the same. Once I was home I would stop all this rubbish about splitting up Elvy assured her. I'd be absolutely fine once we saw each other again.

"Bloody men; think their day is always so important". Well, that was Elvy. This made Bev laugh. Elvy never held back. Bev told her that the worst part of it was that she hadn't seen it coming. There had been no hint of separating before.

She told Cindy that she was going to Gatwick to pick me up from my flight in on Sunday; she looked almost as relieved as Bev was. She gave her a huge hug and told me that I was just running around with my head still up the mountain. "We'll sort him out!" She laughed, positive as usual, obviously word had got out that there was anxiety between us. We're usually a very private couple but it didn't matter, they were friends and wanted the best for us.

Bev went to work that day, which was a mistake. Keith, her boss was marvellous. He had done loads of her work while she was away. He also got in touch with Army Welfare 'just in case'. The chap popped in to see her and asked how she was. She lied to him and said that she was fine now. He asked if she was eating, sleeping, feeling more settled. She could have said no to all three but said yes to all of them. She just wanted calm back and all the drama to go away.

He warned her of a few things she was to expect from me. Erratic sleep, erratic behaviour, brooding, sporadic temper, over-sensitive, memory problems. It all sounded rather dramatic to her and she paid lip service to it all. She decided that none of the behaviour sounded much like me, (the past week had been an exception, surely) so she dismissed it.

She thanked him for coming and he left his details with her in case she felt there was a need.

Bev thanked him for his time and his kindness and tried to get on with work. She put her own behaviour down to a temporary lapse due to tiredness and anxiety. She buried the lot and ignored it was happening and certainly wasn't going to 'share' with a stranger.

Keith hadn't expected a lot of work from her. We think he indulged her all day just so that she could feel a little more of a normal routine by being back in the office. She spent a long time on the phone at work as everyone was calling in wishing us both well and saying how pleased they were that I had done so well with the survival and keeping Carl alive. Bev hardly knew any of this yet but word was getting around and she was hearing lots of things from my friends and colleagues. There were lots of jokes and she didn't get a great deal done.

Trying to stick rigidly to her routine as well as she could to get herself through the day she spent the afternoon photocopying, preparing the forms for the following week and trying to type numerous letters and memos. Keith, bless him, had done all the filing and other administration while she was away so that she didn't have too much to come back to.

Bev had never been much of a typist, but this job had been so streamlined when she arrived, she could go around the office on auto-pilot once she learned the system. Her head still wasn't where it should have been. She had one letter given back four times there were so many errors in it so she gave up and caught up on the bits of filing she had created instead.

She was so tired, she could have put her head down on the desk and slept forever. Bev put work away until Monday. The thing she had loved about this job was that most nights she had empty 'In' trays. On a Friday she had cleared all the work and had set everything ready for Monday, polished the office, watered that over-polished plant and locked up with nothing on her mind but the weekend.

The children appeared to come through it all very well. Their daddy was safe and sound and that was the end of the matter. I wish adults could be so uncomplicated. I would be home in due course as usual to hugs, kisses and wrestling on the furniture with them with Bev half-heartedly scolding us all for screaming and messing up the place but keeping a safe distance in case I grabbed her and dragged her into the fray.

Bev arrived home from work with the children in tow from the school bus and Elvy and Cindy came to see her. She tried on a dress that she was planning to wear when she picked me up. They both sat there and looked blank. They agreed it was awful. Bev was disappointed and asked what was wrong with it, looking down at herself. Elvy and Cindy grimaced at each other.

"You're too skinny for it." They both said in stereo. Bev was miffed with them.

"I've only just bought it." She whined.

"You didn't try it on I take it." said Cindy, grinning and wise-cracking in her soft Scottish accent. Elvy ran home and brought back a lilac and grey dress that was a bit smaller than the blue one Bev had tried. Elvy said she looked better because the other was hanging loose and made her look scrawny.

"Like a bloody rake woman!" Elvy exclaimed.

Cindy was in agreement and said she should wear her hair up and wear the pale shoes not the black and certainly not those 'bloody grubby wellies' she lives in. They agreed nobody would know her without her big 'hippy' dresses and wellies she wears all year. They were enjoying themselves now taking the piss and taking shots at each other. So, having dressed her and told her she looks like a scarecrow in her own clothes, and that she had to do something with that bloody, floppy hair of hers. They sat satisfied and they all gossiped on about nothing. Bev realised she was genuinely laughing and relaxed, not pretending.

As usual, nothing is simple. She was telephoned by Army Welfare on that Friday evening who told her that she wasn't under any circumstances to drive to Gatwick in case she had an accident in her state. God knows what they thought she was going to do with the kids in the car with her. She didn't get it. They thought it was a sensible precaution given the emotional condition she may be in. She insisted she was fine, but she felt a little annoyed that they thought she wasn't capable of holding herself together, especially since she'd been through the worst. She resented being dictated to and having assumptions made about her self-reliance. She felt like giving in was self-pity and she'd already been experienced enough of that with all the other emotions that had dumped on her recently.

She had just negotiated three and half hours of M6 traffic jams and the usual M6/M5 junction trying to get out of first gear. She got back through the remainder of the trip alive, and she didn't think I would appreciate them not meeting me, they were right. Had I known what was going on though, I would have understood if they didn't meet me. The lady said that they would be getting a driver and hire car for them all. Bev actually thought it was an excellent idea.

Elvy and Cindy left and Bev rummaged through the 'Emergency morale kit' that Cindy gave her. There was aromatherapy massage oil, perfume, a big bar of chocolate and bananas to get some carbs into her. Bless her cotton socks!

At 05.00am on Saturday, Andy, Cindy's husband, my friend and colleague pulled up in the hire car to take them all to the airport. She felt sick and couldn't think straight, let alone get a conversation going. It was a gorgeous morning. No traffic, pale blue sky and the sun climbing to where it could warm the ground and set the mist rising. She can't remember what they talked about and the journey seemed to go very quickly. Gemma and Rhys were bursting at the seams to see me. They had picked out their own clothes to wear and been in and out of the shower in a flash at 04:00hrs. Bev didn't have to say a word to jiggle them along today.

The only thing she can remember vividly is seeing a lone car on the opposite Westbound carriageway, still very early on the M4 skid across three lanes and spin around in a big donut into the opposite direction. It was a hell of a skid and the driver was very lucky not to hit the central reservation. She thought 'he' must have fallen asleep. The smoke from the tyres drifted across the carriageways as they drove past and they quickly closed the vents as the car went through the cloud. The car on the other side drove off very, very slowly again. Bev and Andy thought, 'I bet he's awake now!'

Gatwick was busy as usual and they ran around looking for the Churchill Suite. Apparently, it wasn't going to be a quiet homecoming. They were instructed to wait with the other families and let the various media take a turn with thus.

Bev hoped that we could all meet in private first with the kids. She was sick with the worry that she would get a perfunctory peck on the cheek and that I would be cold towards her, she had worked herself up into a real lather. They were shown to a conference suite where there were other families already waiting. Bev tried to look as if she belonged in the clothes she was wearing and hoped she wouldn't fall off the shoes or mess with her hair until it fell out of the clip. I think she looks lovely but she always thinks she is scruffy.

The atmosphere seemed subdued and quiet. Small family groups were sitting at tables, chatting quietly amongst themselves. One lady was reading the paper and eating a bag of crisps. Many of the families didn't seem that anxious at all, indeed she thought some of them looked quite bored. Bev couldn't even swallow. She had expected everyone to be mixing and chatting excitedly. She thought they would be introducing each other, that the officers in the room would say something to break the ice. It reminded her of walking into a cafe full of strangers with nothing in common and the officers hovering about looking anxious as if their train was running late.

Bev, Gemma and Rhys sat with Phil's family. They were lovely. She enjoyed sitting with them. She tried her best to concentrate on what they were saying, but all she can remember is that Phil's brother had borrowed his little sports car and written it off in an accident and was waiting to tell him. Bev laughed heartily and thought it was brilliant; the whole scenario with that at the end for Phil after everything was so comic. They all laughed about it, but she felt so tense, she wanted to be in a dark room on her own with the children, who by now were bored and starting to fidget.

Major Emery came over to them to say hello and ask after everyone. He was very nice and was very attentive. Major Horn from the PT Corps was pacing up and down looking worried to death, Bev couldn't think why. She noticed he didn't look across to her, almost deliberately.

'Maybe he didn't know what to say to me. Maybe he didn't know me', she thought.

After some considerable time, he did go over eventually and introduced himself. He didn't seem too sure what to say or do. He didn't seem comfortable and certainly didn't waste much time with Bev. This didn't rankle her as she was feeling indifferent about most of the people in uniform now. Major Horn went off again before they could even get much of a conversation going. He obviously had something important to do. Bev shook her head slightly wondering what had happened and returned to sit with Phil's family.

Somebody made an announcement that the team would be allowed a few minutes to greet us and then they would be escorted back out to another room to the press conference. (Of course we, being owned by the Army, could let our families wait for us a little longer Bev thought.) Some parts of this machine were looking after us so well and other parts seemed to be keeping us at bay.

They had kindly arranged for my family and I to go out for photos and interviews. That's all Bev needed in her state, especially as she was braced for a cool reception from me, she didn't need to be standing there saying how wonderful everything was and smiling delightedly immediately after, and knowing (so she thought) that I was on my starting blocks to get away from her. Bev had no expectations as far as the Army was concerned now. She was allowed to do this but not that. I was allowed to see her and the children but as soon as visiting time was over I was expected to withdraw again. The family part, Bev decided was now 'window-dressing' by the caring and inclusive Army. By the evening, we'd be back home and dropped like hot bricks until next needed. She didn't feel bitter about it now, she accepted it but didn't like it. She got her mind ready to do her performing poodle act because she couldn't see it any other way for now.

Finally the team arrived. Gemma and Rhys didn't wait to get leave from Bev to go. There was no controlling them and they didn't care who was in their way. They raced out into the lobby, running so fast that they were leaning over as they flew around the corner like a very tight bend on a race track. They sprinted around by the door, raced up the straight towards me and screamed to their daddy.

Bev didn't even want to stand up, she felt rooted and it was with an effort of will that she got up from the table at all and left the waiting room. The children hung off me like monkeys from a tree. Bev's legs felt like she was walking against a strong current as she walked towards me, then suddenly it broke away and released her and she had to stop herself from running too.

I didn't see her at first, and then past the children and other families, I saw her stride out towards me, looking uneasy but smiling. Then she was right in front of me. I hugged her tightly and Bev felt heat rush through her with relief. I had been looking forward to this all the way home. I hadn't the first clue what she was going through. It was as much a relief to her as the news late on Monday that I was down alive. I told Bev she looked lovely and I liked the new dress. She grinned and twitched an eyebrow up and down quickly with a knowing sort of look.

I told her to let go so that I could breathe and get inside. Was this a rebuff? Calm down, calm down. She was trying to keep herself on some kind of mental rails. We returned to the room they had all been waiting in and sat down, which was tricky with Bev's chair pushed right against mine and two children trying to sit on me at the same time. It was just great.

We babbled on for a while and they gave me their little gifts. Gemma gave me a new razor because I had looked scruffy on the telly; I thought it was very funny. Rhys gave me a little game he found that week in a cereal packet. It was one of the ball-bearing games where you have to try and roll it into the little crescents on a route to the bottom. The background picture was a mountain-side and the game was called 'Mountain Rescue' we thought it was very funny too. I also got a really nice 'Animal' T shirt. I still have that although it is thin and threadbare but I can't bring myself to get rid of it.

Bev and I sat close and I never let go of her hand. I never wanted to let go of her hand. She had got herself into a real mess because she couldn't step back and see that I still hadn't mentally come off the expedition. Bev said that I felt warm and thin. She also said I was looking tanned and tired. My beard was new and they all liked it. I felt Bev stare at me while we sat together. I liked it. Both Gemma and Rhys sat on my lap and I held Bev's hand, it seemed important to her too, she gripped onto mine.

The team was called into the press conference, which took some time and was now familiar to us and then we were called outside. There was a wall of camera people shouting at us, and continuous flashing, TV cameras coming up and reporters coming up to us in a constant stream. All Bev could think was, 'It's really alright!', 'It's all fine, none of this matters, they can have their pictures, they can photograph the kids, this is happy.' We laughed at the cameras and the attention, we thought it was genuinely funny watching them jostling and shouting from behind their barrier.

We kissed for the cameras and lots of people said 'Aaah!' Gemma and Rhys thought the cameramen were funny too but wouldn't let go of their daddy. We said a few things for the press that neither of us can remember and just relaxed and enjoyed it. It was after all a happy occasion and we weren't in any rush. We had all the time in the world now. I thought Bev looked lovely and hadn't realised how much I had missed her, even if I had been so pre-occupied and blinkered by work. We were back, confident and happy with each other, just fine.

We went back inside to the other families and swapped lots of phone numbers and addresses and then we were led out to a coach, which would drop us off at the car park away from the press. We said our good byes and went back to the car. Nobody wanted to sit in the front with Andy-bless him. All four of us squashed into the back together. We stopped at Burger King on the way and chatted away merrily. Bev usually has what she calls an embarrassingly huge appetite, but after eight days of not being able to eat. She barely managed half a small burger. She felt very sick after. I struggled to eat mine and didn't feel too great myself with food inside me. The kids were now on their third burger meal in a month and they knew it. They wolfed theirs down and ate anything they could on the table because they knew they had no hope of another one for a very long time.

It was strange to look around and see people going about normally. We all felt far from normal. I looked like I had put my face in front of a furnace. Most of my face was brown but I had white all around my eyes from wearing my goggles and all around the edge of where they had been, the skin was peeling away. I had a line of blooded up scabs on my forehead where the goggles had frozen to my head and the skin had torn when I pulled them away. Bev was looking at me taking it all in.

We slept the rest of the way home, stifling in the back of the car, on a very hot summer's day we daren't let go of each other. I couldn't stay awake after the plane hopping and travelling. We arrived at the house to find Elvy, Gary and Cindy waiting for us. As I got out of the car, Cindy threw herself onto me, hugging and kissing me excitedly. Elvy and Gary had to wait for her to calm down before they got their turn. (Not that Gary was kissing me, just a hug!) It was a great welcome home and great to see them all there.

We finally got into the house and I emptied my luggage out onto the sitting room floor. There was clutter everywhere, but it was immediately evident that there was a lot missing. The insurance would sort that out, but it was a real shame about the carry mat with the message for Gemma.

I braced myself for the scowl from Bev as I confessed that I had been shopping at the REI. Bev knew the REI, (Outdoor Equipment Outlet) in Anchorage. It didn't matter, she had said almost serenely, I didn't trust her calmness.

"No, I've 'really' been shopping!" I said. She said she just couldn't believe I was here, sitting on the sofa chatting away. Bev said I had better phone Ma and Pa, then Wes and Kirsten in Scotland. They were the priorities. Wes was my wing-man and we missed both Wes and Kirsten desperately.

Later Bev sat on the loo seat with her feet up on the side of the bath, leaning back against the wall while I soaked until the water grew tepid and we talked and talked. The kids were in and out the whole time showing me new toys, pictures and bits of school work.

We slept wrapped tightly together and we both kept waking to make sure we were both still there. Bev said I was incredibly thin. She was shocked to see how much weight I had lost. I noticed Bev had shed a few pounds too. She was also shocked when I screamed out in my sleep and shouted "Hold him, don't let him untie!" Bev said I was groaning and mumbling, but the shouting was crystal clear. She was unsure whether to wake me or not. I was suddenly soaked in sweat and she sneaked to the bathroom to get a towel to mop me up without waking me. I didn't even stir as she dried me. She mentioned it the following day but I remembered nothing. All I remembered was that she had put my feet on a pillow and laid a sheet over them.

I can only describe the pain as being like long, hot needles being pushed in through the end of my toes and the arches of my feet. If this is frost-nip, I dread to think what Carl and Steve had gone through.

During the day, I slept on the sofa in between having my feet bathed and massaged. This may sound like luxury to many but anyone with frost injuries will know I dreaded it. Sometimes I could barely let Bev touch them. The skin was peeling away in very thick layers to reveal soft, dark pink skin underneath. The skin on the rest of my feet had blood blisters and clear ones. They looked revolting and again Bev said she felt very sorry for me. My hands were in a similar state, with my fingers peeling deeply down to my middle knuckle, but without the blisters.

I still had the circular wound over the little finger knuckle of my hand where I had been holding the axe against the surface on my way down. It was a hole that took months and months to heal. I was limping on both legs after resting, but insisted I would be fine, as I was sure it would only be a few weeks before I was back to normal. I thought my ankle injuries were just sprains. My mind was on Carl and Steve a great deal. Mostly during those first days, I slept and ate lots of very small portioned meals and drank lots of tea and juice. I was mostly unaware of the demon that had stowed away with me back to the U.K. that manifested in my sleep and hoped it didn't come out in the day.

Chapter 19 - Plaiting fog

Those initial weeks led us into a cocoon of self-reliance in an aspect we had not experienced before. I was becoming increasingly frustrated with being so immobile. I was bored and alone all day when I was at home because Bev had gone back to work and the children had gone back to school. When I returned to work finally, I ended up in the office most of the time. I didn't mind this for a while, as I managed to get away to do a little kayaking some weeks. I was just a couple of offices up from Bev through the double doors, so I would pop in sometimes and get her told off by Keith by making calls from her office and taking up her time. Bev didn't mind and Keith didn't most of the time. The fact remained though that I was grounded and it was beginning to tell on me.

We had a couple of letters from Carl while he was still in Anchorage hospital telling us of his progress and that JD Swed had visited and the discussions they had about Conrad and the kayaking phase on the Susitna River.

Conrad contacted me after I had been back home for some time. He said that following the expedition he needed to clear a few things up and they weren't going well for him. He asked me for a reference regarding his mountain leadership skills. My heart sank. I liked Conrad and thought him more misguided than anything but I had to say no.

Reflecting on how he had been and how fragmented the team was on the mountain I felt the leadership was flawed in that it lacked decisiveness in some areas but was vehement in others where it should have been more flexible, with the route for instance. Also, the fact that Johnny and I were burdened with basic winter skills training on the mountain that Conrad should have not just ensured was in place but thoroughly reinforced before we got on an aeroplane. There was the lack of communication and vagueness at the point when we were stuck in camp for several days in the blizzard early on the mountain.

There were minor things too but that would be nit-picking. The major thing that I felt aware of after these others was the issue of batteries. I knew, I just knew that he had not brought spare batteries and that he had lied to me on the ledge about them. I just couldn't prove it. In hindsight, I saw that one act delayed everyone's rescue and his fall with Steve down the Orient Express would not have happened. Their fall delayed everything even further. I had no choice but to say no. I knew that was probably the end of our friendly relationship. I then received his letter dated 19 Aug 98 written by hand. His letter read as follows, all spelling and punctuation unchanged: N.B. SIB = Special Investigation Branch (of the Royal Military Police - the military equivalent of the C.I.D).

Dear Martin

I have been trying to get hold of you for a few days now but don't have your home number. You will know the S.I.B. is involved now and so I am just writing to let you know I will probably be resigning my commission because of the contents of the investigation team's report. Glyn and the team have basically said it was my fault due to the fact that:

a) The rangers told us not to go on the West Rib cut-off but to do the West Buttress (normal) route due to the team's inexperience. We were all at the briefing and I do not believe Joel said that at all. I'm sure he stated that we would do well as we were strong and well prepared. We did agree that if conditions were bad at the Rib due to excessive snow etc. we could always switch at 14,200, however.

b) I failed my JSMEL (W) and was therefore too inexperienced to lead on the mountain - which I think is bollocks because of my experience. They cite my poor navigation and security on steep ground as reasons why the accidents occurred.

Anyway, this note is just to say that I really appreciated having you on the trip and hope we can climb again together. I still want to go and do the whole climb and kayak trip without incident! Maybe a two man trip or three man private trip with Johnny could be a lot less hassle!

I hope to see you soon and will make an effort after my quick operation on the 20th. All my regards to Beverley and the children.

Cheers Mucker

Conrad

I felt really bad for Conrad but Carl was proving to be right. I didn't want to get swept up in the political aftermath but the tide was coming in my direction.

Then a telephone call came that changed everything. I spoke to an investigator from the accident, an old colleague who could see what was happening.

He told me outright that Conrad had indeed failed his JSMEL (W) and wasn't qualified to lead a rope team on the mountain. Of course it all made sense now but I don't know how he got the ATFA through to get the team out of the country.

The investigator said that wasn't all. Conrad had failed the course so badly that he was the worst candidate that the assessor had ever had. This report would have been seen by Major Edward Simpson at 'Tywyn'. The shock hit me then. So Simpson had seen Conrad's report and that neither of them had informed Colonel Harrison at 4 Div. Conrad must have somehow convinced Colonel Harrison that he had passed his course and he had then secured his ATFA. I couldn't believe it had gone so far. Even with Conrad's letter I couldn't believe he had tried to take a rope team without his JSMEL (W). He must have been desperate to make this expedition work.

There was one thing in Conrad's letter that I had to agree with, that I felt very important. During the one briefing that I attended at the Ranger Station in Talkeetna before the expedition, Joel did not advise us 'not' to go via the West Rib Route. Joel was mistaken in remembering exactly what he had said. He had spoken mostly about the West Buttress, that is correct but he did indicate to the West Rib route on the slide saying 'but this is the route that your team will be taking.' This indicated to me that there had already been discussions with Conrad and the Rangers that had taken place at the previous briefing when I wasn't present. I found the talk interesting and did ask Conrad later after the expedition had started. "If the West Buttress is the route the Rangers recommend, then why aren't we going that way?" Conrad had made his mind up and planned for the West Rib, that was it. My feelings about Conrad were still not bad but I just couldn't reconcile the ambition of the man and how Edward Simpson had managed to let the ATFA slip through.

Bev was still working in the office down the corridor and I would make those visits to her that got her ticked off by Keith from time to time and we would cycle home together for lunch. The company was nice for both of us as Bev worked alone much of the time as Keith drove up and down the valleys looking after his 'patch'. Bev's job however was coming to an end soon as the office was moving all its operations to a place that was the best part of sixty miles away near Swansea.

Bev was almost on her last day in post when the Special Investigation Branch (SIB) of the Military Police told my boss, Ray, of a visit. We were a little apprehensive when the day arrived and I asked if Bev was allowed to attend, as her memory was more reliable. Both Ray, my boss and Keith, Bev's boss were understanding of the situation and gave us leave to attend. Poor Keith was up to his eyes in packing boxes and mess as Bev's office was dismantled, and he continued to pack and man the phone for the rest of the day alone as Bev abandoned him to keep me company. She thought she'd only be gone for an hour and leave me to the rest of it.

The interview, we were told would probably take a couple of hours. It went on from around 10:30hrs to about 17:30hrs. We had to get Elvy to take the kids after school. As usual there wasn't a word of protest from her.

Bev listened intently to me, as did the policeman, (Jim) who was quick to try and put us at ease. Although Bev had heard parts of the saga over and over; from my private account to the interviews that were more restricted for the media, she had never heard every detail from start to finish before, and not ever in such graphic detail.

Although I could remember quite clearly, what happened all the way up the mountain and conversations that took place, I was having trouble remembering the actual timings. I thought that being snowed in for three days was significant but whether I had noodles or grits for supper on the second day wasn't, so couldn't recall timing details. I found myself apologising again and again for this, but assured Jim that it was all written in the diary I made on the expedition, even if the entries were very brief. Jim didn't mind and said it could all be checked if need be anyway.

Bev was writing reams of notes furiously, trying to keep track of all the questions. She has no shorthand so she was concentrating hard. She noticed a subtle change in the questions. They had become much more specific as Jim was obviously trying to pinpoint a particular detail. The same questions were posed in a different way on occasion and received a different aspect to the similar answer. She found it all very clever as she had never seen this in action before (we don't tend to watch soaps and cop shows) and I didn't seem to be aware of it at all. I was so busy looking down and closing my eyes to remember tiny details.

Jim needed to clarify something regarding my Mountain Instructor Certificate qualification. Bev telephoned Glenmore Lodge outside Aviemore and spoke with Nigel Williams. He was extremely sympathetic towards us and offered his help if it were needed. He gave Bev the information and wished me luck. Nigel and I knew each other from our time in Scotland, and by coincidence, was an ex-Army Captain in the PWRR. Bev passed on the information and the interview went on. The question then came regarding the fall. "What happened next?"

Bev said that at this point the scene in the office on those awful easy chairs around that coffee table with all its paperwork on became surreal. She saw me focus at a point that wasn't in the room. I was looking beyond to the incident that was now happening in front of my eyes.

Jim and Bev were no longer in the room, I was back under the cornice and it was the early evening of 18th June 1998.

I began to describe the fall; Jim was leaning over the table, pen in hand ready to write. As I continued, Jim leaned back in the chair listening and watching. Bev closed her eyes as if it would close her ears as well to the description of me clawing at the ice with my hands and feeling myself falling away from the slope. The tale went on in all its appalling detail. I had become intense and animated. As I was describing what was happening, I was miming it with my whole body from leaning on the table to kneeling on the floor showing how Phil pulled tangled rope from himself.

Bev said it was alarming to watch and she could feel herself shaking. She looked away and I continued on as if I could actually see it in our time and place. I was consumed by the incident replaying in front of me.

Bev felt such horror and pity at the whole thing. Tears fell onto her note pad and she wiped them away quickly and pulled herself together. She had nothing to blow her nose with so she held the back of her hand over it, quietly waiting for me to finish. I looked up and was brought back to the present momentarily.

They urged me to carry on. I seemed to be transported straight back there and hardly broke the stride of my story. As I trailed off not knowing what else to say, Jim and Bev were both spellbound by what they had witnessed. They just sat and stared at me for a few seconds. Bev smiled and winked at me to tell me 'Well done, you're O.K!'

Jim just wrote, "Then we fell," We laughed and it snapped the tension and I apologised for going on. Jim said, "Not at all, I was engrossed!" We needed a short break then. Bev collected the children from school, dumped them with Elvy, apologised to Keith for leaving him with all the ghastly packing all day and went back in to the interview.

After the description of the fall, there were a lot of questions about the radios posed in different ways. I confirmed that Conrad had indeed hired two C.B. radios locally and that I had told Conrad at 14,200ft that even though I had kept my batteries next to my body, they had still gone flat. I had asked if he could sort some spares out and he said he would. I had one radio but I don't recall who carried the other. My own avalanche transceiver was working but the radio was dead. Then we discussed the radios on the ledge where we had landed from the first fall. I told him that as soon as I realised we couldn't get ourselves down with our injuries I asked Conrad, who I now assumed had the new batteries to call in and summon help. I told him that Conrad had said that the batteries were no good but I didn't believe him, although I had no evidence to support this so I didn't pursue it at the time.

I was then asked a question that came up a lot over the coming months with various people. I was asked if I had seen Conrad boil any batteries at the scene or at any other point on the expedition. I was rather astonished as I hadn't come across this myself. I was thinking 'what a dangerous and stupid thing to do.' I didn't think of anyone on the team who would try such a daft stunt. We even had Steve on the expedition who was an electrical engineer, he would have made a right song and dance about it if he'd seen it happening. I confirmed that I did not see Conrad boil batteries, nor did I see anyone else do it during the whole expedition to my knowledge. I also confirmed that nobody had mentioned it being done. I wondered where that suggestion had come from. Jim said he couldn't say.

The theory behind this is that the heat on the chemicals in the batteries gives an increase in their output but it won't re-charge them. It will only help squeeze the last drop of juice out of them. I'd rate this theory as a waste of time with electrical items like radios. Also I would have thought that the fluctuating extreme temperature would cause them to leak so they'd be no good. It may have been used here and there with farmers or fishermen but I've never seen or heard of anyone in my profession doing it.

The interview was just winding up and the conversation went on to general chat. Jim was a nice chap and made the interview as easy for me as he could, but I was worn out. I joked that I would rather climb Denali again than go through another interview like that. Jim then offered us a copy of the statement.

Bev laughed and told him her hand was nearly falling off from writing all those notes. She wished she had known we were allowed a copy of the statement at the beginning. Jim gave us his card and wished me well. He shook Bev's hand and told her to look after me.

We went back home feeling shattered and hoping that nothing I said could cause any problems for anyone else on the team. We read back through the statement and thought it was fine. Bev told me that I could only tell what happened, if the police chose to use it or pass it by it was out of our hands. She said she couldn't see that there was anything bad in there about anyone, even Conrad didn't get the same jabbing he was getting from Carl.

Bev, sadly left her job the following week and became a lady of leisure. She hated it. The first few weeks were a novelty and it was nice to catch up on things around the house and the garden. Sam our Labrador/cross was getting a good long run nearly every day now, and at least a couple of short runs if Bev couldn't be bothered to go through all the farm land. I taught her to Kayak at beginner's level, which she loved and we went to the boat moored at Hayling Island as often as we could. I was back at work though, as she left her job and she was bored.

Bev's new routine carried on and I was back to work either in the office or kayaking. I was going to my regular physiotherapy appointments and seeing the medical officer whenever he needed an update. At home, things were different. My ankle had not improved at all. It was painful and often swollen. I was bored and frustrated at the restrictions the injury imposed. I became frustrated more easily and quick tempered. This had got gradually worse over the past three months since my return. Bev tried to understand, knowing that I was bound to need time to recover. My sleeping hadn't improved, nor had the yelling, throwing myself around in bed and sweating in the middle of the night, if not every night then several nights a week.

I had come home to the U.K. feeling guilty that I had left Carl and Steve in the hospital. I had spent much of my time after the accident doing what I could to look after them along with crowds of others who all wanted to help and comfort them. I suppose I felt that I was abandoning them. I didn't have much choice, if I had, I would have stayed the six weeks with them.

Bev, I thought was O.K. at home, even if she was nearly out of her tree by that time, which I didn't know about, at least she was at home. Carl and Steve were left behind and it bothered me a great deal. There were numerous phone calls to Alaska over those weeks and on top of the phone calls made after the accident and the following week, Bev said she regretted not having shares in British Telecom. I was just frustrated and restless.

In those weeks before Carl and Steve returned, there was a surreal feeling of detachment from the world around us. Apart from wanting to see Carl and Steve, I also had an aura of peace about me that sometimes changed to euphoria. It was the most comfortable feeling of contentment Bev and I had experienced before.

All the problems we ever had before faded into the place they should be. The commitments in life, the day to day problems and restrictions that seemed to bind us were no longer important and we felt good about everyone and everything. We completely relaxed and let the euphoria of this new feeling wash over us. There was only the night that showed how deeply I had been affected by the whole experience when I was dreaming and thrashing around and shouting in my sleep. The pain I suffered as a result of my physical injury was something we could understand and deal with. It was what was hiding beneath the surface that was causing the big problems.

I had insisted to my Medical Officer, (M.O.) that I was still in a lot of pain and that I felt something was very wrong inside my joint. I was prescribed more anti-inflammatory pain killers and physio sessions. I had at least a dozen appointments and was becoming despondent. I had to return to work and I was happy to get back into the hills and back into the crowd at work. When I returned home, I was clearly in pain. Sometimes in the mornings, I could barely put my weight on my ankle to get out of bed. Still the M.O. said I had nothing seriously wrong with me.

Carl and Steve were flown back to Gatwick. I had hoped to meet them there, but I couldn't make the timings fit in with my appointment. I drove to HMS Haslar, which was an antiquated military hospital in Southampton, in the hope of seeing them there. I was anxious to welcome them home and to let them know the team was still thinking about them.

As I entered the hospital, it gave me a shudder. I was never comfortable with this environment, but this place had a very dated and depressing atmosphere. It was like a time warp. I felt like it was the 1950s.

I wandered around from reception, then ward to ward, asking the staff at the nursing stations for information. They still hadn't arrived at the hospital and I was very pushed for time. I should have been on the road again by now. I made way to the exit feeling very disappointed at having to just leave a message. I pushed the exit door open as a mini-bus pulled up in front of me. I was over-the-moon, as Carl and Steve stepped out in front of me. I chatted with Carl as Steve got himself organised with his bags. I spent a while with them, catching up on news and finding out what their further treatment was likely to be.

They were both in fairly good spirits, especially Carl, who was just glad to be alive. Steve was a little more subdued; his amputation had hit him hard. It wasn't surprising as he was a technician and had very serious doubts about his future. Still, he seemed glad to be back. The same surgeon, who had come out of retirement to help Carl and Steve in Alaska, had trained the doctors due to be treating them here at Haslar. They felt they were in the best hands they could be, if they couldn't stay in Alaska. They had both been told it would be far better for them to be treated in the U.K., that way they could be closer to their families and it would be good for their morale.

Steve said they weren't stupid. They were well aware of the fact that they had left Alaska six weeks, almost to the day after being hospitalised. Steve put it down to the terms of their insurance policy and the Army wasn't going to be too happy with incurring any further medical expenses in the United States by keeping them in the lap of luxury in Anchorage Hospital.

Some members of the public in Anchorage were asked for their opinion of the cost of the rescue. Some remarks were scathing, but sadly predictable. A lot of mention was made about the American taxpayers covering the cost of the vast operation. One remark was completely inaccurate and cutting. The lady said that if these people could afford to go and climb mountains, then they should pay for the rescue.

The facts were clear to the Army and the team. Everyone struggled to make the £600-£1,000 contribution, which covered rescue and medical insurance. The US Government could get their money back if they wanted to claim on the policy Conrad had taken out. It had to cover rescue expenses, so the hospital and the rescue services resources would not be depleted as a result of rescuing the Brits. We were told that the rescue had cost over $75,000 and they were right, it was way over and closer to $230,000 according to local news sources in Anchorage and was a record high.

The Rangers themselves, having an understanding of what drives climbers to visit the mountain are of the view that individuals should not be held accountable for using their services if they are needed. On a personal note from Bev, she's sure the lady concerned would take a different view if one of her loved ones was on the brink of death and required the help of the National Parks Ranger Services.

Also, we hope it may placate some to know that although our insurance and/or the British Government, through the British Army we were able to reimburse the U.S. taxpayers. The offer was not claimed and we will always be in the debt of the people on the mountain who had a hand in helping to get the team off the mountain in more ways than just financial. We are also grateful to the U.S. citizens who all wished us well. We are all appropriately humbled by this.

The three years following the accident seemed to go on forever for us three injured men. The Training Accident Investigation Team (TAIT) that flew to Alaska immediately in the days following the accident, had interviewed everybody at length. The problem with this was that emotions were still high and the team was on the defensive, not wanting to implicate anyone. We all knew something, or several things had gone terribly wrong, but nobody had time nor the inclination to dissect and analyse what it was.

There was a general feeling that among the investigators, that there was a reluctance to talk. The good thing about the investigation at the time was that everyone was still a little bewildered by what had happened so there was no finger-pointing or time to think what 'may' have happened rather than what 'did'. Given time to analyse what happened and what was said, the S.I.B. investigation was very different to the TAIT investigation.

The TAIT had arrived, as I said, within a few days of the rescue and conducted interviews with the team members, Rangers, guides and hospital staff. I knew one of the investigators well and was very pleased and relieved to see a friendly and familiar face in all the chaos that surrounded us all. However, even to my friend, I seemed cautious and was reluctant to be too open. There was a strong feeling within the team that we had gone through something very important in our lives and we must stick together and not let each other down. There wasn't anything to hide anyway as far as most of the team were concerned, but nobody wanted to be the one to say something out of turn that would bring a disciplinary down on the head of an unfortunate team mate.

Carl and Steve were booked in and settled into their ward at Haslar in the grim-looking building. It was a far cry from the bright, cheery hospital they had left behind. The staff had been wonderful in Anchorage and the hospitality had been very warm and friendly. Here in the UK, military people surrounded them. Many of the staff appeared stoic, officious, disinterested and perfunctory.

Carl and Steve found that some of the nursing staff were OK, but on the whole, none of them seemed to want to be there, and they couldn't blame them. Carl described one or two of the nurses as absolute streaks of misery. The whole place was oppressive. If it was all designed to get bums out of bed and back to work, then it was a method that would work to great effect. They couldn't imagine anyone wanting to spend any more time there than they had to.

I came back from Haslar with my spirits lifted far more than they had been in the month previously. It was not such a happy story for Carl and Steve. The treatment that they got in Haslar was appalling. I was upset by the apparent neglect of the M.O. to help with my medical problems, but the treatment Carl got was nothing short of barbaric. It was ironic that Haslar is a naval place. What he went through there was what one would have expected on HMS Victory in Admiral Nelson's day.

Carl's treatment was particularly harrowing. A television company had asked to film his treatment and at first, the hospital agreed. A doctor treating Carl later told him that it wouldn't be possible, as it could leave them open to litigation. Carl soon realised why. Within a couple of weeks, the skin grafts that had caused him so much pain and been so carefully put into place to make a flap of skin that would fold over where his toes had been became infected since he had been admitted to the hospital. The infection was bad enough for the doctor to decide to remove them altogether. Carl was understandably very upset about this, as he thought not enough care had been taken to prevent the infection The grafted skin was removed that had been so carefully cared for in Alaska. All that pain and all those weeks of healing wasted.

As the new wound began to heal a new problem became apparent. Carl noticed he was still in a lot of pain and where his little toe used to be, the wound had become infected again. He was given the usual anti-biotics but the wound was now swollen, hot, still weeping fluid and very sore. He was taken to have the sutures removed where the area was particularly sore and so he asked for a local anaesthetic. The medical staff were very flippant and said that a grown man like him wouldn't need one and not to be silly.

He became quite alarmed when a male nurse laid himself across Carl's body and another helped to hold his legs down. Two of the sutures had healed over with new skin and were now buried underneath the infected part of the wound. The nurse removing the sutures grabbed the skin where the stitches were buried, sliced the skin open with a scalpel. The nurse put the scalpel down then rummaged a little with the tweezers until the stitches were gripped and ripped them out one at a time. Carl couldn't breathe with the intensity of the pain. He had had the pain of the frost bite and the demarcation as the foot split, the surgery and skin grafts, the infections and now this barbaric treatment. There and then he made his decision to sue the bastards.

Steve's decision had been made long before. He was very bitter about it all and who can blame him. He wasn't a mountaineer and he had been through both horrendous falls on the mountain. Both Carl and Steve had a lot of time to discuss matters on their own together and had found a lot out about the expedition preparation, which they came to share with me now that they were back in the U.K.

They gave Bev hand-written versions of their experiences before, during and after the expedition. They gave her photos of their frost-bitten hands and feet. She took long notes, recorded, photocopied and compiled month after month of everything that came our way.

Although Steve can't remember anything at all about the first fall, he accepted that he must have fainted and suffered enough for Conrad to decide to take him down the Orient Express. Here, being belayed from below (a bad practice for steep ground), he tumbled into Conrad and they fell 1,500ft and lived. With Conrad lying in the snow screaming, he went off for rescue and fell down two crevasses. There had to be something wrong with an expedition that goes that badly wrong. He was an electrical engineer by trade, a fat lot of good he would be now with no fingers. Steve found out that he should have, in best practice been belayed from above if Conrad was qualified as a rope leader and JSMEL (W). That would have been good 'security on steep ground.'

We all kept in touch and within a few months we had all decided to collaborate and pursue a claim against the MoD. At this point I still didn't know the extent of my own medical condition. We still didn't even know what case we had against them but Carl and Steve were getting information thick and fast from their advisors. It was all starting to get very political and complicated and far from moving on, we all got sucked back into the black hole of the expedition.

I still felt a bit bad for Conrad although I felt he'd made foolish mistakes in his ambition to get that mountain ticked off his list but he was helped somewhere to get the expedition under way and I knew where this help was. I couldn't prove it though.

Carl was discharged from hospital once his infection finally went and was back in the PWRR unit at Howe Barracks in Canterbury but had been keeping in touch with me as much as he could and sometimes came to stay for the weekend with us in Wales.

He told me he wasn't getting on very well with Conrad but neither he nor I were surprised. They didn't appear best buddies in Alaska. I asked him to pass on my regards to him all the same, which he did.

I thought if Conrad was in trouble he would probably get carpeted by his boss and fined. Some people have recovered their careers from a whole lot worse and still managed promotions. Nobody has a glowing career when it lasts for decades, we all make mistakes.

My problem was a little deeper than the investigations and failing friendships. Bev came to keep clean towels by the bed every night. I would lie awake not being able to sleep for an hour or so. When I had been asleep for a while I would begin jerking my arms and legs and speaking, sometimes shouting, "Hold him, don't let him untie himself" Bev told me that my speech was often crystal clear and sometimes barely mumbled but always the same thing that I yelled

I would be asking where something is or shouting that we were going to go over the edge. I would often shout or mumble incoherently about Steve going over the ledge. Sometimes I would jump awake and not remember anything, thinking that Bev had woken me from the recurring playback I was going through, whether I slept through or woke during this cycle of dreaming the incident again and again, I very rarely re-called anything the next morning for many weeks. Bev used the towels most nights to mop my body dry of the sweat as I dreamt on. She tried not to wake me if she could. The morning was the same routine. I would wake and go to the shower, Bev would pull the sheets off the bed and change the pillow cases and dump everything in the washing machine. She had it in a routine that only took her a few minutes each day now. We got used to seeing bedding on the washing line every day or slung over doors and banisters.

I was so tired. I bathed late at night to relax, didn't drink and watched movies in the evening to steer my mind away from any stress. It didn't work. There was obviously a demon that had come home with me that was going to find its way to the surface one way or another, so it comes in my sleep, even now occasionally after all these years. Now I simply say, "I dreamed about the mountain last night." Bev will put a hand on my arm and say nothing.

We talked about how I was feeling but didn't know quite what to do about it. I had mentioned it to my medical officer but he had said that I seemed OK to him so we let the matter drop. I suggested to Bev that we look forward to being posted to the South Coast where we can make a fresh start where there was nobody around that was associated with the accident and didn't know me.

As the weeks and months went by, I began to recall my dreams and seemed to be disturbed by them. I suppose I began to withdraw into myself at this point and would become agitated and annoyed over the smallest trifle. Neither of us had any idea at this point that we were to be on first name terms with post trauma symptoms. It is a phrase that is banded about all over the place now, but back then it certainly was not.

It was now the end of October and I wasn't improving. Bev was bored at home now and never saw anyone unless she went shopping or met me from work. Elvy and Gary had been posted to Aldershot and our new neighbour kept to herself and so did Bev. She became quiet and guarded with me over things we would never even consider before. She said I was constantly finding fault with her, criticising the smallest thing, being sarcastic and generally treating her as if, yes, I loved her but didn't really like her much. We both wondered what had happened to that 'euphoria' we were bathing in during the weeks after I arrived home.

She got to the stage where she was struggling with frustration and didn't know why. She was crying very easily lately and that irritated me too. I tried talking to her. She explained that although the accident hadn't happened to her, she couldn't cope as well as she thought with what had happened and how it had left me. She wanted the Martin she had before Denali, not a streak of misery who had turned into a pessimist. She said that it was not the nicest thing to say, and incredibly selfish considering it was mostly my suffering that was bothering her. I came to understand a little of the effect the accident had had on those around me. I wanted her to be happy again, I really did.

My personality at home became more withdrawn as time passed. I couldn't say why but acknowledged this and knew that it should have passed by now. We talked a lot and tried to find a solution. Bev tried the local doctor, but was told that they were not allowed to see soldiers as the Army refused to pay the small fee and they do not like to release the medical documents. She explained the problem to the doctor and he agreed that I was suffering some kind of trauma and that I was burying it. The doctor very kindly agreed to get into contact with my medical officer. Bev explained that she had tried, but got the impression that she was just seen as a neurotic wifey, who was poking her nose into military business.

I saw the M.O. eventually and was told again that I was fine. I was at least given an appointment to see a specialist. This happened eventually in early March 1999, eight months after the accident. This was my first full medical de-brief from the expedition. It had taken four months from first asking for help to finally getting an appointment. Bev thought it was a good job I didn't have to wait much longer; she thought I'd have been walking the streets, wielding an axe like Jack Nicholson in 'The Shining!' She used to joke and call me Jack Torrance if I got moody with her.

During the same period, I had also approached the M.O. with regard to my ankle. The pain was still acute in a small range of movement after seven months. The doctor didn't examine my ankle at all but said he would refer me to the specialist from rehabilitation centre at Headley Court near London. There would be a clinic held at St Thomas' hospital in London that I could attend. I was about to leave the medical centre when I decided to go and see if the physiotherapist had a few minutes to spare to give me some ultra-sound pain relief.

I took off my sock and the physio said, "Oh my God, they've popped." She called in the M.O. who agreed. It appeared that the ligaments that hold the fibula to my tarsals had completely snapped and the lateral side of the fibula was free at its base. The ankle bone that shows on the outside of the foot was about a centimetre further out than it should have been.

Even after examination by a military orthopaedic surgeon at St. Thomas' in London, I was sent back for re-hab. In the end, we decided through our solicitor to try to push for a CT scan to find out what was really going on in my ankle, which confirmed that the ligament had been completely ruptured and the mechanism of injury was consistent with me digging my crampons into the ice face to slow the fall. Basically, my ankle was completely detached from the foot and the outside ankle bone was still coming away to the point that it looked like a golf ball stuck onto the side of my ankle instead of set into it.

After my appointment I came home in low spirits. I said in one way, it's very good news. I told Bev that the specialist spent a good deal of time with me and told me that I didn't need surgery but two weeks of rehabilitation at Headley Court. I said I was down because I didn't feel that it was correct and that my ankle was so unstable.

I went back to work pondering the diagnosis. We pursued the new posting, wondering why we hadn't been given a decision when we had applied in September 1998. We were told that the decision hadn't been made yet. We approached SSAFA, (Forces charity that helps service men and women and their families), as we had been through so much in the past months and no matter how much we helped ourselves, nothing happened.

We had never asked for help from them before, but when we had done, that it seemed to come to nothing either. The only thing that seemed to happen regarding me over the past months was the requests for media interviews. This was becoming an issue with me now and I only did later interviews because I felt manipulated into it.

I was sent to Headley Court Rehabilitation Centre for four weeks intensive therapy. It is a superb place and a real credit to the military. I went through the motions and worked hard, enjoying the physical training again, but I knew my ankle was never going to repair. I could not prepare in any way for the fact that I was unlikely to return to any serious climbing again. I didn't want to go back to the mountains and only be able to cope with the foothills. Still, I was enjoying Headley Court, the hard training and the banter, having a few good laughs along the way.

Back home there was still quite a lot of media interest. It was frustrating for us both, as I would sit there in front of the camera singing the praises of the Army and how great everything is, when really, I felt a little let down medically. I felt very badly for Carl and Steve who were now likely to be medically discharged and end up in the dole queue at some stage.

The interviews came and the help didn't. Trying to get anything done to get a move to the South Coast was like plaiting fog. We worked away at it from every possible angle for months. I decided to get a diagnosis for my ankle privately by going through our solicitor. He made the contacts and I got an appointment.

The consultant took a stress X-Ray and manipulated my foot until I nearly shot off the bed in pain. The X-Ray came back to show that my tarsals were out of line and that the previous diagnosis was incorrect. It would definitely need surgery to prevent further damage. Did I need another blow to my situation?

The PT Corps obviously felt I did. Whilst away at Headley Court where I could do very little about it, I found out that I was posted to a basic training depot in Surrey. I would be practically desk bound in my new role. Surrounded by London, Guildford, Aldershot, Basingstoke and all the other places we loath, we began to despair. This wasn't the bad move we thought it was and a well thought out one by the Army but we didn't know that yet.

Bev went into orbit, she called my immediate boss and my Master at Arms to see if anything could be done. I was really quite disappointed but Bev was very upset. She is a South Saxon born and bred but she had no intention of going back to the South East surrounded by cities again.

Besides, she thought nothing would ever be as good as living in Brighton again as she did as a kid if she did have to live like a 'townie'. She called SSAFA again, hoping they would be able to help even though the PT Corps ignored them last time. We were at our wits end.

I then received a telephone call from a friend who was involved somewhere in the proceedings that followed the accident. Apparently, some of the team members had been recommended for bravery awards. It was suggested that I be recommended for a bravery award by some of the investigating team (TAIT) that went to Alaska and by the S.I.B. of the Military Police. The PT Corps officer that was approached, Major Horn who had a fleeting presence at Gatwick Airport the day we arrived back said, "I don't feel that it would be appropriate pending investigation." So, that was the end of that.

I shrugged and said that it was no surprise from them, as they obviously felt I had been responsible for something that had gone wrong up there on the mountain and were probably waiting for the inquiry to hammer me; besides, my concerns were more with my injuries at this stage. That close to the end of my career, a gong, (medal) isn't going to make much difference. I was puzzled why the inquiry would be bothering the P.T. Corps., my conscience was clear.

My other underlying concern with the whole affair was whether the climbing world would still back me up, even if the PT Corps didn't. I knew I had done nothing wrong, in hindsight, I would have still done everything the same on the mountain with the information I had at the time.

All the team members had been back in the U.K. a good while now and over time half the team were separated and some lost contact with others for good. There were interviews with the media, telephone calls and a dozen different versions of what happened between the team members, investigators, organisers and the media.

By the time the S.I.B. investigations started a couple of months after the accident, suspicions had been aroused amongst the team that all had not been as it should have from before the outset. The TAIT report was said by one S.I.B. investigator to be, 'Not worth the paper it is written on.' Another source said it was very good, because it captured everyone in the

269

aftermath before the team had time to think about what they were saying, they just reported. There were many errors in the content of the report, but there was still a lot of confusion at the time. What it boiled down to was how did it happen and what happened?

The facts were sifted through and put into order later by the S.I.B. investigation and the following Board of Inquiry. The S.I.B. had no doubt that there were parties to blame for the accident and even a TAIT member told Bev when she was researching for the legal case that the team should never have left the U.K.

Conrad wrote and submitted his Post Exercise Report, usually freely available, I was never allowed to read it. It quickly became 'Restricted Pending Inquiry'. Though said to make interesting reading, the team will not see it. That was as far as I got in obtaining a copy. Bev tried again and again and as mentioned earlier her final attempt was as late as 2013 but the Army Records Office wrote back to her saying that they had no record of it and that nobody had heard of The Summit to the Sea Expedition.

Bev found out that not only was Conrad not qualified but that most of the team had not done their summer mountaineering nor winter mountaineering qualifications. Also, that nobody in the team apart from Martin and Conrad had a kayaking qualification. The only two that went to Scotland, when it should have been the whole team only did the summer qualification because there was no snow. The team was not safe to be on the mountain and that they certainly weren't safe for the kayaking. She asked me when I'd found all this out. Obviously we knew about the failing of the JSMEL (W) from Conrad's letter but I told her it had been around the same time, a few weeks after arriving back home. She sat thinking for a moment.

Bev told me to sleep with one eye open because this whole thing stinks now. I tried to reason with her. She argued that if I was not getting information but they were then they could say and do anything before the Inquiry. I protested that Conrad wouldn't just dump me in trouble as he had nothing to blame me for.

She said, "I'm not talking about Conrad alone. Who rubber-stamped the exped. before it went to Colonel Harrison at 4 Div? We need to speak with Chris Cotterill."

"Why does he need to be involved?" I asked

"Because, if they try to make you culpable for what happened in any way from any angle, you don't even have your gammy ankle to stand on."

Was she really that paranoid? I thought it was only me getting unnecessarily suspicious. She kissed me on the forehead and had a self-confident grin on her face as she turned her back on me and strode out of the room. She went to the kitchen and made lunch. Chris Cotterill was our solicitor and thought it an interesting twist but said I had little to worry about. He would very much like to attend the Inquiry with me when it started. We agreed this would be a good idea. Bev's paranoia was starting to rub off onto me.

He asked if we were still in touch with Lightwood, (Conrad) and Bev said no, we had been up until a little while ago. We had received a letter from him telling us how much trouble he was in and that he had phoned and asked me for a 'positive' winter mountaineering reference and although I was friendly with him at the time, I couldn't give him the reference he was after.

Chris was of the same opinion as the Investigation Team member he had been in touch with. He said I had done the right thing and that I could have ended up in serious trouble because that reference would have been used by Conrad at the Inquiry and all the evidence would contradict my reference. I would have no credibility left, especially in the mountaineering world. I did say that Conrad had not asked me to do anything under-hand at all, he simply asked for a reference.

At this point Chris asked us if we had heard of the 'No win, no fee.' scheme. His firm were licensed for it and it would save us a great deal of money. He was quietly confident that we had a strong case. We declined, as we didn't know enough about the system. He said it didn't matter, as we could sign up for it at any time. The legal bills piled up at alarming speed but Chris wasn't troubled at all if we only put in a little here and there. It was a lot here and there to us but if we were successful, we would get it back later.

271

Adventure trainers are not in the forefront of promotions boards and often go up the ladder slowly if the stay in that role for a long time. I also had my spot of bother in Canada a few years ago to recover from but it came as no surprise to find that after all the media coverage, I was promoted. I can't say that I wasn't pleased, it didn't matter to me either way. My job would stay the same. I had already done the job of yet another rank above me in Scotland, so apart from the pay rise it made no difference to me. I had ceased to care about many things but the money was helpful for keeping the boat.

Chapter 20 - Gym Queen

Our request not to go to the Guard's depot at Pirbright in Surrey was declined. We packed, made lists, labelled and cleaned and Bev filled in and painted over picture pin holes and cleaned electrical sockets with cotton buds. She carefully washed light bulbs and replaced them and stripped the cooker into so many pieces it took us an age to find where all the screws went. She covered everything with cling film and paper and the removal men were only allowed to collect everything from the garage until she had laid the paper path around the house so they didn't mark her shampooed carpets. This had been the routine 9 times in the past 16 years and it wouldn't be the last. The house was immaculate but it stank of bleach. Most clean quarters do and we hoped our next house would be clean at least.

We arrived in Brookwood, Surrey an hour or so before the removal lorry. The house was tiny, it was the smallest house we had ever had. It looked scruffy and a bit tired. There was no garage but there were some on camp but there was a long waiting list. We wondered what we were going to do with all our gear.

We had the week to sort out the house but we realised we had to hope the ceilings wouldn't fall in as we heaved and sweated getting repacked box after repacked box into the loft space. We had so much stuff crammed up there that we had to make sure we put the heaviest stuff over where we thought the walls were below. We were laughing about it really, physics should have brought the whole lot down into the rooms below. We had no idea how the ceilings didn't bow and crack.

There was a tiny shed at the front that we could fit our bikes into if we stacked them on top of each other, (a recipe for a tantrum) and a couple of boxes we had to wrap in tarps that stayed in the garden.

The children had no school. They just wouldn't take them anywhere. They had weeks and weeks at home when they should have been placed somewhere. In the end, Rhys got into the local Brookwood Primary School and Gemma went to her high school in Camberley some miles away. Gemma's school was a success but she got bullied sometimes on the bus. Rhys' school was appalling and he got stabbed with a pencil in the shoulder and the carbon tip snapped off under the skin by a boy who had been excluded previously. The headmistress back then said the Army kids were no better than gypsies. Elvy was a gypsy, her mother had been a traveller for many years until she finally settled in a house and Elvy was one of Bev's truest friends. Rhys got 'sick' at every opportunity. He took up karate and we carried on as the rest of the families did, making the best of a bad school system and cramped accommodation.

Gemma took up riding at the stables near Camberley and she made lots of nice friends. Rhys stayed close to home, made a few friends and kept his head down. He and Gemma were very close and seemed to become closer so that helped because even though Gemma was coming into her teens, they played together a lot. It wasn't so bad. One great thing for us was that Gary and Elvy, our old neighbours had been posted to Aldershot nearby so we could see them sometimes and Gemma could see their daughter Stacey.

The move here wasn't our idea of a good posting at first but it was working out. In the Corps, if you're an Adventure Trainer, you're a 'Woolly Hatter' and if you work in a Regiment then you're a 'Gym Queen'. The names could be a lot worse given some nicknames I've come across.

When I first arrived I had to go into camp for the introductory meeting with the Commandant. As one could imagine, the Guard's Depot has a reputation for elitism (and bullshit). It is the boot camp for the Household Division of Footguards; the Scarlet-Tuniced and Glossy Bear-Skinned School for the Extremely Polished who drill so immaculately outside the grand palaces of our esteemed capital city. They are also very tall infantry soldiers in times of conflict, (even without their hats on.) Bev's elder brother had been in the 2nd Battalion, Coldstream Guards and heard many stories of the 'killer' assault course here or how they 'drilled' so much that the tarmac on the parade square had to be re-surfaced every year, (that's bullshit too).

I had my current uniform on from my previous job in Wales, which was navy blue polo shirt, (a bit thin and worn out and the collar had gone a bit wavy) and navy blue mountain walking trousers, (a bit thin, faded and baggy at the knees). Bev had given me a pretty short and tight haircut ready for the C.O.'s interview. I suppose I did need to make an effort. My hair hadn't been long but it hadn't been this short in over a decade. I was unable to wear shoes because since the accident I was unable to get them on and I still limped.

I arrived at the Commandant's offices and a very polished, pressed and smartly-razor-edge-creased Drill Sergeant attempted to bring me to attention. Screaming out the time in perfect Guard's Depot fashion 'marched' me into the office, as if he were being constantly scalded in time to a swiftly paced metronome. "Luf, 'ight, luf, 'ight, luf, ight - halt!" I ambled in ignoring him utterly and instead of slamming my feet to a halt; I gently and casually brought my left Teva-sandalled foot across to meet my right. The Drill Sergeant's eyes nearly popped out of his face and his complexion grew deep red. I looked at him out of the corner of my eye and raised an eyebrow. I thought to myself, 'What a twat.'

The Commandant watched this little scene and grinned slightly to himself while he looked down at my file.

"At ease, morning staff, how are you?"

He already knew my problem from the records so didn't expect anything else. The Drill Sergeant was nearly popping and sparking next to me. I could almost see his nearly invisible Peter Pan shadow grabbing me around the throat and giving me a good kicking. I continued to ignore him and enjoyed it and went on with my meeting. It was quite formal, as it is a training establishment and the meeting didn't last long. It was the usual introductory routine. The Commandant seemed to be in-the-loop as to my needs and was prepared to be quite accommodating. He was also aware of my long back-ground away from formality and military uniform. He was pleasant and wished me success. It was a good start. However, his passing shot as I was dismissed was, "One more thing staff,"

"Yes Sir?"

"Get your hair cut."

"Sir!"

I went to work as the APTC Instructor, supervising a team of instructors and co-ordinating competitions, facilities bookings etc. I was right back where I started in Dortmund after I first passed in to the Corps from the Royal Engineers.

My immediate boss was a colleague from the P.T.School, Geoff Chapman. I was very pleased to see him because we always got on so well. We talked a lot and caught up with years of experiences since 'The School'. We had lots of gossip about the other guys we came across. I really enjoyed his company and was glad to have him around. He was very supportive throughout my posting and understood my mis-trust, though he hadn't experienced the same things that I had. He had chosen a different path and I was pleased such a really nice guy was doing well.

Bev and I attended just a couple of Mess functions at Pirbright. It was a pleasant enough Mess and much smaller than the Mess we had in Germany many years ago, which had long refectory tables, upholstered chairs and more Regimental silver adorning the tables than I have ever seen anywhere.

I attended one alone, as it was a members only and no partners function. My Mess dress was a red, cropped cavalry jacket with black lapels and high waisted, black trousers with a broad red stripe down the outside length of each leg. Also, dress shirt, black silk bow tie and 'bulled' (highly polished) Oxford, black shoes. Remembering that this was the Guard's Depot, I couldn't wear shoes. My hair had grown a bit since my arrival and my gym staff were ready to help. I turned up at the Mess having done my best to look presentable. I had to wear sandals with black socks. As I entered I heard one member say, "Who's that scruffy bastard?" Straight on my defence, one of my friends disappeared and came back a few minutes later with a roll of black 'gaffer' (duct) tape. He tore off several short strips and taped them over the front of my socks so that I had 'shiny' feet. I thought it was a great piss-take.

I seem to have been forgiven by the 'Guards' as by the end of the night, although I couldn't walk on my feet very well, I managed to have enough to drink to go into a handstand on top of a row of dining tables and 'walk' the length of them on my hands. I got home at 04:00hrs feeling quite triumphant, as Bev knelt down and undid my taped sandals and took them off. I sat swaying on the seat by the door and could only co-ordinate my mouth to say, "The cat wants to come in." Bev reached up from her kneeling position, pulled down the front door handle and the cat sauntered in rubbing her body against my legs as I tried ineffectively to pick the cat hairs off my trousers. Bev knelt there shaking her head and smiling at my attempts. All she had to say was, "I'll get you some paracetamol, don't try to get up the stairs by yourself".

Even though my job role was tortuous to me, it was a very good move medically, as I was close to Frimley Hospital that was staffed jointly by National Health Service, (NHS) and the Army. I also had a large medical centre on the barracks that I could go to without notice and my medical appointments could be attended because I now had staff under me again to cover my duties. I couldn't complain about any of them in any way. They were a really good crew and I liked them all. I warmed to them pretty quickly and we all gelled in work and socially.

We were also only an hour away from the boat at Hayling Island, so we could go there over many weekends and work on her. I settled in and went through my treatments and worked in the regiment. It was pretty dull but in other ways very good for me.

I finally had my surgery at Frimley, which was called an 'Evan's tendonesis'. As my sprain was a Grade 3 it had meant that there was a lot of swelling, and acute pain on weight-bearing. It had not been recognised for a very long time so it was quite messy in there.

An incision was made behind my lateral malleous or the big round bit that sticks out. There were more incisions made inside to get round the sural nerve, and the talofibular ligament is reached. This is where the foot is attached to the fibula. The anterior tissues are cut to allow access to the front of the ankle joint. The ligament that runs transverse is cut and opened out then after some more fiddling with sinews, the peroneus brevis tendon gets split length ways over about 5cm and after a hole is drilled through the lateral malleous, one half of the split tendon is threaded through the hole. The ankle is set in a neutral position and the half tendon now replacing the ligament was tensioned and secured. As the ligament was torn through, it could never heal and there was nothing else at that time to do with it. I was set in a cast and sent home with pain-killers and a lot of Temazapam to stop my muscles from stressing the area in the cast. That wasn't going to happen as it was too painful even to move my toes.

Chapter 21 - Inquiry

After the investigations finished, we waited for the inquiry to get under way. We made enquiries about it but heard nothing. Finally, we heard about the Inquiry just two days before I was called to add my testimony. We were pretty annoyed about it, as we had nobody to turn to for representation at short notice and our solicitor, Chris Cotterill was particularly cross about it.

He was in South Wales and told us it would cost us about £1,200 for the day for him to attend and at such short notice he would be unable to attend anyway. In his entire career, he had never been given such short notice nor been refused an opportunity even to submit for a postponement for a client's interview. It was extremely bad manners professionally.

The Inquiry would last a while, so he couldn't see why they couldn't interview me just a couple of days later and change the order that everyone was questioned. He would have been able to attend then. He knew we couldn't afford it and wrote and told the Board of Inquiry too. He also stated that the astonishingly short notice we had received was unacceptable. He wasn't surprised that he wasn't even given the courtesy of a reply.

We understood there was no way he could make it to Aldershot on such short notice, so we had to rely on the text of the interview. We wanted Chris there because we saw that Major Brack of the Intelligence Corps was on the Board and we knew he wouldn't be objective, in fact I found him to be the most partisan man I have ever worked with.

We knew that Major Brack was a friend of Edward Simpson and he, (Brack) did not like me at all. We had been posted together in Scotland and from the outset, he made my life as difficult as he could. Even the staff there wrote statements to our Commanding Officer at Grantown-on-Spey to complain about his conduct not just to them but to me. Nobody could understand why he particularly felt and demonstrated such a venomous attitude towards me.

I have kept a copy of the statement from one staff member who wrote about me and how Major Brack treated me in front of other staff and students. I was just glad to get out of there and get posted to Wales. I found him peevish and spiteful. I knew there would be no objectivity with him. I made my feelings and opinion clear but they weren't going to change the panel for me, I knew that. I just wanted them to know I knew he wouldn't be objective.

Carl was due to be interviewed the day before me, so he came to stay with us. I accompanied Carl and I sat in on his interview, which produced a surprised glance from Major Brack.

Carl came away feeling cheated. He felt that the questions were leading and he wasn't given the opportunity to answer in the way he wished. He had to give almost monosyllabic answers and was prevented from explaining the truth of the answer. He felt many of his brief answers could be misconstrued and manipulated. I could see why. There was no leeway to explain anything, as if they wanted the conclusion to head in one direction only.

He didn't get to say any of the things he wanted to tell the Board. He was flustered and frustrated when he came back to the house. Carl had remembered especially that Conrad had accused him of boiling the batteries in order to restore a charge in them. Not only had Carl not done this, he had never heard of such a practice. I too thought it sounded like fantasy to try such a hazardous trick when I first found out about it. I'd never heard of it either before the expedition. The first I had heard was when I was questioned by Jim from the S.I.B. back in Wales and he only asked if Conrad had boiled batteries, he didn't mention Carl at all.

It seemed to Carl that to Conrad it would be a reason not to have any live batteries with him when they all so badly needed a radio for the rescue after the first fall at 19,000 ft.

I don't blame Carl for feeling so despondent after that. It was a bit of a grim evening we had over supper and a few beers. I had seen the way the Board of Inquiry was being conducted. It was barely an Inquiry at all. It was brow-beating questions to everyone. Team members and others involved in the background were interrupted, not able to put things into context and made to feel extremely uncomfortable. This is not what an Inquiry is supposed to be.

The next morning I got my 'Mufti' out of the suit cover, the black woollen blazer with regimental brass buttons and heavily embroidered, colourful P.T. Corps badge with its golden threads on the breast pocket, good quality, white shirt, grey flannels, one highly polished, right foot Oxford shoe and the regimental tie. Bev folded the left trouser leg back and yanked and forced it over my plaster cast as well as possible as I wobbled on the crutches with my toes exposed.

I arrived in Aldershot and entered the building and met up with many of the team that I hadn't seen since we departed Gatwick. It was great to see everyone. Some were glad to be there and hoped to have a chance to have their say and some were annoyed at being dragged into something they felt they didn't have much involvement with. Anyway, we were all glad to see each other. Steve Brown I remember was scathing and couldn't wait for his chance to tear the Army off a strip. He was not intimidated by the high rank uniforms everywhere.

The Inquiry room was laid out like a court room with the Board panel in front, various clerks, other officers and a chair set out for each witness. Major Brack looked as if he were going to enjoy it so I made sure I was going to as best I could but I still felt uneasy. It didn't trust this. Major Brack was introduced as the Subject Matter Expert.

We won't go down that path too far but he was no expert as far as any other instructor I know was concerned either military or civilian. He had compiled the Army Adventure Training Compendium so he had some work on paper but out on the ground was the most idiotically, reckless and immature soldier I have met of any rank. If Conrad had been misguided or foolish, Brack was off the scale. Adventure Training wasn't 'playtime' but that was how he treated it, an opportunity to pull dangerous stunts and show off to students. I just thought it was the icing on the cake and looked upon the entire panel from that moment with complete disdain and didn't attempt to hide my disgust at them or my temper. I knew I wasn't in the wrong so I dug myself in. If they could allow a man like that on a Board of Inquiry, it didn't mean a thing to me.

So, here was I about to have my future in mountaineering picked to pieces by the officer who hated me from the moment he stepped through the door in Kingussie three years earlier and had tried before to ruin my career with a report from him I later successfully redressed and discredited.

It wasn't so much Brack's attitude that bothered me, I am a MIC with over twenty years of climbing experience behind me. Major Brack had only fairly recently gained his Mountain Leader (Winter), (ML (W), which is a military qualification for low-level mountain walking. He had never done any serious mountaineering or had experience of altitude. Conrad, although he failed his JSMEL (W) had higher qualifications and an awful lot more experience than Brack. We didn't see how we could be questioned by someone who was less qualified and experienced by a very long way. We all, every member of the team thought it was flawed.

I was ready for a good forty-five minutes or an hour of being interviewed. I spent three hours being interviewed by them. I was assured that my conduct and the decisions I made would not be questioned. The questioning by the Board President and the Army Legal Branch representative went as I expected. Similar questions to the S.I.B. specific in places, short explanations here and there but unable to answer fully on very much at all.

Finally, came the ML (W) Subject Matter Expert, Major Brack, Int. Corps. and he took a hostile manner in the way he posed the questions right from the start. There were a few raised eyebrows as I glanced around the room at the tone he took. This was the Board of Inquiry not the Magistrate's Court or a Court Martial and he should have been brought back in line immediately but they let him run. I think some were as surprised as I was at his tone.

I have never been intimidated by this kind of conduct and fired everything back, including the way that he might be trying to use my qualification as a way of making me a scapegoat for an accident that was the Army's responsibility. He was really trying to nail me.

I had to reiterate my position on the team regardless of my qualification. The other Board Members accepted that I was neither the expedition leader nor the 2i/c. I shot back at Brack that I was there to advise and lead a rope, that's all. If my suggestions were not taken up by the Leader and 2i/c, it was for them to answer why. Nodding heads from others on the panel and Brack glaring at me, as if he wanted to leap over and grab me. I almost hoped he would. I thought he was making a fool of himself in front of his peers.

I threw everything back at him over and over with as much sarcasm and disdain as I was receiving. I threw it all back including having to train half the team with Johnny when we got there. I raised my voice almost to a shout. "If it was anybody's fault it was the person who allowed the team out of the country." This was met with sudden silence across the Board and a glance across to Brack from the President. There was a pause. I hoped they knew I was referring to Major Edward Simpson who must have signed off on Conrad's failure at JSMEL (W) and held back information from H.Q. 4 Div. It was heated enough to see we were fighting fire with fire on both sides. I think even now that they expected that I was going to point the finger at Conrad but he was only part of it and that wasn't going to happen.

When I was questioned about whether I knew that the team wasn't qualified to be there until they got to the glacier, Major Brack called me a liar. At the time it didn't register because we were so heated. Bev read it herself in the transcript. I had said "No"

Brack replied, "You did" and then carried on with the questioning. The comment from Brack was almost an undertone in its delivery and appeared to go unnoticed by the other Board members but it was there in black and white. The stenographer had got it. The recording had got it.

It wouldn't surprise me though if that page disappeared if it was ever questioned, along with other things that don't seem to exist anymore. I was disappointed that the other Board members allowed the remark to stand or didn't notice it as it slipped into the dialogue just as I didn't at the time. He was not allowed to do that, it was an Inquiry, not a disciplinary court, as I've said.

Bev was in an absolute rage when she read for herself what happened and as soon as we returned home she telephoned an old friend of mine at Glenmore Lodge for advice. She spoke with my friend there who assured her that my credibility in the mountaineering world would not be affected by the findings of a Military Inquiry. The Secretary of the Mountain Leader Training Board for the UK also said that it is unlikely that if I acted within the remit of my qualification, that I should not be worrying about my future. As far as they were concerned I was 'clean as a whistle and had done well in very poor and trying circumstances.'

It's maddening to know that even if someone is of no consequence to you any more, they can have the ability to get under your skin. I was annoyed at myself for letting Brack get under mine during the questioning.

Our minds were put at rest, as we are convinced that if Major Brack could find any means, fair or foul to implicate me in any way for being responsible for the accident, he would. We didn't trust him and we were now both fighting against a system that was set up to find the truth. I felt betrayed and was not happy with the A.P.T.C., my own Corps for allowing me to be thrown at an Inquiry like that. I was sitting amongst all the heroes of the PWRR with their gallantry awards and their hierarchy around them supporting them all and still, the PT Corps was very quiet, was I a goody or a baddy? The Corps still waited but it was too late for me now. I felt that I was somehow an embarrassment to them and I didn't see why I should have to prove otherwise now? I'd done my job.

To add to the fun, my transcript of the interview was not produced for signature. Everyone else had had theirs and approved it, signed it within a day or two at the most and was done with it. Mine was held back. I asked again why it wasn't produced after a week and I was told not to worry, it was being held by Major Brack, (for over three weeks).

Fortuitously, Steve Brown came to stay with us, as he was due to be interviewed the following week. The Inquiry interviews were adjourned for a good while, we didn't know why at first. Then crucially, Carl phoned to tell us that Conrad had left and was going to the Himalayas with Major Edward Simpson, the other Subject Matter Expert who had had serious loss of memory during the investigation of his part in sanctioning the expedition. Steve said that if they were as thick as thieves together, good friends then nobody will ever know what really happened. There was some damage limitation going on for Conrad Lightwood and Edward Simpson and they were probably contriving a 'slap-on-the-wrist' for Conrad as an outcome to satisfy everyone.

Steve had his interview, which was even more interesting. His contempt for Conrad had given him a new perception of the military. He was a man with nothing to lose, as he saw it at the time. He had lost his fingers, and he thought his future livelihood as an electrical technician and his Army career. Major Brack had no idea Steve was friends with me and had been staying with us on occasion. Steve told us that he found the opportunity to chat to Brack informally outside the conference room and to question Major Brack about his climbing experience. Major Brack, in the three weeks that he held my transcript, told Steve that he had recently been on a trip to the Himalayas and flew out on the same plane as Major Edward Simpson. We assumed at the time that Conrad, who was yet to be questioned by the Board was also present, as Carl had told us, though Brack would never mention Conrad being there.

So, we have presumably, Brack, a Board member and 'Subject Matter Expert, Edward Simpson, a Subject Matter Expert for the expedition and possibly Conrad, yet to be interviewed, all on the same plane and likely, though we can't prove it, my transcript from the Inquiry that was absent from 'Records' for the duration of the trip. Whether or not the transcript was on board, or a copy of it, it didn't look good. The timescale that they were away and my transcript was not yet available fitted together perfectly. It was an astonishing piece of information that this could happen.

Steve's and Carl's stories made us very wary. We just didn't trust any part of the system now. It didn't matter where the transcript was, we felt the three of them were talking just as we were but they were in a powerful position and we were nothing and on the defensive and shouldn't have been. I do firmly believe that the transcript was with them and they all had an opportunity to work their questions and answers for their parts in the Inquiry around it. It then occurred to me what a small world the Army is.

If the tale of my punching the Warrant Officer in Canada seemed irrelevant earlier in this tale it isn't. Brack and Simpson were on friendly terms, we knew that so it is likely that Brack knew from Simpson what I had done. However, on its own this should be no reason to have such venom for me on Brack's arrival in Scotland and would, indeed seem a tenuous connection.

It suddenly dawned on me that the Warrant Officer in Canada was also Intelligence Corps, the same as Brack. It is extremely likely that they knew each other and could have been friends too. He was only in Canada for one week and had to get back to the U.K., so there was some urgency about his visit. The reason it kicked up such a stink that I punched him wasn't just that I punched 'up the ranks' it was that he had to have several stitches in his forehead and spent three days of that one week in hospital.

In the P.T. Corps, it is feasible to directly know or know of a very high percentage of its members. The Intelligence Corps isn't that big either and especially as the ranks get higher, there are fewer and fewer personnel. Why wouldn't Brack and the Warrant Officer know each other? It didn't seem like paranoia now. It was very likely to be fact.

When I was called in eventually to read my transcript, it was after the time they would have all returned from the trip to the Himalayas. I was told to make any spelling or punctuation corrections, but not to alter the text in any way. We thought this odd. As my leg was in a cast from my recent surgery, it was too good an opportunity to miss. Bev asked if she could go in with me and wait, as she had to drive for me. The Legal Branch clerk said that she shouldn't really, it was strictly Martin only but to go ahead. We were very glad she did come in. She looked at it very slowly and in a different way to me. We read the text together, the wad of pages so thick; we thought we would be there all afternoon. Bev's memory is so much more reliable than mine and she concentrated intensely on the dialogue.

It was a frustrating experience and wondered why we were asked to do the clerk's job. We questioned twice what we were allowed to do with the text. Twice the answer was specific, spelling and grammar only. It was ridiculous, why would we be expected to correct that? There were empty gaps in the text of several words long that made important answers seem ambiguous. We hoped that the audiotapes were truer than what the stenographer had missed in the transcript but if the audio typist couldn't pick up what was said, why should anyone else be able to?

Bev couldn't believe what she was reading. The questioning even on paper was completely different in its tone when Brack was doing it. I, as usual didn't give an inch in any direction with anyone, probably reinforcing my reputation for being 'difficult'. Needless to say, I decided I would refuse to sign any of it and after an hour we had given up trying to correct anything. Whatever the findings of the Inquiry, I was confident that even if a finger was pointed in my direction, I had excellent grounds to redress. Bev agreed. Brack had been so hostile and it was so apparent on paper that we felt a lot better.

Bev told our solicitor, Chris that there were so many long spaces of dots in the dialogue, it barely made sense. They could do anything they wanted with it. It wasn't worth the time typing it up certainly, that was a spelling and grammar mess itself but had it hardly been worth the time we spent reading it.

The Board of Inquiry wouldn't have been a problem at all if Major Brack had not been involved. But, I had lost confidence in the system and didn't know whom to trust anymore. The opinions I hold of these people have only been confirmed by the Inquiry. There was one statement that confirmed it for us, and that was when Conrad and Carl were back at the regiment following the Inquiry interviews and everyone was awaiting its outcome and reports. Conrad turned to Carl and said. "I hate that Spooner; he's ruined my life!"

According to one senior officer Bev spoke to about the Inquiry, he said it was Lightwood who had ruined my life. Conrad after all had a lot of sympathy following the Inquiry, he had his career and his body intact. He would probably be dealt with summarily and be allowed to get on. There was certainly going to be no reason for him not to do further expeditions and it is unlikely to delay any promotion much.

I shrugged at this and it didn't bother me drastically. I was always conflicted about how I had felt about Conrad. He was a likeable chancer in some ways and made incredulous decisions in others but he was still younger than I was and still had plenty of time ahead of him. I completely understood how Carl and Steve must feel about him. I didn't hate him but I wouldn't help him now.

We weren't looking for anyone to get nailed for this, we didn't care about that. We just didn't want to be blamed ourselves. Carl, Steve and I kept in touch and waited to find out what was happening. Carl and Steve heard nothing for a while. Quite a long time later, I didn't know how long, a couple of months I think, I heard that I had been completely exonerated and that general opinion was that I had done very well. It was a relief but it was something I already knew and I felt a bit flat afterwards.

Geoff Chapman, my boss who had been my friend from the start of my posting never wavered and was pleased that that part was all over for us.

Carl came to stay again and showed us a clipping from a local newspaper that told how Conrad had been fined £750 for negligence for not taking batteries with him on summit day. He had got off extremely lightly, as expected. We later heard that he had been given a Regimental tie to show he was back in favour with everyone. We did have a bit of a giggle about that bit. That's more than could have been said for the three permanently injured who were trying to redirect their whole lives as they prepared to leave the remnants of their active careers and livelihoods in the photo albums.

The Board of Inquiry findings were supposed to be completed by the end of February 2000, almost two years from the expedition however, the Post Exercise Report (PXR), had not been asked for during the Inquiry, as they had amazingly 'forgotten to consider it'. It had already been withheld for the Inquiry.

The PXR is usually a freely available document and all team members usually get a copy. However, due to the MOD's concerns about the litigation that has followed the expedition, it was still classified, 'Restricted - Inquiry' so hardly anyone has seen it or knows any of its contents. Bev spoke to a TAIT member who told her that they, (The Army) would bury it as deep as they could as it was sensitive to litigation. There was no way we would see a copy until everything was settled and it was published freely. He was proved to be correct. So two, three, four, five years after the accident, the saga continued.

Bev was very lucky to persuade the officer involved in sanctioning the expedition to allow her to interview him on my behalf. Colonel Harrison seemed to her to be greatly disappointed by the turn of events and I don't blame him.

Even when she questioned him directly about the accident he refused to confirm that Conrad or Edward Simpson had deliberately withheld information from him. She and I thought it was loyalty to post and his ethics in the extreme to deflect her questions of two men that between them could have ruined his career. He did not have any loyalty to them as individuals on a personal level.

The way she built the picture up, it seemed that Conrad had lied and withheld information from Colonel Harrison and Edward Simpson had left him, (Colonel Harrison) to take all the responsibility. Regarding the mystery of the Conrad's PXR he too said it made interesting reading but was now restricted and was confident that nobody will see it, ever. That confirmed from the 'horse's mouth' so she moved on. He seemed to have little sympathy for Conrad and regretted that his actions had ruined the careers of three men. I did understand up to a point why Conrad wanted to do what he did, I just don't understand why he took it so far.

Colonel Harrison was right for the job he did and was very good at it. He had a real empathy for Adventure Training and gave very convincing statements regarding its relevance to military training. He said "It makes soldiers more robust by putting them at risk. There is an element of risk to every single Adventure Training expedition, there has to be by definition. To be able to put soldiers at risk safely we run what is called the Joint Services Adventure Training Centres (JSATC's) where instructors go to be trained to whatever level is appropriate at the time. It is a very good, very comprehensive scheme and it's all laid out in a publication called the 'JSB 419', which covers every single level of instructor qualification. In addition it lays down the remit at every level for expeditions. If a guy goes on a Mountain Expedition Leader (Summer) course he has to have done certain other things in order to do that course in the first place. When he comes off that course, he is quite clear in his mind what he is able to do and that is laid down in black and white."

When Bev asked him about Conrad failing his Joint Services Mountain Expedition Leader (Winter) course, JSMEL (W). He told her what he had told Conrad before he went to Ballachulish. He needed the qualification to be a rope leader or he must find someone else, it was as simple as that. The report of his failure had not been passed to him. It appeared to us that the communication seemed to grind to a halt at Tywyn in North Wales with Major Edward Simpson and as little as possible got through to 4 Div. in Aldershot.

4 Division alone deals with between 400-450 expeditions a year from low level walking or dinghy sailing in the U.K. to the big overseas expeditions like Summit to the Sea. Around 1/3 are very simple expeditions. These include individual expeditions where an individual person is going off to join another expedition. To make sure that person is properly accounted for, they are counted as a single expedition, so that in its own right counts as 'one'. In addition to that they have the level II, which is still very simple but will be multi-activity challenging pursuits and camping, that sort of thing. The level III expeditions are voluntary and again cover about 1/3 of all the expeditions. The UK expeditions can be dealt with pretty quickly as we have access to all the information that we need. There are greater problems with overseas expeditions with the visa, access, politically sensitive areas and permissions."

Bev asked about the coffers available for the expeditions bearing in mind that 4 Div contributes 1/3 of the funding for each one. We were astounded to hear that it was as little as £100,000 for all of them. Colonel Harrison had to spread his money very thinly.

Asked about the overseas exercises, he answered,

"I guess I deal with around 150 a year. Some, as I said are easier to deal with than others, some are very easy to clear because the Service Attachés in theatre are very cooperative. Others are more difficult. What we have now is a scheme in place where certain military qualifications are accepted to be the equivalent of the required civilian qualification. We have a scale of equivalent qualifications for example with the BCU (British Canoe Union) etc."

Colonel Harrison clearly didn't want to be drawn on the matter of the expedition and Inquiry but he did volunteer that the Inquiry had been an unpleasant experience for him. He is a fair man and could do nothing more than go by the book regarding any of Conrad's future expeditions.

Bev came away admiring Colonel Harrison for his candour, honesty and professionalism and felt very sorry that such a personally nice bloke had been dragged over the coals for others' slippery dealings. I had known of Colonel Harrison before and heard nothing but good of him from everyone. He also reassured us that the findings of the Board of Inquiry would seal any of these kinds of loopholes in the future. Bev knew I would be pleased that there was someone else out there that held the same opinion and it was not my own paranoia. I was torn between my loyalty to a system that had seen me through a career I loved and the mistrust I had come to experience in the past few years.

Chapter 22 - Moving On

I found myself under the wing of a Brigadier in Aldershot who helped me start to come to terms with what I felt was a betrayal by the PT Corps. I felt they had left me utterly unsupported at the Inquiry and had kept an uncomfortable distance since the accident so long before. The dreams and night sweats continued in their intensity, as did many of the other symptoms. Some demon had definitely stowed away with me back to the U.K. and was going in and out of hiding.

I didn't expect anything much from the P.T. Corps anymore but had expected them to stand by me with at least some visibility and have some faith in my conduct during the expedition. I trusted almost nobody now and wouldn't even answer the telephone unless I really had to. I was aware that I had become anxious of contact with anyone outside my family and friends circle. I did everything I could to cut myself off from the Corps. I 'hated' them at the time as an establishment. I felt I represented them well, saved lives, not just on this expedition. Not a word, not that I expected it but if it came now, it would be too late for me. Nobody even wanted to shake my hand. It had been my impression that they had been suspicious.

I owed a lot of my good experiences to them but it was still my own hard work and dedication and the family making sacrifices at home at the end of the day that got me through them. I had also had a great deal, and I mean a great deal of support from my boss in Ripon, Tom Parker after the Canada incident and from my bosses in Wales Ray and Billy and Geoff in Pirbright. I could see that the medical support I got from my posting to Pirbright with all its nearby facilities was to help me but it rankled that the PT Corps officially kept their distance.

The Princess of Wales Royal Regiment walked off with the medals and glory, which they deserved to and all that wonderful publicity for them even though it was one of their own that had been instrumental in much of what happened and I felt the Corps buried its head.

It is a great pity that this happened because the APTC is not easy to get into. It develops instructors extremely well and there are many specialists doing a sterling job through the Corps education and opportunities for experience. It isn't all about sport, it has a great deal to do with developing the character and spirit of soldiers. They also work closely with rehabilitation and medical issues and are adept at dealing with injuries of all kinds to get people moving comfortably again. This is anything from being overweight or my sort of injury to amputees, head injuries where a soldier has to learn to co-ordinate again and burn injuries, there is so much they know.

My experiences in Adventure Training have been superb and I can't take that away from them but as a Corps it was 'cliquey' then, it was something one accepted. I also accept completely that this is not everyone's experience of them. It is mine. Bev and I are square pegs you see. We don't care for the ball gowns and silver service, although we don't disgrace ourselves if we had to attend and I don't think we were prepared for the competitiveness and ambition for success in a small Corps amongst so few, which of course had to include people who were friends and we understood that but it wasn't that easy. Of course, by its nature the P.T. Corps with its international sportsmen and women, Olympic medallists some of them, was competitive, we had to instil that drive in our staff and soldiers but it was still difficult to see friends contriving and driving for the same postings and promotions as their friends.

There were individuals of course that were falling over themselves to congratulate me on a job well done and wishing me well, I appreciated this more than they will know. It was reassuring and I needed that. They were genuine and full-hearted about it. Waiting for it from the P.T. Corps was like wanting approval from a father. The Corp kept quiet. I was torn between doubting myself and staying true to what I believe.

Nobody in an official capacity in the hierarchy uttered a word. They were waiting for the outcome of the Board of Inquiry we were told. That made me still worry in case someone had implicated me in something but I didn't know what it could be. I had already been told I was exonerated but the findings were still not released. I had nothing in writing. By the end of the Inquiry, it would be too late.

"If they can't take a chance on me after all the years I've put in then I'm not interested." I was upset and Bev said she didn't blame me but "Wasn't I looking into it a bit too deeply? I was left in the dark and we were left to deal with everything ourselves.

There was only one APTC officer I remember who took me to one side, I think it was in a corridor at the Inquiry. That doesn't matter but I clearly remember that he shook my hand warmly and told me, "Very well done staff, you were right at the cutting-edge of Adventure Training." I really appreciated that and he phrased it perfectly for me to appreciate it. I was very grateful for that much at least, even if it was behind the scenes so to speak. I only wish I could remember who it was. I want him to know it gave me some comfort during a dark time in my mind. Where were the ones that I knew?

I met the Brigadier Wickenden as part of my medical treatment. The operation on my ankle seemed to have worked out as well as it could have and was grateful to the surgeon for giving me a bit more stability. I was in constant pain or discomfort but that could be managed. I knew it was a permanent state. I was now having a different kind of medical treatment.

Brigadier P.D.W. Wickenden M.B., B. Chir., F.R.C.Physc., (474160) late R.A.M.C., former Director of Army Psychology was a completely different area of expertise. I knew I was extremely fortunate to have been given even 5 minutes with this man but he was now my regular counsellor, therapist, confidant and doctor.

He talked to me of the accident, asked about the family, my general well-being and seemed to spend a great deal of time getting to know me as in what type of person I was. I also got to know him as a gentle and calming personality, the big drawback was that he was the Brigadier, although retired, and therefore the military, not to be trusted. Why couldn't I overcome this distrust? It was a privilege to be here and I couldn't let go of this wariness.

Bev met the Brigadier on my second visit with him. He was friendly and calming to her also. I seemed to say little and felt distracted for the two hours we were there. On many subsequent visits with him there was a marked improvement. I felt much more comfortable with him and felt able to draw out more detail in my problems or what I thought them to be at the time.

We were astonished to hear him tell both Bev and I that he had been a consultant psychiatrist at 'rather a high level' (modest description for 'top'), for over 30 years and had dealt with soldiers from the Northern Ireland troubles, the Falklands Conflict and the Gulf and in that time he, personally had only diagnosed and treated what he found to be just 5 genuine cases of Post Traumatic Stress Disorder. We thought it was more common but there are varying degrees of it. He went on to say that out of those 5 in 30 years, I was one of them. He expected it to be chronic so he couldn't give us any good news at this level on how it could fade or if it would always stay with me to some degree.

It explained a great deal and we took the treatment more seriously. I reluctantly took my meds and changed them and took them diligently again. The problem here was that I felt horribly stigmatised. I hated the idea that the medical centre at the Guard's depot would know about it and that I would have to keep going to them for my meds. I almost had the excuse I needed to be bad tempered and unreasonable if I wanted and to most of all to shut myself away from everyone. The problem with this aspect is that I wanted everyone to know how 'normal' I was and my many medical appointments were all to do with my ankle. This put more pressure on with the pretence.

That Christmas, 1999 was awful. I was in a crisis about my career and my health. Everything around me went from irritating to intolerable, even my family. I was angry, so angry at everything that happened. I couldn't bear the family being upset about me or the attention and because of me with my increasing temper and frustration but it was overtaking me. I felt a kind of freedom in the crystal clear thinking the emotion gave me. I had a kind of reasoning behind my behaviour that was perfectly clear to me but to nobody else, I could barely tolerate anyone at all around me.

Christmas day Bev ran around the Country Park as she had done the morning she found out about the accident. I had been sullen and unresponsive to all the fun and excitement that had been going on with the children that morning. Pa had noticed the change in me as soon as we arrived. He said that it was if I had to try the entire time just to be civil to everyone. I barked at Ma a couple of times until Pa had to tell me "That'll do!" I was angry and feeling guilty about it all and just wanted to isolate myself altogether.

I had been prescribed medication to help me sleep, something to kick me back into a regular pattern as the previous medication didn't suit me. Bev had put them into her handbag, which in turn got left at the Welcome Break service station on the M40 near Oxford. She had cancelled the cards in her purse right before Christmas, which was even more inconvenient but it didn't help the medication problem. I was furious. She knew all along this wasn't me but sometimes she was emotionally exhausted and weary of it. Today was one of those days. She didn't want to come back, she ran on.

In the Country Park just along the lane from where Ma and Pa live it was cold, overcast and very muddy. On a path above the fishing pond she went over on her ankle very badly. She heard a crunch and she felt as if a cold liquid had been poured down the side of her shoe. She knew she'd done something but in what she called her self-pitying tantrum she ran on. Her anger with me kept her going. She ran out of the park, up the steep gravel steps, up the steep, narrow lane and down into the next village of Cheddleton.

The bells of St. Edwards on Hollow Lane were ringing out calling people to church. She felt suddenly comforted by the sound and ran down past the church. She ran along the towpath of the frozen canal and back towards the bottom of the garden at Wall Grange. She paused at the gate to the iron bridge that crosses onto the land there and braced herself to come back inside. She got back to the house, showered, changed, tarted up her face and hair and stomped defiantly into the kitchen to start the cooking.

She was wearing high black shoes and as she stood there peeling swede and carrots she felt the pain creep into her ankle. She blamed me for it of course. If I hadn't been pulling a 'moody', she wouldn't have gone running. Everything was turning into my fault.

By the beginning of January we were back home and I went to work. Bev phoned Brigadier Wickenden to tell him what had happened to the medication so there had been a break in the treatment and that things were not good. In fact they were pretty bad. He asked to speak with me. She told him that I was at work and he was very stern with her for the first time. She was told in no uncertain terms to get me back home at once and if anyone had issue with it, they were to speak with him directly.

She phoned to tell me that Brigadier Wickenden had given an explicit order for me to return home. I told her that I couldn't. I'd at least have to wait until lunch-time. She just said, "No, he means right now. It was an order."

That was that really. I never went back to work in the Army again.

After months of therapy of all kinds, physiotherapy, Headley Court Rehabilitation Centre, pain-management, surgery, different pain management, psychiatric appointments, cognitive behaviour therapy and sleeping tablets, it was all over. It was really hard for me to be at home and idle, so sometimes I went to the boat. Bev would leave me there all week alone sometimes. Whatever I did it was in almost complete isolation. I couldn't dig myself out. I didn't understand it. I was utterly ashamed of it. I was determined that nobody should ever know, even decades after. I did spend some weeks at home with Bev and we enjoyed the time together for the most part but there were lots of appointments of all kinds. All anyone was ever allowed to know for years and years was that it was my ankle.

Bev wondered at the time if she would ever get me back. I had a hidden dilemma with what had happened on the mountain, which was exacerbated by the mistrust around me after I got back. I didn't know if Bev and I would ever be the same again and sometimes I wasn't really bothered about it. Other times I didn't want us to be apart at any time of the day or night.

Bev too shut the world away. She had got to the end of her rope with it all, including my temper. I came back from the boat and went for an appointment with Brigadier Wickenden again and then after a day or so at home went back to the boat for another week or two. I begun after a period to feel better in myself, to sleep a little better on occasion and Bev responded very positively to the change. We attended the Brigadier's appointments together and soon were communicating in a way we had never done before.

There was a tiny light in the distance and we were struggling towards it together. Several weeks later I went for another appointment with him. I liked the appointments, they unravelled me. He was a really lovely man. Very gentle and very bright, very fatherly and astute. He was also very funny and used gentle humour when he found it appropriate. I went on my own this time. Bev waited in the car. When I came out again, I said "Just call me Mr. Spooner!" I smiled at Bev and she burst out laughing when she realised what I meant. She pulled out of the parking space teary-eyed but happy. We had no idea what was going to happen to us. The Army had been our lives for so long, we didn't know how to move ahead on our own at first.

It was relief that everything was over or so I thought. I was coming into a new world that I wasn't prepared for. Bev was more than ready. She was worn out with Army life now. I was to be medically discharged. I was an Adventure Training Instructor and Physical Training Instructor in the P.T. Corps and I had ankles that wouldn't let me run for a bus. I was to be an ex-soldier, a veteran. We had mixed feelings as we drove home. It was the end of everything I had known all my adult life, before even, as I had joined as a Junior Leader at 16 years old, barely 5ft tall. This really was going to be new.

The medical discharge process didn't take very long and there was a lot of information we had to take in. We were on the brink of losing everything we owned after all we had gone through with solicitors fees and borrowing money to cover a bit of them. There was a change in me with the family. I was warm and open again, patient and approachable again. I could be chaffed without taking offence. I felt I was coming back, at least from time to time. The first thing 'Mr Spooner' did was grow a beard.

Carl wanted to thank me for what I had done on the mountain. He had said it over and over and didn't need to, I knew how he felt but now he came up with an idea that I couldn't refuse. Carl offered to pay for me to take me back to Talkeetna to shake the hands of our rescuers. I jumped at it.

We flew out to Los Angeles first, where Carl was to meet up with a documentary producer called Tom Beardmore. I went along not knowing what to expect. Bev sent her 'Dictaphone' along with me in case I met George Clooney, (who is apparently a friend of Tom's). She didn't want just an autograph, she wanted his voice too! Sadly, she heard from Steve Wright on the radio that George was just flying into the UK and was to be interviewed by Steve's side-kick presenter, Janie-Lee Grace. Hey-Ho!

Tom's place was eventful enough, he had a barbeque party, which was attended by popular Hollywood people and lots of lovely girls. I tried to be gallant and offered a couple of girls a drink. They wanted a beer, so off I trotted with Carl to the kitchen to get the beers out of the fridge. With a beer bottle in each hand I strode out through the doorway ready to impress, hit the screen door that I couldn't see for the sun and knocked it straight off the frame. It made such a clatter as it came down with me stumbling over the top of it, trying to keep my balance. The thing was, it didn't land on the floor. It hit a large shrub by a wall that dropped down to the lawn below. I staggered over the top of the frame, stumbled over the shrub and dropped off the wall on the other side and landed on the grass.

The whole place was silent and all eyes were on me in disbelief. Trying to compose myself, I stood up, with the beer bottles still in my hands walked over to the embarrassed girls who were shrinking in their seats and announced, "I'm the entertainment." Nobody smiled or laughed. They looked away hoping I would vaporise. I slunk off to the kitchen where Carl was lying on the floor unable to stand or speak, tears streaming out of his eyes. I shrugged and giggled, then fell about laughing myself when I turned around and saw the state of the veranda and the shards of timber and ripped screen fabric that were all that was left of the screen door. We weren't invited back. We felt like 'Dumb and Dumber.'

We flew on to Anchorage and met up with Margrite again. She was the same as ever and very pleased to see us. We travelled on up to Talkeetna and went around looking for Roger, Scott or anyone else who may be around. To our surprise, a lot of people still recognised us years on. Lots of people waved or shook hands. I discovered Roger sitting on the edge of the boot of his estate car (station wagon) eating his sandwiches. Roger was very pleased to see us. I was very grateful to be able to shake his hand long after the events and say a real 'Thank you'. We went back to the Ranger Station for a while and chatted about things. I wished, ungraciously that I could stay right there, as Carl wanted to move on after a while. I felt quite at home there and enjoyed being in Roger's company. I felt we could have swapped a life-times worth of stories

I discovered that Conrad had been making enquiries and indeed wanted to work as a volunteer Ranger himself. Roger reassured me that it wasn't going to happen. Carl met up with C.C., one of the nurses from the hospital who spent so much time and effort on him. They were to meet for a beer later but something went awry with the trip and sadly they missed the reunion. I would dearly have loved to have driven up to see Jay Hudson but that didn't happen either, I was here on Carl's itinerary and I was grateful for that, so I hope I can thank everyone through this story.

Scott Darsney who worked hand in hand with Roger on that epic weekend, Liz, Pete and all the others that worked so hard for us are often thought of and maybe one day we can have the privilege of shaking hands with them.

Jim Hood who did such an extraordinary job in flying in those appalling conditions to bring us supplies and finally rescue us is fondly thought of too and we were really happy with the news that he had been awarded the 1998 Trimbel Award for helicopter pilot of the year. Apparently, he is the only pilot to have won it twice. Bev would love to meet them all but fears she would just blub through the whole thing and embarrass them all.

We told Carl and Steve the news about the medical discharge. They were pleased for us. Steve's case against the MoD was on-going at the time as was ours. Carl had given in on his. He just wanted to move on in life. He got engaged and went on holiday to Australia. We heard from him later that he married Jane so we couldn't be happier that life is going great guns for him. Later we heard they had a family. Life does move on. We hope he has put the mountain behind him.

Steve was progressing with his career and taking on more courses. He did a tour of Sierra Leonne and was hoping for promotion. So, El Gato had managed to salvage his career afterall. He is a sound guy and had bought a little house to renovate. That was all good too.

As part of my Army Resettlement I was allowed a full nine months and the maximum financial allowance for tuition and accommodation for a residential traditional boatbuilding course in Lyme Regis in Dorset by way of an attempted career change. I lived away during the week and I returned to dreaded Surrey at weekends or the family came to stay with me. Lyme Regis was gorgeous. Refreshing, relaxing and CIVILIAN. We loved all our weekends there.

I was paid my end of service entitlement by the Army, which went down on all the debts we had built up from the boat and the aftermath of the expedition. We were made homeless due to the fact that we were no longer entitled to live in Army Quarters. We scoured the South West coast for social housing so that I could continue in boat building. We couldn't get anything, as we had no connections in those areas. The house prices in the West Country were far too high for people like us. Anyway, we enjoyed the visits around there.

We looked at Hastings with Bev's family connections and after a brief visit, decided – 'Not a chance!' it was big, noisy and no place to bring up our kids after so long in rural areas although I hear it is improving rapidly. So we applied to the Staffordshire Moorlands Council. After a few months, we had to give up the Army house, as we no longer had the salary and the non-subsidised rent and were on our way back to Longsdon to live with my parents until we could find a house to rent somewhere.

We were officially homeless and jobless. Six weeks on and we were still out of work with our belongings in storage and living out of suitcases. We eventually rented a shell of a house, no spare money at all, no job and an increasing sense of despair again. Bev took a job getting up at 04.30hrs in the morning to get to work by 06:00hrs to clean toilets in a factory and in the evening stack shelves in the Co-op. Bev got anxious about the money sometimes but we were as happy as larks.

In time we heard that we won our case against the MoD but would have to wait for who knows how long for them to settle any compensation payment, it could be a year or two. We both got jobs as IT Trainers to fill the gap and made our plans to move on. Teaching Microsoft packages all day was so alien to me. I stepped out of the IT centre after a near death experience of being sucked into a computer screen – it was so boring and unfulfilling I couldn't cope.

We got back on track with our finances so the suit and tie came off and I finally got the remainder of my 22 year service retirement payment from the Army and a small pension, so we bought Wall Grange, the derelict pumping station and the surrounding land at Ma and Pa's with a plan to run an underground diving centre. If I can't climb up, I'll dive down. We still needed to earn a living. We did that, ran a country cafe where Bev had to learn to cook properly, quick sharp and ran that with the diving for about 8 years. I somehow ended up in arboriculture through my old school pal, Rozzer on the side at the same time. We did anything we could to bring the pennies in. When Rozzer left to live and work in New Zealand I thought I'd get the rest of my arboriculture 'tickets.' Before I had completed them all, I had a truck and chipper and a start-up load of kit including chainsaws and climbing gear. This was 2007.

The climbing systems are similar to mountaineering and we ran a small tree surgery company for about another 8 years with Bev as my groundy and when Rhys was old enough, he worked with us too and sometimes Gemma and Matthew, her then fiancé. During that time I was asked to shadow arboricultural training courses as an assistant instructor then and instructor. Before I knew it I had folded the 'Tree Surgery' side and was an industry instructor and assessor. The diving and country cafe closed and Arboriculture Training and Assessments became our business. I work in the forests or sometimes travel the U.K. to different centres for training and assessing and Bev and I do the occasional industry inspections of climbing kits, Lifting Operations and Lowering Equipment Regulations, (LOLER). We got our licenses for this a few years ago. The course content would put a glass eye to sleep but it's useful knowledge for us with a climbing background and a very old boat with lots of rigging to keep in good nick.

The kids grew up just great. We are grand-parents and in-laws now. Our old boat Last Freedom was dismantled a few years ago and we got our Royal Yachting Association qualifications. We learned to sail traditionally on the Pilot Cutter Amelie Rose and made very good friends along the way. I had wanted to sail for decades and now Bev was keen, especially after so many summers with our friends Kev and Marney who live in Cowes and are sailing crazy, we were away!

We had already bought a stunning old Cornish fishing boat in 2014, which was built in 1903. She is on the Historic Ships Register and we spent 2 years on an initial restoration, which continues. We sail her short-handed with two of our dogs aboard, enter the 'Classic' regattas with big plans for big passages. We made a 2nd life sailing out of or just bobbing about on the Helford River near Falmouth with friends coming along or other river users rowing, paddling or sailing up for a chat. As with all old wooden vessels, she will always need lots of work but that suits us.

We have a social life there that sometimes overtakes us and we love the wilds of West Cornwall. Cornwall has been good to us and the people are very open and friendly. We enjoy the ease of the Helford River Sailing Club and we enjoy our times with our friends that live aboard in Gweek at the top of the river. We have friends near Penzance we met in Longsdon, who we don't see enough and helped us get to grips with the boat on our first trips out. We take our dogs and they love it. They were born on a boat so we can't keep them out of water. We spend nearly all our time in between work in Staffordshire, family visits, sometimes catching up with our friends who used to live in the village and moved to the city and going to the boat.

My lust for travel is partially satisfied by an outfit I mentioned earlier, Explore Trees, who facilitate conservation projects world-wide. I have had a few trips to South Africa, the Bijagos Islands off West Africa and to Brazil, literally working with birds and bees and trees. The people I work with are my friends. I couldn't be luckier.

The years since the accident have been spent trying to stay as busy as possible. Years on, my ankle has recently had to have more surgery. Scraped clean, peppered with tiny holes to try to encourage new cartilage growth. I may not be able to walk far or climb mountains with my re-strapped and reconstructed cartilage. But I can't get away from ropes and clinking climbing gear.

My little boy is a man and climbs up trees with a chainsaw too. He also rock climbs, disappears with a little expedition tent sometimes along with his friends and comes back for a visit to tell us he just went up 'such and such' in Wales as if he'd just popped to the shops for some milk. He makes forest shelters and fires, rigs up rope constructions of various kinds for fun and watches wildlife. He has been drumming since he was 11 years old and our neighbours are blessed by the sound of his 'Metallica' kit thudding and crashing its echoes down the valley. He hasn't decided where he's going or what he's doing. He goes with the flow and is very laid back.

Gemma and our son-in-law, Matthew have children of their own, run a gardening and arboriculture business and like us, like nothing better than to get their hands in the earth, stand in falling leaves and get constantly delighted by nature, wildlife and the outdoors. Rhys works with them quite often and they all love each other.

We don't have any cash to throw about, we don't live in a big, smart house or have a lah-di-dah car. We have a nice, very modest little business in a beautiful spot and I appreciate every day I am with my family. We have dogs, kids and grandkids and we are all close, an old boat, an old work van and each other all of which are in fairly good nick. That makes us extremely wealthy.

We still like the Adventure Training when we can get away for a couple of days here and there, just to keep us in practice for the future, mostly sailing now. I say even now that I have no regrets about going into Adventure Training or the expedition. There are many ways that I miss the Army, the Royal Engineers and the P.T.Corps and as an ex-soldier I always will.

We don't question why things happen on this roller-coaster ride anymore. Our fortunes are extremely good or extremely bad, just like everybody else. We are very rarely going through a stale patch. We just fight our way back up from the troughs so we are together at the top again. We don't really care about the twists and turns to come, they're not here yet. The ones behind us are too much of a strain to even bother trying to look back at. We learn from them and put them away.

Time does ease that strain and pain to the point where some great events eventually feel not so significant. We can only plan as far as we can see and when the next drop comes we won't be doing it on our own. Bev and I are in this together. (Except the Transatlantic solo sail I want to do in our boat, but don't mention it to the Mrs.)

Some bad and stressful events feel like they go on forever when you are in the middle of them but they really do pass. Just don't continue to live there if the past hasn't been kind. It does help shape us but we don't have to make bad experiences in the past be who we are. It is a choice to step away and leave it behind and live with what is happening now. You can walk out of a door and become whoever you want. It just needs a bit of work and commitment but soon becomes a habit and you can be, for the most part the person you wish to be.

We hope 'everyone' has moved on and that they remember how they did what they could at the time and that the world is lucky to have people like Roger Robinson and his team, Jay Hudson and Jim Hood and the engineers who built that fascinating and amazing little Lama helicopter. There were so many that did so much good. Total strangers wished us well and sent prayers, whether we believed or not, they did it anyway.

The Summit to the Sea team was:

Captain Conrad Lightwood - Continued career and later promoted, subsequent civilian career in adventure training
Captain Phil Whitfield - Continued career
Sergeant Martin Spooner - Promoted and medically discharged from service
Sergeant Johnny Johnston - Continued career
Corporal Gary Keep   (Gaz) - Continued career and later promoted
Corporal Carl Bougard - Medically discharged from service, lives and works in Guernsey
Lance Corporal Steve Brown - Continued career
Lance Corporal Nigel Coar - Continued career

Private Luke Mills   (Millsy) - Continued career
Private Ian Haywood   (Tory) - Continued career
    In the background:

Major Edward Simpson (APTC) Joint Services Mountain Training Centre Wales - Continued Career, Retired. Later became involved in adventure training advisory body.

Lt. Col. Harrison (PAT 4 Div) Aldershot - Continued career, we hope he retired very happily. Remained involved in rugby

Major Brack - Don't know and don't care

    In the United States:

Roger Robinson - Still in touch from time to time. Longest serving U.S. Park Ranger. Involvement in promoting mountaineering.

Jim Hood - Still send messages occasionally. Won more awards. Still flying!

Jeff Munroe – Survived and spent over a year recovering his speech and being able to walk unaided. He eventually returned to outdoor activities of all kinds, such was his energy and enthusiasm, in spite of his incredibly hard recovery from his injuries. The tragedy is that on the 22nd February 2001 at just 28 years old, he died in Mexico. It is said he was a man worth saving and he was missed by so many. I can't possibly do him justice here but I do remember our brief meeting and the very happy impression he made on me.

Billy Finley is doing well with a web and graphic design company and is still a very active climber in Denali National Park.

Denali will always be with us and so will all those involved but now that the worry and confusion is over, there is no bitterness. We often wonder how everyone is doing. We hope they all moved on happily. We never thought it would pass but it all did. There are still so many years left to work and play and things that will go right and go wrong but we look forward.

It is not the end.

"Climb if you will, but remember that courage and strength are nought without prudence, and that a momentary negligence may destroy the happiness of a lifetime. Do nothing in haste; look well to each step; and from the beginning think what may be the end."

— *Edward Whymper, <u>Scrambles Amongst the Alps</u>*

Acknowledgements

Our very special thanks must go to all the Rangers, guides, pilots, medics and other climbers who had a hand in all the rescues, we don't know who you all are but every little bit of help eased the operations, most especially to Roger who was so supportive and helpful with the editing of the story and to Jim whose story adds the most spectacular drama. Their efforts and bravery will always be appreciated by us.

I also must thank John Dyson who was a prolific author of his own works and contributing author to many well known magazines who advised and encouraged me to write the story and gave me a lot of helpful guidance. Always patient and helpful at the end of the phone. John passed away in 2012. R.I.P. John.

Thanks also to Nigel Williams of Glenmore Lodge in Aviemore for helpful advice and lots of reassurance and to our friend on the TAIT, who gave careful advice and reassurance also.

Big thanks to Carl Bougard and Steve Brown for their friendship and the interviews on a project that brought back painful memories for them. Brigadier (Ret'd) PD Wickenden, for all his help getting the Spooners back into the realms of normality. John Cousins and Captain Glynn Shepherd for helpful advice regarding the remits and policies and many thanks too to Zeb Spring for invaluable help, time, information and his friendship, also for his Extreme mitts he lent Martin for the mountain that helped prevent frostbite and that he let Martin keep. Noel Godfrey (formerly APTC and Welsh Rugby Team physiotherapist) for information and advice on a person we had no access to.

Thank you to Johnny Johnston and Phil Whitfield for being on the expedition, we hope we conveyed how much you did. Martin's special thanks go too to Sandy Sanderson, mentor, confidant and friend for so patiently and diligently passing on so much of his wisdom, experience and knowledge with gentleness and such good humour.

Thank you to Mike Wotton for taking such painstaking care and diligence in editing the book and for his good advice.

Also thanks to Martin and Beverley Spooner for sharing their experience and time.

To my family who wholeheartedly supported and encouraged me to continue with this work over a long period of time.

Sources

Various reference publications on Denali National Park, Climbing Guides for Denali and the U.K.

Medicine for Mountaineering, Acute Mountain Sickness, specifically cerebral and pulmonary oedema regarding Jeff Munroe.

John Krakauer, Into Thin Air, comparing the effects of AMS in behaviour and decision making abilities.

Roger Robinson, Head Ranger Denali National Park Service, (USNPS), Denali National Park. Technical advice specific to Denali, Roger's version of events. Also editing the book for accuracy and technical data.

Jim Hood, Lama helicopter pilot contracted by USNPS by Evergreen Aviation. Jim's version of events as related to John Dyson from donated notes and interview.

John Dyson, freelance author. Interviewed Jim and Roger in Alaska and many of the soldiers involved, where permitted. Donated all of his notes from the interviews in the U.S.A. and the British soldiers back in the U.K., timelines, all other notes regarding the expedition and advice after publication of his own works for free use. Worked for well-known publications and wrote works on tall ships, The Spirit of Sail, Columbus et al.. I acknowledge his valuable contribution, advice and an entire very enjoyable day of talking about sailing.

Staff Sergeant Martin Spooner, A.P.T.C., M.I.C, expedition technical advisor, rope leader on expedition. Involved in first fall of 300ft, Left injured and stranded at 19,000ft for four nights and three days. Assumed dead by day two. Provided lecture notes on technical Alpine climbing and mountaineering skills, cold weather injuries, first aid, Acute Mountain Sickness, (AMS) and medicines, weather and other technical advice. Interviews regarding the events.

Beverley Spooner, wife of Martin. Related the events at home, including experiences with investigations, medical treatments, Board of Inquiry and interviews with media. Conducted interviews of her own with many key, U.K.-based personnel. Collected and collated information for documentaries.

Corporal Carl Bougard, 1 Princess of Wales Royal Regiment. No mountaineering experience, part of the guided group for training. Partnered expedition leader. Not involved in falls but remained on ledge with Spooner and stranded. Assumed dead by day two. Lost parts of both feet to frost injuries. Contributed comprehensive written notes, interviews information and friendship.

Corporal Steve Brown, Royal Engineers, (AKA: El Gato'). No mountaineering experience, part of guided group for training. Member of Spooner's rope team. Instigated accidental first fall of 300ft. Involved in second fall of 1,500ft and other crevasse falls. Lost many fingers to frost injuries.

Lieutenant Colonel Harrison, (Ret'd) O.B.E. Former 4 Division Head of Adventure Training, Aldershot. (Serving 4 Div, S.E. England). Subject Matter Expert. Authorised expeditions and funding following correct completion and compliance of the requirements of Adventure Training Form, (Alpha), (ATFA). Interview on Army Adventurous Training policies and procedures and the value of adventure training in the armed forces. (Probably the easiest, most enlightening and informative interviews conducted for the book relating the system to the lay person).

Supporting documents lent or donated:
Army Adventure Training Compendium 1995, which provides guidance on all Adventure Training activities including blank templates of all documents required to be completed and submitted. Also contains an example of a completed 'ATFA'. This document ensures that all organisers and participants have the information required, not just recommended to work within the remits of their training and experience. All administrative requirements are covered for U.K. and overseas expeditions.

Expedition Information Summit to the Sea 1998. Expedition information, aims and objectives, team profiles, press release, expenditure forecast and other logistics and information. Mostly an 'Unrestricted' document doesn't just suggest but cites greater abilities and experience amongst the team members.

Special Investigation Branch, Royal Military Police – statement Staff Sergeant Martin Spooner. Statement of events submitted for investigation and subsequent Board of Inquiry. Questioning regarding the background of the expedition, the events during the expedition and knowledge of the team's experience.

United States Department of the Interior, Denali National Park Incident Reports x 2. Submitted by Head Ranger, Roger Robinson. 1 x 5 page report on Jeff Munroe and Billy Finley and 1 x 9 page report on the British Army, Summit to the Sea incident. This includes an accurate timeline that ties in with Spooner's diary entries. Report provides rescue details, personnel involved, services used and their own conclusions with the information they had at the time as to why the incidents occurred.

Letters, Handwritten by Carl Bougard and Conrad Lightwood

Photographs (if published) with thanks to Steve Brown, Margrite van Lakke, John Dyson and Scott Darsney. Front cover, shows Martin holding onto Carl, slung across his body on the 100ft short haul line under the Lama helicopter. Taken by unknown team member with Steve Brown's camera. Rear Cover if shown, shows Chinook flying into Ranger Camp at 14,200ft, again by unknown team member with Steve Brown's camera or maybe by Scott Darsney. All scanned from originals and/or processed from negatives donated to the author. All pictures credited correctly where possible.

Inset rear cover if shown, RAPTC cap badge.

Various U.K. national and local press stories.

GLOSSARY

AMS   Acute Mountaineering Sickness (Altitude Sickness)
APTC   Army Physical Training Corps.
ATFA   Army Training Form (Alpha), mainly concerned with any adventurous outdoor activities in the UK or worldwide from a simple ramble to extreme activity. It is pronounced 'At-fer'.
Mountaineering Qualifications in order both military and civilian:
UEL   Unit Expedition Leader
ML (S)   Mountain Leader (Summer)
ML (W)   Mountain Leader (Winter)
JSMEL (S) Joint Service Mountain Expedition Leader (Summer)
JSMEL (W) Joint Service Mountain Expedition Leader (Winter)
MIA   Mountaineering Instructor Award
MIC   Mountain Instructor Certificate
MoD   Ministry of Defence
MO   Medical Officer
HACE   High Altitude Cerebral Oedema
HAPE   High Altitude Pulmonary Oedema
PXR   Post Exercise Report
SIB   Special Investigation Branch (Royal Military Police)
TAIT   Training Accident Investigation Team
USNPS   United States National Park Service

Before the MIA, a JSMEL can be taken; this is pronounced 'Jes-mel'. Each qualification must be supported by a completed logbook with minimum criteria of experience in terms of time, breadth of experience, weather and terrain conditions and assessments. If an assessment is failed then a minimum time must pass before re-taking the assessment with the logbook further supporting extended training.   This list is typical of what would be expected in the profession at the time of the expedition.

Virginia Buchanan comes from an 'Army' family and has had some of her own experience of Army life on a part-time basis. She has a background of recreational outdoor activities, which include rock climbing, hill-walking and sailing. Professionally, Virginia has worked in systems analysis and quality assurance administration, alongside creative works as an artist, illustrator and writing short children's stories under a nom de plume. Virginia Buchanan lives in Staffordshire, U.K.